eGAIA

" The problem is essentially that people don't understand each other or themselves. It's in this area of learning to understand ourselves, and therefore learning to live together, that we are defective in the world. So learning to do that is constructing an adequate model of man.

If we are looking for a model of man, it has to be a cap that fits; and if it is a cap that fits, then people are going to put it on. That is why the problem is open to solution – a solution in which people's behaviour changes because they become progressively enlightened as to their own nature"

Professor Mike Hussey

Gary Alexander

eGAIA:

Growing a

peaceful,

sustainable

Earth through

communications

LIGHTHOUSE
BOOKS

Illustrations and cover by Beverly Curl

Cartoons by Sarah Guthrie

Design by Linda Rodgers

First published in England by

Lighthouse Books

Field House

Thrandeston

Diss, Norfolk IP21 4BU

ISBN 0907637248

Printed and bound in Great Britain by

Micropress Printers Limited

01986 834200

27 Norwich Road, Halesworth, Suffolk IP19 8BX

*Dedicated to
the late Professor Michael Hussey,
for many years my closest friend
and mentor. He deserves credit for
the deepest ideas and for the
fundamental changes in my
worldview reflected here.
His sudden death in 1990 left a
huge hole in my life
and in that of many others.*

*This edition is also dedicated to the
thousands of people attending the
Johannesburg World Summit on
Sustainable Development in
August/September 2002, who are
my allies and the best hope in a
generation of making a difference
towards the visions in this book.*

Acknowledgements

A special thanks to the team of good friends who helped me put together this Earth Summit edition: Linda Rodgers whose graphic design made it look so good (and whose ideas over many years helped shape it), Brian Guthrie, my editor and publisher who put my prose into shape, Beverly Curl whose cover and illustrations in Chapter 4 helped evolution to come alive, Sarah Guthrie whose wonderful cartoons made it a little less serious and captured some of its key points.

Many people have read and commented on this and earlier attempts at writing this book. Many of the ideas were clarified through their comments and in conversation with them, so special thanks to Godfrey, Howard, Allen, Stephen, Tony, and all the others I have forgotten to mention.

Table of Contents

PREFACE

This book is a journey we will be taking together – you the reader and me. We'll be exploring lots of ideas and possibilities. Some of these will be far from conventional wisdom, so if we are to stay together, I would at least like to be clear about where we start.

However you have come to this book, I imagine you are likely to be in general sympathy with my starting points.

- *A worry about the natural environment.* You have a strong sense that human activities are destroying natural habitats, that plants and animals are going extinct rapidly, the climate is changing, the weather is becoming more unstable, the air and seas are polluted, and more. These issues have been in the public consciousness since the 1960s. A lot more is understood now than then, but nevertheless it still seems to be getting worse, not better. You find this upsetting and would like to see it change. You do what you can in your daily life, but feel that that is probably not much more than tokenism. To a large extent you feel caught in an unsustainable lifestyle.

- *Worries about the economy, local and global, and where it is going.* For a start, it seems so unstable. Very few people have much job security. Recessions come and go, and a real economic crash, like in the 1930s and affecting the whole world, could happen at any time. This despite the efforts of politicians, central bankers etc to keep it stable and prosperous. And so many people get left out. Even in places where times are good, there are lots of people who are struggling. You may be one of them. Or you may see your children or your friends struggling. As for the really poor people in famine areas or in shanty towns, it is almost too painful to think about. And you probably have a sense of resigned cynicism about all the awful things which are done purely in pursuit of money, whether it is arms and tobacco sales, or the corruption that affects business and politics.

- *A sense of hopeless despair about wars and ethnic cleansing.* Yes, the cold war has ended and the shadow of a nuclear war between the west and communism has largely cleared. But you feel that so many of the conflicts which are left are just as appalling.

- *Nagging doubts about your government.* You may live in a country with a parliamentary democracy amd free elections. But somehow it doesn't feel like 'government by the people and for the people'. All sorts of special interests seem to get in the way. Taxes always seem very high and public services underfunded, and the large mass of public employees underpaid. You probably vote against the party you think is worse rather than for a party you genuinely identify with. You are sure this kind of government is better than the old feudal system it replaced, or modern totalitarian equivalents. But you imagine that there could be something much better, much more community-based and with a much more human face.

- *Concern about the decline of relationships and community.* If you haven't been part of a broken family yourself, either as a child or an adult, you are likely to know lots of people who are. You know of the damage it causes to all concerned. You probably know about strong communities from your childhood, or from your parents, or from people who have come from other countries where 'they were poor but cared for each other'. You worry about the effects on so many children of both a broken family and a non-existent community. Perhaps you think this has some connection with the rate of crime which seems to be getting higher.

This book is for people who would like to see major change in these areas, who want to be clearer as to what is desirable in their place and what kind of change is possible. You may already be devoting some or much of your time to creating change of this sort, and are interested in another perspective on it. Perhaps you are looking for change in your life and are exploring ideas which may help in that. You may simply be keeping a watching brief on what is going on and are interested in a book which tries to make some sense of the larger picture.

Our dialogue

I try to imagine the people who are reading this book so I know what I can assume as I write. It sometimes seems that it would be easier if this could be more of a dialogue than seems to be possible in a book. I would like to know how much you agree with what I have just assumed about you. Have I got it right? Are there areas I have missed out?

> **You** Well, perhaps it can be a limited sort of dialogue. Yes, you have more or less got me right, but I might not express it in the same way. And what about issues of health and diet?

Don't those concern you? Anyway, hello.

Me Well hello. Yes, I'm sure there are lots of other areas which we could explore.

Perhaps the first issue we should look at, before the book starts, is whether or not you are open to the possibility that there might be very dramatic changes for the better over the next few generations, if enough people want it and work for it.

You That's not an easy question to answer. I certainly would like to see dramatic changes for the better, but I tend to be quite cynical, especially about people. This book is already sounding somewhat utopian, and I might take some convincing.

Me What worries me is that you might mean utopian in a dismissive fashion – too good to happen.

The book is very much utopian, in the sense of trying to figure out what kind of a society and what kind of relationship with the earth would work best for us all, humanity in all its diversity, and the rest of life on earth. That's the big question.

Can we imagine a society in which human activities preserve and enhance rather than destroy the natural world? And in which all the other issues raised above were at least significantly better, if not fully resolved? What might it be like? What sort of jobs would people do? What kinds of social structures would be needed? What would their relationships with one another be like?

What I am hoping to offer more than anything else is that large-scale picture, and to clarify it as fully as I am able. How do the different problems reinforce each other? To help do that, I will need something to compare the problems with. I will try to imagine some possible futures.

You Are you trying to wriggle out of saying you think these possible futures will actually happen?

Me Alright, let's be clear about that from the beginning. I wouldn't be writing about something I believed couldn't happen. What would be the point? But that's not the same as saying I think it will happen. I don't know and don't believe the future is knowable. Sometimes I feel very positive about the future and other times I think everything is hopeless. I do think it is very important to look at what is desirable, and to understand what might stop it from happening. The necessary changes might not happen simply because not enough people take them seriously. Where do you stand on this? How open are you to change?

You I want notice on that question, but I have a lot of sympathy for change.

The miracle question

My preferred approach to looking at the future is similar to that used by 'solution-focused brief therapists', a school of personal and family therapy that works by exploring the positive in people's lives. They say to their clients 'Imagine that you went to sleep, and while you were asleep, a miracle happened so that all your problems were ended. What would you notice when you woke up? What would be different?' This is a technique to bypass their clients' habitual defences, negativity and preoccupation with what is wrong. It allows them to look at what they really want. The therapist can then ask 'What first steps could you take to make that happen?'

So it is in that spirit that I will be looking at possible futures. What do we really want? And later in the book I'll look at steps in those directions.

You Well that sounds a little better. But anyway, why should I believe you? What is so special about your view of the future? Who are you?

Me I don't want you to believe me. When I find a book I like, it is generally because it has clarified something I was already generally sympathetic towards. I hope you will come to agree with me rather than believe me. The ideas will then be as much yours as mine. And as for who I am, perhaps a potted biography will suggest where these ideas came from.

Who am I?

I was born in New York City in 1943, in a family of immigrant Romanian-Jewish origin. My family and friends were aware of the troubles and conflicts in the city. There were racial problems between various cultures, and lots of crime. We were very aware of the wars, conflicts and hatreds that had afflicted people in the past and that still left their legacy in our multi-cultural city. In particular, we knew about pogroms, Nazism and the holocaust, and residual anti-Semitism. Some of our grandparents were concentration camp survivors, with numbers tattooed on their arms. We were also aware of slavery, the American civil war, and the residual racial prejudice around us. As an older child and teenager, it was only natural that I should join in with some of the social and political struggles around me, which were, first, the campaigns for racial integration and later the anti-war and anti-nuclear weapons movements.

But I grew up with liberal American values, and viewed New York accordingly. We enjoyed the many cultures that made up the city. We liked each others' food and would join in the celebrations of each other's holidays. We went to Little Italy for the Festival of San Gennaro, to

Chinatown for the Chinese New Year. Each year the line down the centre of Fifth Avenue was painted green for the St Patrick's Day parade. We went to midnight mass on Christmas Eve.

It seemed reasonable and normal that we could all retain the forms of our ancestral cultures but at the same time see ourselves as New Yorkers and Americans with all that implied. It seemed reasonable and normal for different cultures to live mixed in together for the most part without difficulty.

In school, my greatest interests were science and mathematics. This led me into an undergraduate degree in electronic engineering from Columbia University. Later I did a Master's degree and then a PhD at Purdue University in Indiana, doing research into non-linear circuit theory. The research was virtually pure mathematics and highly abstract. Although totally removed from my earlier social and political interests, it gave me very useful ways of thinking about the dynamic behaviour of complex systems – a set of mental tools which underpins the social views in this book: How feedback processes can create either stability or instability. How systems may have characteristic ways of behaving which involve 'flipping' from one somewhat stable pattern to a quite different one.

This was just the time when a new wave of ideas was sweeping the Western world, and in particular, the young. We were excited by New Left ideas of decentralised socialism, angered by the discovery of the environmental problems industrial societies were causing, and began taking a new look at the relationships between men and women.

> **You** Yes, I think I get the picture. You're an ageing hippie. But isn't all this a little self-indulgent? I wasn't expecting an autobiography.
>
> **Me** Please be patient. I'm getting quite near the time when the

main ideas in this book began to emerge, but I think this background is necessary for you to understand how they came about.

In early 1971 I moved to England, with my wife and daughter. I was a Lecturer in Electronics, Design and Communication at the Open University (OU), just formed as the first distance-learning university and aimed at adults who had missed their chance to go to university and were learning at home.

Many of us young academic staff were determined to bring our new environmental insights into teaching. We felt that part of our mission was to produce a much more integrated form of education to our students, especially as we saw that advanced technology was intimately involved in the environmental destruction that disturbed us. Our first-year course had a strong environmental flavour to it, quite unlike conventional engineering courses of that time.

When my friend and colleague, Peter Chapman, formed the Energy Research Group, I eagerly joined as a founder member. When Peter Chapman resigned as Director a few years later I took his place.

During the mid-1970s a group of us decided to produce our 'grand course', which we referred to as the Human Ecology Course. We wanted to put environmental issues into their context: show their historical and social roots. We were clear that it wasn't just ignorance that was the problem. We saw a great contradiction between what was considered desirable for the economy and desirable for the environment (and social well-being).

You Isn't that still the case?

Me Absolutely. That remains the big issue and will be central.

We didn't believe that contradiction was a law of nature and wanted to display the social processes that led to it, in the belief that only by doing so could the root problems be understood and corrected. Our team set about researching and developing the background material from many disciplines. There was no obvious niche for a non-linear circuit theorist, so I began to look into processes of social change and into the roots of economic behaviour. I read extensively in the anthropological literature and was fascinated by the variety of human cultures. Many were warlike, but many were extremely peaceful and gentle with crime unknown. Clearly, the aggressive, competitive nature of human nature as it now appears in western cultures was neither inevitable nor the full extent of human possibilities. The forms of economic behaviour were very varied too, with systems of formalised gift giving very prevalent, and many systems of symbolic exchange with money-like features. Clearly, the idea that monetary exchange came about basically as a great advance over primitive barter totally misunderstood the nature of early cultures and the forces that held them together. All of this will come up later.

For many reasons, personal and otherwise, the human ecology course was never produced, although several of us produced first drafts of the written material. I've always thought of the it as unfinished business, which this book is an attempt to complete. The course leader, Mike Hussey (to whom this book is dedicated) took extended study leave, with the intention of writing a book that would form the basis of the course at a later date. He collected material on economics, development, psychology and many other areas. One day in the spring of 1976, he had what he experienced as a tremendous breakthrough. Suddenly, in a momentary flash of insight, all the pieces fitted together.

You Are you saying he had a mystical experience?

> **Me** Perhaps in an earlier age it would have been seen that way. I'd rather leave it as I've described it.

Any previous ideas about blaming groups or organisations as the cause of environmental or other social problems fell away. Instead, he could see people caught in chains, or perhaps webs of circumstances, each of which led to other circumstances, endlessly recreating the same patterns. A key element in this was the way in which people's ideas and relationships were formed and shaped by the words and concepts they used. Communication and conversation were at the root of the problem.

The flash of insight was far more than an understanding of what was going wrong, for implicit in that was the possibility that it could be put right. Getting the communication right seemed to hold the possibility of getting relationships right at all levels. Mike immediately began talking about a 'semantic unity network' where people had a shared understanding of critical issues between them.

> **You** Hold on! You are going much too fast. I have a general sense of what you are saying, but it certainly isn't clear.
>
> **Me** Sorry, I'm anticipating some of the key ideas of the book here. It should get clearer.

During that period I spent a lot of time helping Mike develop his ideas. For many years I expected Mike Hussey to write his own book, but that never happened. Then he died suddenly in 1990, leaving a mass of notes but no book.

During the 1980s and 90s, my career took on a new direction. I had become one of the OU's pioneers in the use of computer communications for distance learning, specialising in collaborative learning on-line. I saw this as an opportunity to try out some of our insights into the communications process. I foresaw the possibility of on-line communities linking like-minded but isolated people, like our distance learning students.

I produced experimental computers, on-line environments, and experimental courses and fed their results into real courses. All OU courses are developed by teams, and my role generally included teaching students to form on-line educational support communities. From small beginnings, this led to around 100,000 OU students being on-line each year, mostly learning to do so using material I developed.

This book brings together those two parts of my career: the interest in social and environmental change and the use of computers to support collaborative communities.

Up to date

This book builds upon one further part of my life that is personal rather than professional. In the early 1990s I started going to various festivals and camps for music and dance, mostly in the south-west of England. I met a new partner at one of these. She was in the process of setting up a similar music and dance camp in eastern England. We worked on these together for several years.

About 500 people would attend these events. They camped in groups of between 20 and 40 people in a circle around a common campfire for about 10 days. They cooked communally and socialised around that fire. They lived much closer to the elements than they were used to. The social setting, with its tribe-like camp divided into band-like camping circles, was much closer to that of their pre-historic ancestors than they were used to.

Among the various special qualities of these camps was that they encouraged a sense of instant community. A culture grew up among the campers of self-organising mutual support. A mixture of music, dance and creative play pervaded the practical work of preparing the food, keeping the place clean, caring for the children – and even cleaning the toilets. Some of the people who came to these events felt it changed their lives. Many felt they wanted to extend the kind of community there more widely into their lives. I thought of those camps as the nursery schools of the new culture I was dreaming about, and which this book explores.

INTRODUCTION TO eGAIA

The problems which humanity has created for the natural world and for itself are extremely severe. They are bad enough that the metaphor of a global cancer seems appropriate. Although our environmental problems have been in the public consciousness since the 1960s, it is only now that their full severity is becoming appreciated.

Many people are writing and working to counteract this global cancer. This book introduces the image of eGaia. It is an unashamedly Utopian image, of humanity living in harmony with the planet and in harmony with itself – a genuinely peaceful, sustainable world based around co-operation and community through enhanced communication rather than conflict, competition and war.

Massive problems require radical solutions. Tinkering around the edges won't have much effect. The radical Utopian image of eGaia both clarifies the present problems and provides a pointer to practical steps in that direction: co-operative social groupings, information systems, improving human skills of communication and relationships.

The image of eGaia is of the Earth coming to function as an organism with humanity as its nervous system. An organism has wholeness and coherence. Its parts don't fight each other or destroy the health of the whole. Its nervous system is as much controlled by its body as it controls the body. It is part of the body and responds to its needs.

The e in eGaia is there because a nervous system is a communication system. If humans are the nerve cells of a global nervous system, then our electronic communication technologies will enable us to connect to each other in a way rich enough to form locally and globally self-organising and self-regulating social structures.

To convey a first sense of the overall message of this book first demands two metaphors – global cancer and global nervous system – but most of the book will be much more concrete.

> **You** Yes, they are quite emotional metaphors, and they don't quite fit together. How can a cancer turn into a nervous system?
>
> **Me** Well, it's the best I can do. And even though I really want to separate the question of what is desirable from the question of

how we might get there, I'll try to give a first answer to your question by mixing my metaphors even more. Do you know how a caterpillar changes into a butterfly?

This is a metaphor for the possible transformation, or metamorphosis, from global cancer to global nervous system. A caterpillar is completely unlike a butterfly. It is a soft, fat creature, with a body of many segments and a pair of legs on each, which crawls slowly along plants spending its life eating. A butterfly has a small, hard three-segmented body with a pair of legs on each segment and wonderful colourful wings. It flies about pollinating flowers and looking for a mate.

> **Me** You could say the caterpillar lives for food and the butterfly lives for love!

How could such a radical transformation happen? When conditions are right, the caterpillar creates a cocoon around itself and starts its metamorphosis. Triggered by hormonal signals, small areas of its body called 'imaginal disks' begin to grow into the various parts of the butterfly. Simultaneously, the rest of the caterpillar begins to dissolve into its component chemicals, providing the raw materials for the growing butterfly. All this is carefully co-ordinated so that the growing parts link up to form a coherent organism.

The analogy with the Earth is only loose. Unfortunately, there is no protective cocoon. The dissolving of the caterpillar body is analogous to many of the breakdowns caused by the global cancer. It is well underway and is probably irreversible. The imaginal disks are the huge number of organisations and initiatives working to create a sustainable world and a peaceful world. Their influence is only marginal now, but their growth is stimulated by the breakdowns. This book is about how to inspire their growth and help them link up through the development of a communications-based global nervous system.

The metaphor also implies that the results of the transformation will be something completely new, neither a return to some mythical ancient golden age nor business-as-usual but with more environmental awareness. There is no doubt that most of humanity desires a transition to a genuinely peaceful, sustainable earth. Of course, many caterpillars don't make it through to the butterfly stage, and there is no guarantee that we will succeed in transforming the earth. But what else is there to do which is as important or exciting?

Outline of the book

As the overall message of this book is more important than any specific idea in it, this outline will provide some context. Like many books, this one will not necessarily be read from beginning to end. This outline is something of a guide to those readers who wish to cherry pick. The book is in four parts with part 1 laying out the main ideas and parts 2 – 4 filling them out.

PART 1 From global cancer to global nervous system

Chapter 1 Humanity as a global cancer uses a series of quotations from experts in various areas to give the bad news:

- how we are destroying the natural world
- the ways in which humanity is at war with itself
- how our money-driven, globalised economy perpetuates the first two problems.

Chapter 2 eGaian principles picks up on those three aspects of the global cancer and turns them into organising principles for an eGaian world.

Chapter 3 A taste of an eGaian future suggests how these principles might be implemented through an imaginary community of the future – 'Pinecone Network'.

> **You** So if I want to see what you are proposing I could jump straight to Chapter 3?
>
> **Me** Well yes, but I wouldn't recommend it. The intervening chapters begin to explain why it is like it is. Also, remember that it is only my image of a desirable future, not of how to get there.

PART 2 The five-billion-year story

Chapter 4 Symbiosis and competition is a history of the Earth and the evolution of life on it. It lays out the evolutionary progression towards which this book is leading, from the first simple cells to the living-Earth-as-organism. Its second function is to counter the crude view of evolution as shaped by competition, 'nature red in tooth and claw'. Competition is only a small part of the evolutionary process. Chapter 4 shows the key role of symbiosis in the evolution of life. The third reason for this chapter is simply that it's a very good story. The Big Bang plus evolution is our modern, scientific creation myth. It is a real shame that the popular version of it has conflict and random change as the central image. This re-write puts symbiosis, collaboration and the growth of order at its centre, so that it provides a sense of direction and hope for the future.

Chapter 5 The co-operative ape favours a positive view of human evolution – collaboration rather than competition. It describes some early systems of co-operation and exchange which provide a useful vision for the future. It counter-acts the notion that the ideas in this book aren't possible because 'the world isn't like that …people aren't like that … conflict and competition are inherent in the way nature works and the way people work'.

> **You** Yes, I bet people think you are completely naïve!
>
> **Me** Sometimes they do. And if you look at the world today and read about past civilisations it doesn't surprise me. But I think that there is more to the whole picture than most people realise, as I will try to show. There is a difference between the ways things are now and have been recently, and the way they are inherently and necessarily.

Chapter 6 Towards the global cancer traces the stages in the transition from the co-operative ape to global cancer – in agriculture, civilisation, industrialisation and globalisation. It shows how human societies have progressively lost their connection with the natural world and even with human needs, resulting in out-of-control growth which is the hallmark of a cancer.

PART 3 An eGaian guide: philosophy and principles

Chapter 7 eGaian relationships sets out the basis for the progressive type of relationship characterised by the Pinecone Network in Chapter 3 – supportive, and embedded in a social structure that nourishes it. It describes communication principles necessary for collaboration and conflict resolution.

Chapter 8 A peaceful earth: conflict resolution compares cultures in which conflicts are rare and easily handled because conflict resolution is built into the culture, with those in which conflict is endemic. It describes basic principles of conflict resolution based upon the experience of practitioners.

Chapter 9 A co-operative economy describes organising principles for co-operative economic structures in which information systems provide better measures of cost, of people's social contributions and the other ingredients needed to organise an economy than are provided by conventional money.

> **You** A economy without money? I will read that chapter carefully. This seems to me to be most far-fetched point you are making. I will need a lot of convincing.
>
> **Me** Well I can only try. I think this is one of those issues which seems mad at first, but then becomes so obvious you see evidence of it everywhere you look.

Chapter 10 A sustainable earth is a largely practical review of ways in which the sustainability of the earth might be improved if humanity made that a real priority. It pays special attention to food production, as the basis of human health and human connection to the natural world and also takes a careful look at sustainable methods of production and of energy use.

PART 4 Making eGaia happen

Chapter 11 Starting points is about current 'imaginal disks' – what is happening now that is consistent with the ideas in the eGaian guide: the beginnings of a global communication system, of a global sense of identity and of a sense of symbiosis or mutual support between human cultures. It concludes with a telling case study, of the Damanhur community in Italy that embodies many of the eGaian principles.

Chapter 13 eGaian co-operative networks is a practical guide to enacting eGaian philosophy and principles: how to use communications technology to create a limited, virtual eco-village within an existing community – starting up, dealing with food, transport and so on.

Chapter 14 Towards an eGaian Earth looks to the near future – the Johannesburg summit – and beyond, in terms of further projects. It describes six practical initiatives that would form the beginnings of a co-operative economy, reduce poverty and conflict and work towards an education system centred on sustainability.

You You really expect the major corporations, democratic governments much less repressive ones to voluntarily join your co-operative world?

Me Who knows what could happen? I don't believe it is actually knowable; the future will be what the future will be. My speculations might turn out to have some truth, or we may take a quite different route towards a future that feels similarly eGaian. Or we may not. The global cancer that is our present human culture may make the planet a miserable place to live for most of humanity or may even lead to the extinction of humans among the many other life forms that are being lost. Those who understand the possibilities at least have the choice to work for an eGaian future.

PART one

FROM GLOBAL CANCER TO GLOBAL NERVOUS SYSTEM

CHAPTER one

HUMANITY AS
A GLOBAL CANCER

The world is certainly not like the eGaian image today. Nor are the dominant trends in that direction. Humanity is now more like a global cancer than a global nervous system. The cells in an organism are normally in communication with each other. When their growth is sufficient it stops. Cancerous cells lose that controlling communication. Their growth continues until the body supporting it dies, taking them with it. This chapter looks at several aspects of the global cancer, which underpin motivations for eGaia.

You So this is the gloomy chapter.

Me I'm afraid so. Let's get it out of the way early. You will find lots of horrible facts you can use to shock your friends. But at least it ends on a hopeful note, by arguing that the problems are socially created and are thus not inevitable.

A cancer of the natural world

"At some time in the 1970s, humanity as a whole passed the point at which it lived within the global regenerative capacity of the Earth,…"
World Wide Fund for Nature [1]

A hundred thousand years or so ago we were one medium-sized mammal among many, with no more effect on the planet than any of the others. We were (and are) one of a handful of species of great ape. Life flourished throughout the seas, the land and the air – forming forests, grasslands, aquatic and other ecosystems.

The planet as a whole has had a limited stability over its five billion year life. Major ecosystems maintained their general form over long periods of time as a result of feedback effects such as predator-prey relationships. Food webs and decomposers acted to recycle the raw materials of life indefinitely. The effect of life as a whole on the physical Earth was to maintain the general conditions it needed to continue. The presence of life kept the composition of the atmosphere, the surface temperature and the presence of liquid water far from chemical equilibrium as needed for life's survival. [2]

This relative stability was punctuated from time to time by periods of very rapid change. There have been five mass extinctions in which most of the species alive at the time were wiped out. The best known extinction was 65 million years ago when the dinosaurs disappeared. There have been major rapid changes of weather and climate such as the start and end of ice ages. These ideas are developed in Part II of the book, The five-billion-year story.

We are now in one of those periods of very rapid change. This time it is due to human activity, which now dominates the world physically and biologically. We are certainly no longer one medium-sized mammal among many.

3

The concept of 'environmental footprint' has recently been developed to measure the area of land needed to support a person at a given level of technology. On this measure, the wealthier countries already consume on average three times their fair share of sustainable global output.[3] Human population growth and the prospect of development in the poorer countries will make this worse.

4

Extinction of species

> "My greatest fear for our world is that global warming may produce an increased rate of extinction and eventually reach some threshold point, triggering a cascade of mass extinction, a free-fall of death. Each species on the earth is like a tiny piece in a four-dimensional jigsaw, interlocking with other species," *Peter Ward* [4]

It is not just the odd pretty butterfly that is in danger. The rate at which species are becoming extinct is comparable to that of the great extinctions of the past. All of the other great apes – the chimpanzees, gorillas and orang-utans, our closest cousins – are threatened with extinction within the next 20 years or so. The normal background rate of extinctions is about 10 to 25 per year, while now it is probably in the thousands. Expert sources agree:

- "The World Wide Fund for Nature (WWF) said unless there was co-ordinated action by governments in central Africa and south-east Asia there could be no halt to the dramatic decline in the numbers of great apes – chimpanzees, gorillas, bonobos and orang-utans – and their eventual disappearance."[5]

- "A total of 11,046 species of plants and animals are threatened, facing a high risk of extinction in the near future, in almost all cases as a result of human activities. This includes 24 percent (one in four) of mammal species and 12 percent (one in eight) of bird species. The total number of threatened animal species has increased from 5,205 to 5,435."[6]

- "Cascade effects occur when the local extinction of one species significantly changes the population sizes of other species, potentially leading to other extirpations."[7]

Loss of natural habitats

- "Forest cover has been reduced by more than 20 percent worldwide, with some forest ecosystems, such as the dry tropical forests of Central America, virtually gone. More than 50 percent of the original mangrove area in many countries is gone; wet-lands area has shrunk by about half; and grasslands have been reduced by more than 90 percent in some areas. Only tundra, arctic, and deep-sea ecosystems have emerged relatively unscathed."[8]

Damage to agriculture and fisheries

- "Agriculture, forestry, and fishing are responsible for 50 percent of all jobs world- wide and 70 percent of the jobs in sub-Saharan Africa, East Asia, and the Pacific. ...Although crop yields are still rising, the underlying condition of agroecosystems is declining in much of the world. Soil degradation is a concern on as much as 65 percent of agricultural land. ...About two-thirds of agricultural land has been degraded in the past 50 years by erosion, salinization, compaction, nutrient depletion, biological degradation, or pollution. About 40 percent of agricultural land has been strongly or very strongly degraded."[9]

- "…freshwater ecosystems are far and away the most degraded, with some 20 percent of freshwater fish species extinct, threatened, or endangered in recent decades. …[for coastal ecosystems] Almost 70 percent of the major fisheries are fully fished or overfished,"[10]

Change to the physical world: climate and weather

The scientific evidence for climate change, increases in severe weather, and changes to the composition of the atmosphere are becoming much clearer, as presented by the IPCC:[11]

- "The atmospheric concentration of carbon dioxide (CO_2) has increased by 31% since 1750. The present CO_2 concentration has not been exceeded during the past 420,000 years and likely not during the past 20 million years. About three-quarters of the anthropogenic emissions of CO_2 to the atmosphere during the past 20 years is due to fossil fuel burning. The rest is predominantly due to land-use change, especially deforestation. …several centuries after CO_2 emissions occur, about a quarter of the increase in CO_2 concentration caused by these emissions is still present in the atmosphere."

- "The atmospheric concentration of methane (CH_4) has increased by 1060 ppb (151%) since 1750 and continues to increase."

- "Globally, it is very likely that the 1990s was the warmest decade and 1998 the warmest year in the instrumental record, since 1861"

- "…over the latter half of the 20th century, it is likely that there has been a 2 to 4% increase in the frequency of heavy precipitation events."

- "The globally averaged surface temperature is projected to increase by 1.4 to 5.8°C over the period 1990 to 2100. …Glaciers and ice caps are projected to continue their widespread retreat during the 21st century. Global mean sea level is projected to rise by 0.09 to 0.88 metres between 1990 and 2100."

- "Global mean surface temperature increases and rising sea level from thermal expansion of the ocean are projected to continue for hundreds of years after stabilization of greenhouse gas concentrations (even at present levels), owing to the long timescales on which the deep ocean adjusts to climate change."

7

Effects of environmental degradation

The World Bank has distinguished the effects of the major environmental problems on both health and productivity:[12]

- "More than two million deaths and billions of illnesses a year are attributable to water pollution. ...Urban air pollution is responsible for 300,000 – 700,000 deaths annually and creates chronic health problems for many more people."

- "Diseases are spread by uncollected garbage and blocked drains; the health risks from hazardous wastes are typically more localized, but often acute. Wastes affect productivity through the pollution of groundwater resources."

- "Ozone depletion is responsible for perhaps 300,000 additional cases of skin cancer a year and 1.7 million cases of cataracts. Global warming may lead to a shift in vector-borne diseases and increase the risk of climatic natural disasters."

Humanity at war with itself

Humanity out of communication with the natural world, and so acting as a cancer upon it, is only one part of the bad news, and doesn't even get near to the root of it. The environmental disruption is merely a side effect of a fundamental fragmentation of human culture. In many ways, humanity is at war with itself.

8

We are not even living well at the expense of the planet that supports us. Those parts of humanity with the largest material consumption generally also have little sense of spirituality or community, high mental and emotional instability, unstable families and relationships, high drug use and crime rates, economic insecurity, political corruption and so on. And that is only the richer parts. The poorer parts are beset by wars, poverty, famines, harshly repressive and highly corrupt governments etc.

For most of our evolutionary history, humanity lived in small bands that were communities based around extended families. Language and culture evolved to enable us to take advantage of the resilience, flexibility and sheer enhanced ability that support from a group gives to an individual. Our bodies, brains, minds and hearts are adapted to being part of that kind of a community structure. The inherently collaborative nature of humanity is developed further in Chapter 5.

The culture of traditional communities gave people a sense of who they were, what they could contribute and what they could expect from life. Children grew up with role models and support from adults other than their parents. All productive activity was clearly in support of community needs, desires and culture. Crime was rare because of community pressures. Moreover, those huge classes of crime and corruption motivated by obtaining money (which we think of as inevitable today) simply couldn't happen before a monetary economy developed.

You So are you saying that we need to return to that primitive way of life?

Me Not at all. For a start our population is now much too large. We also don't want that limited, culture-bound view. Moreover, early cultures were not the eco-friendly paradises some myths would suggest. What I am saying is that we need to re-create the sense of connection and community support from that way of life in our own. It is the key to happiness. And we also need to re-create the direct connection between production and needs/wants.

To be clearer about how bad is the condition of humanity as a whole, here is a series of quotations from experts who have looked at different aspects of it. Mostly, it is about the appalling way people can treat other people, sometimes deliberately, and sometimes as a side effect of other activities. The statistics give an impression of the extent of this, but do not convey the full horror of it, which we can glimpse from the more personal stories we see in television images of genocide and famine.

Wars

- "There were 27 major armed conflicts in 1999, there were 11 in Africa, 9 in Asia, 3 in the Middle East, 2 in Europe and 2 in South America. All but two of the conflicts were internal. Most of the major armed conflicts registered for 1999 are protracted (17 have been active for at least eight years) or recurrent (4 conflicts). Seen against the 19 conflicts in 1997...there was a sharp upturn in the last two years of the decade.... Foreign military intervention occurred in only 5 of the 27 conflicts waged in 1999, suggesting that it remains the exception and is not becoming the rule.

- Total world military expenditure increased by 2.1% in real terms in 1999 and amounted to roughly $780 billion. While this is almost one-third less than 10 years earlier, it still represents a significant share of world economic resources: 2.6% of world gross national product (GNP)."[13]

Human rights abuses

According to Amnesty International, human rights were abused by governments all over the world, democratic or otherwise, on a very large scale.[14] See their reports for details. Here is simply a table indicating its scale.

Type of Abuse	Number of countries
Extrajudicial executions	38
"Disappearances"	37
Torture and ill-treatment	132
...leading to death in custody	81
Prisoners of conscience	81
Unfair trials	51
Detention without charge or trial	63
Death penalty	34
Human rights abuses by armed opposition groups	46

Crime

Crime is endemic all over the world, affecting large proportions of the population. The table below shows the percentage of the population victimised each year in a range of countries.[15]

Country & year of survey	% of population	Country & year of survey	% of population
Netherlands, 1995	31.5	Italy, 1991	24.6
England & Wales, 1995	30.9	USA, 1995	24.2
New Zealand, 1991	29.4	Sweden, 1995	24.0
Australia, 1991	28.6	Malta, 1996	23.1
Switzerland, 1995	26.7	Germany (west), 1988	21.9
Scotland, 1995	25.6	Belgium, 1991	19.3
France, 1995	25.3	Finland, 1995	18.9
Canada, 1995	25.2	Austria, 1995	18.8
Spain, 1988	24.8	Northern Ireland, 1995	16.8

11

The cost of crime is not just the direct costs to the victims, but also includes the cost of running services like the police, customs, courts and prisons.

- "The annual cost of crime in Britain is £60 billion – more than £1,000 for every man, woman and child in the country."[16]

Hunger and poverty

- "Thirty million people a year die of hunger. And 800 million suffer from chronic malnutrition."[17]

- "Until 1996, the number of poor people was on the decline, but by 1998 it was on the rise again. Today there are more than 1.3 billion chronically poor people in the world."[18]

- "In over 70 countries, per capita income is lower today than it was 20 years ago. Almost three billion people – half the world's population – live on less than two dollars a day."[19]

Inequality

- "The total wealth of the world's three richest individuals is greater than the combined gross domestic product of the 48 poorest countries – a quarter of all the world's states. In 1960 the income of the 20% of the world's population living in the richest countries was 30 times greater than that of the 20% in the poorest countries…in 1995 it was 82 times greater".[20]

Family and emotional problems

The family within a community has traditionally been the basis of human societies. In many countries now, much of the sense of community is gone and even the family is in very poor shape.

- [For the United States] "Cherlin compares the likelihood of marrying, divorcing, remarrying and redivorcing of four cohorts of women (born 1908-1912, 1928-1932, 1948-1952, 1970). …The marriage rates are quite similar [but the] likelihood of divorce is dramatically different for each of these generations. The lifetime chance that the first generation would divorce was 22% while the lifetime probability for the great-granddaughters born in 1970 is 44%."[21]

- "Overall, about 25% of children live in single-parent households. It is also estimated that about 40% of children will EVER live in a single-parent household while they are under 18 years of age."[22]

- "40 population-based quantitative studies, conducted in 24 countries on four continents, revealed that between 20% and 50% of the women interviewed reported that they had suffered physical violence from their male partners. In addition, surveys also indicate that at least one in five women suffer rape or attempted rape in their lifetimes."[23]

The same source shows that mental health problems are the largest cause of illness and disability for women throughout the world, and it is actually far worse in the developed regions as the following graph shows.

The ten leading causes of disease burden for women, aged 15+, 1990

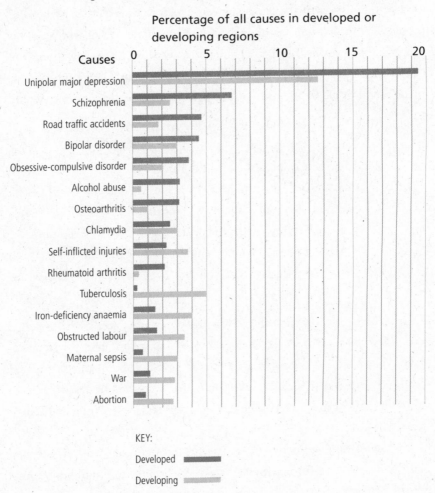

Percentage of all causes in developed or developing regions

KEY:

Developed

Developing

The problem with money

" Money is institutionalised mistrust"
Professor Mike Hussey

One further aspect of the global cancer, which links the other two sets of problems (cancer of the natural world and humanity at war with itself) is central to the reasons they perpetuate themselves. An increasing amount of people's activities are motivated by money, and the inherent problems are made much worse by the form of our current globalised economic system.

> **You** You have come to the conclusion that money is the root of all evil!
>
> **Me** The actual quote is from the Bible,[24] (*I Tim vi 10*) "The love of money is the root of all evil things." but no, I don't agree with it. The root is social and spiritual fragmentation, the loss of connection with the Earth and sense of community between people. Money enables us to carry on dealing with each other despite that. It looms large in the global cancer but is not at its root.

Instead of being constrained and controlled by the needs of humanity, much less the natural world, our modern globalised monetary system has taken on a life of its own. Flows of money have become relatively isolated from physical constraints. In 1995, only 2 or 3% of money flows were to do with trade or investment. The rest were speculative – buying and selling currencies.[25]

Most of our productive effort is now through paid work, motivated largely by our need for money. If the work is beneficial to our community, to the planet, to ourselves and if it gives us prestige and social standing, that is a nice side benefit, a luxury for some rather than the immediate and direct motivation for that work. The global economy is driven by money flows, not need. This is a major source of our environmental problems and social problems.

From the statements of most politicians and the media, with their emphasis on economic growth, globalisation and the dominance of the market, it is easy to believe that our present economic system is inevitable and is more or less optimum despite its apparent flaws and instabilities. This despite the fact that it is continually changing and has been in its present globalised form for only a few decades.

Doing things for money is a relatively recent invention, and even barter is not the original form of exchange. For most of humanity's evolutionary history we lived in small bands where people worked co-operatively and did things for each other in ways for which the terms 'primitive money' or 'barter' miss the point. Sometimes various commodities were used in ways modern people have called 'money', but actually it was more like gift-giving, often highly ritualised and subject to custom and tradition. Various human cultures have invented other systems of organising the ways in which they exchange and do things for each other (see Chapter 6). Our present economic and monetary system is actually one of the strangest, but happens to have grown to dominate the planet.

As Chapter 9 demonstrates, a co-operative economy can produce a synergy where the result is greater than the sum of people's efforts. This produces the qualities of a group functioning as an organism, which is the fundamental eGaian image. In a competitive economy people feel that they are in a war. Other organisations are trying to take their markets. Other people in their organisation are trying to get their position. This creates a sense of oppression.

In a war there are lots of losers. Most the of world's population are economic losers. It is only the Western developed nations that have a substantial part of their population that isn't poor, and even they suffer the psychological effects of the economic war – insecurity and stress. Wars favour the powerful, so it is not surprising that poverty is so widespread.

The problems become clearer when expressed in the language of communication and control. What are the goals of an activity or organisation? What is it trying to accomplish? What information does it have to enable it to reach those goals? Is it inherently stable or unstable?

The wrong goals

Having money rather than need or desires as the motivation for activities simply means the economy is upside-down. The best companies try to put their customers' needs first, but even then there is an underlying conflict. They want and need you to patronise them, even if it really isn't in your best interests to do so. Huge amounts of productive work are devoted to encouraging people to want more of anything. Shopping has become one of our most popular leisure activities. Governments encourage their citizens to consume more.[26]

We are told we must increase production – not so much because the public is in desperate need of genetically modified foods, digital TVs, the next generation of computers or a new theme park, much less because we need to preserve the health of the environment – but because we need to produce more to safeguard jobs. Consumption serves production, not the other way round.

As money became the dominant mechanism of exchange, the connection with real needs and desires became looser. It has become highly abstract, with money flows taking on a life of their own. Survival has come to depend upon maintaining the flows of money. Bankruptcy generally means the end of an organisation, regardless of whether it is corrupt or dedicated to the public good. Charities need to maintain their cash flows to survive too.

This creates an inherent contradiction between the need to survive and any other goals, such as serving the public or looking after your staff. The 'bottom line', the effect on the financial balance sheet is widely used to mean 'that which is real, undeniable'. In fact, it is just a convention, an artefact of the way we organise ourselves economically. In a co-operative economy the only 'bottom line' is everybody's well-being.

Once society's goal is maximising – or simply maintaining – flows of this abstract entity money, all sorts of madness become possible.

- A rainforest can be cut down for short-term economic gain because its vital biological contribution has no economic value.

- The food and drink industry promotes junk foods that emphasise profit not nutrition, producing a huge increase in chronic and degenerative diseases.

- An airport or a railway station becomes a shopping mall, trying to extract as much money as possible from the people who use it, because its inherent function doesn't provide enough revenue.[27]

- Television channels appear that are fully dedicated to advertising, with no programme content at all.

- Companies will produce new versions of solid, useful well-loved, well-understood products and convince consumers that the old ones are obsolete or old-fashioned.

Since it is money and not service which motivates people, many 'legitimate' activities are actually more like people preying on people: making and selling shoddy goods, hard selling on your doorstep or your telephone. And then there are the downright damaging activities, such as corruption and organised crime. In traditional societies crime is quite rare and tends to be mostly to do with interpersonal conflict.

- "Corruption diverts perhaps 30 percent from billions of dollars spent annually for international development loans. Importantly, this illegitimate cash flow becomes the primary reason why funds are requested."[28]

- "By most estimates, the traffic in illicit drugs is one of the world's most substantial money earners. The retail value of drugs, at around 500 billion US dollars a year, now exceeds the value of the international trade in oil and is second only to that of the arms trade."[29]

> **You** So the world's two largest industries are the arms trade and the illegal drugs trade?
>
> **Me** So it would seem. How's that for an upside-down economy?

Sustained economic growth, that hallowed goal of politicians, central bankers and business people, appears sensible only in the context of an economy following local goals which are disconnected from physical reality. No natural process can ever grow indefinitely. It will always find some natural limit. A recession may actually be good for the environment because production and consumption are lower.

If there is to be any hope that our economy will take on a sustainable form, such as that described in Chapter 10, the goals of individuals and organisations will have to be aligned with that, and not with the abstraction of money flows.

The problems with balanced exchange

We are so used to balanced exchange – you pay for what you receive and get paid for your work – that the more generalised exchange of traditional societies doesn't appear to be a serious alternative. It doesn't seem suitable for 'real' work.

> **You** Yes, it is a matter of fairness. Why shouldn't people be rewarded for what they do, and be more highly rewarded if they do more?
>
> **Me** Fairness isn't usually an issue when people know each other well, appreciate each other as individuals and are pleased for each other's well-being. It is much more of an issue when they see their goals as opposed.

We have become blind to the major difficulties with balanced exchange. In the competitive world, the supposed fairness of being paid for your work and paying for what you receive is often illusory. Because people don't share the same goals, because they are not working for each other's well-being, prices and wages are often contentious. They are set not so much by considerations of fairness, but by considerations of power and of what the market will bear. Much effort goes into bargaining over pay; major disruption can result when there is no agreement. For many, payment for work is so low as to be exploitative and keeps them in permanent poverty. So coming to agreement on pay can be a major cost to an organisation.

The comparative 'value' of different forms of work is highly arbitrary. Does fairness explain why a company director, a famous entertainer or leading athlete earns hundreds of times the income of a nurse, a teacher or a street cleaner? Why should a factory worker in a western country be paid many times what someone in the third world gets for doing a similar job?

Some people have a say in what they will get paid for a job – the more so the higher their earnings in the first place. However, most people must take what is on offer, regardless of whether they can live adequately on it, and regardless of any considerations of fairness. So the reality is that working for money, where the goals of employer and employee are opposed, is often grossly unfair.

In the monetary economy all kinds of special arrangements have to be made for the many cases when balanced exchange breaks down.

- Insurance is needed because balanced exchange breaks down in emergencies.

- Welfare systems need to be set up (in more progressive countries) for those people on the sharp end of monetary exchange.

- Pensions are needed to look after the elderly, who are no longer cared for by their families and the community.

Misused and misleading information

An economics textbook will tell you that, theoretically, in the conventional economy all information should be public and shared for a perfect market. "The assumptions of perfect competition… [include] …perfect knowledge, we assume that everyone knows what is happening in every part of the market in which he is interested."[30] In the much simpler markets that existed a few hundred years ago, that might have been approximately true. It certainly isn't now.

If two organisations are in competition, it is certainly not in their interests to provide full and public knowledge of their costs. That information is usually part of their competitive advantage and is jealously guarded. As to a knowledge of the strengths and weaknesses of their products, a company will try to provide the best gloss on it rather than full and public knowledge, as otherwise consumers will patronise their competitors. So simply because of competition the information consumers need to make the best choice for their own needs is hidden.

The price of goods is in many cases the only way to distinguish one product from another. It is often the main factor determining whether and which product someone will buy. In principle, price should give some measure of quality and should be related to the cost of production. In practice, the monetary price is a very poor indicator.

21

- How much of the price of that luxury perfume represents the cost of making it and how much is mark-up because it is meant to appeal to well-off people?

- Can you tell from the price which pair of trainers was made by children in a third-world country working for almost nothing?

- Can you tell from the price which furniture was made from wood grown sustainably and which wasn't?

- Can you tell from the price that that low cost chicken spent its whole life in a cramped battery cage?

> **You** Probably yes! Why else would it be so cheap?
>
> **Me** Ok, but that's perhaps the only one you could work out – and some wouldn't be able to

One particularly clear example of the difference between information available in a competitive and co-operative economy is in the software market. Competing brands of similar software jealously guard their features, taking their competitors to court if they copy their best features too closely. Often competing software produces files that are not compatible with each other. Worse still, an old version of a word processor will not be able to read files produced by a later version. The manufacturers of the best-selling brands encourage this, because it forces people to buy their products if they want to share files with others using that brand. The result is a natural monopoly of the product that got the biggest market share early, regardless of whether or not it is the best. Anything else is restricted to a niche market supplying special needs or interests.

22

In contrast to the competitive software market, there has also been a co-operative software sub-culture that traces its origins back to before the days of personal computers. Unfortunately, it has always served people who are computer professionals or serious amateurs, rather than either the general public or business users.[31] It has spawned the Free Software Movement , "dedicated to promoting computer users' right to use, study, copy, modify, and redistribute computer programs." The essential point of the free software movement is that programmers should have access to the original code that created the software. That way, all the original author's best ideas and clever tricks are freely available to later authors. Instead of software that has copyright protection, the Free Software Movement[32] provides 'copyleft' protection, which says that

> "This program is free software; you can redistribute it and/or modify it under the terms of the GNU General Public License as published by the Free Software Foundation."[33]

Over time, the efforts of members of the free software community continually improve their software, building upon the best ideas and discarding the second best. All their efforts combine synergistically. The result is usually software that is extremely solid and reliable. Any problems that appear are quickly removed. The new improved version is distributed to all that want it. Probably the best example of this is Apache, a 'web server' used by more professional web sites than any other program.[34]

In contrast, competitive software companies work against each other. Much effort goes to stopping competitors. Software is sometimes designed so that competing products won't work with it, and distribution arrangements prohibit retailers from including competitors software on machines sold with a leading operating system. Programmers spend a lot of effort re-inventing features that are desirable, but try to make them slightly different so as not to infringe copyright. Any problems that occur are not corrected until the next version of the software, for which consumers are charged whatever the market will bear for an upgrade.

It should be pretty clear which of these approaches better serves its users and makes more efficient use of its developer's time and effort.

Inherent instability

The business cycle, in which periods of relative prosperity and recession alternate, is often taken as a fact of life, as though it were a law of nature. Actually, it is an artefact, a side effect of a world economy based on money and competition. In a co-operative economy it simply could not arise in the same way that money-based crime and corruption cannot in a society that doesn't use money. Worse, as globalisation developed through the 20th century, the world became increasingly linked so that downturns in one part of the world are likely to lead to downturns elsewhere. A large organisation or a small farmer can find their survival determined by events in some remote part of the world which have nothing to do with how well they are doing their job or how well they are satisfying their customers. A major steelworks, said to be among the most efficient in Europe was closed because exchange rate fluctuations made it unprofitable.

We are now in a position where a global economic crash is not only possible but likely. It could make the 1930s depression look like a minor blip. It could be triggered by wars, by disruption and fears due to terrorism, or by environmental disruption. For example, global production of oil is expected to peak and then decline within the present decade. That will have a huge economic effect which is largely unappreciated. Climate change is creating extreme storms and flooding which could put insurance companies under impossible pressure. It may change agricultural patterns, and even lead to runaway global warming with catastrophic consequences.

In general the causes of economic instability and what limited cures might be possible are assessed in terms of the existing system. Should there be more government regulation or more deregulation? Might accounting procedures or changes to taxation improve stability? Could changes in the banking system help?[35] For example, writing about the 1990s Asian crisis and others, Chakravarthi Raghavan writes:[36]

> "The root of these crises can be traced to imprudent financial liberalization and the subsequent failure to adequately manage and control the resultant capital surges."

Never questioned is whether this chronic instability is actually inherent in the basic structure of the economy. The inherent instability comes from a combination of:

- the loss of natural controls in our upside-down economy, where the goals are the producer's need for money rather than the consumer's needs and the health of the environment

- a competitive economy in which everyone's goals are set against everyone else's.

The dynamics of an economic downturn usually reflects a separation and non-alignment of everyone's goals. For example, some event may cause fear and a loss of confidence among the public or businesses. They postpone planned purchases, since of course they are not part of an ongoing relationship with those they are buying from. Since less is purchased, companies postpone their purchase of supplies and may let go of staff – again, because the company goals are not the same as that of their suppliers and staff. This means that people have less to spend and more companies' income is reduced. And so the downward spiral feeds back upon itself and continues.

> **You** Of course, in planned economies, such as 20th century communism, there were no business cycles either.
>
> **Me** Exactly. That was a radically different economic system, and it shows again that business cycles are simply an artefact. However, centrally planned economies have other fundamental problems. Their information flows are even worse. How can a centrally produced five-year plan match the ever-changing needs and conditions of a population?

Even central bankers and finance ministers recognise the instability of the global financial system:

- "As we all know, the financial crises of recent years, first in Mexico in 1994, then in Asia in 1997, and in Russia and Brazil in 1998, have clearly demonstrated that there is inherent instability in today's liberalised market economy."[37]

- "Since 1980, over two-thirds of IMF member countries have experienced at least one serious banking-sector difficulty...And, as we all know, national financial crises have been transmitted to other countries, threatening not only the economic well-being of those countries but also the stability of the international financial system as a whole."[38]

Is the global cancer inevitable?

The picture painted so far in this chapter is pretty bleak. No-one could doubt the desirability of dramatically reducing the global cancer. So are these problems inevitable, inherent in the nature of things? If so, there would be no point in even thinking about eGaia.

Take two examples. In most countries people drive their cars on the right side of the road, but in quite a few they drive on the left. If you live in a place where people drive on one side, no individual can choose to do otherwise. It is a behaviour pattern that is strongly locked in. You risk killing yourself if you violate it. There are laws and police to ensure compliance. Vehicle design, road design and signs are all consistent with it. It is a complex pattern of behaviour that regenerates itself as new roads are built consistent with it, and new drivers are trained. Yet change is possible, given sufficient will and social co-ordination (basically, passing a law to enable and enforce the change). A few countries actually have changed.

On the other hand, if we decided to change the law of gravity, so that we could fly unaided at will, thus reducing fuel use, traffic congestion, etc no amount of will and social co-ordination would enable us to do so.

The question is whether the global cancer is more like the first or the second example. The answer is neither easy nor obvious, but this book is predicated on the assumption that it is the former.

You Sure, you just pass laws against wars and that's the end of them.

Me Very funny! Getting the will and the social co-ordination is not simple and is, of course, the key issue. We'll get to that. For now, it is simply the possibility I want to establish. The global cancer seems inevitable because there are so many interlocking factors that combine to regenerate it. But I believe it is an open question.

Simply in environmental terms, is sustainability possible, given current and future human population levels? And if physically and biologically possible, would it mean either continuing inequality with plenty for a few and poverty for most, or at best a life of great austerity for everyone?

Firstly, will the human population rise indefinitely, making any kind of adjustment to the Earth impossible? It doesn't seem so. World population is now about 6.1 billion and is still rising, but the rate of increase has peaked and population may stabilise towards the end of the 21st century.

- " the global annual increment -- that is, the number of people added to the world's population each year -- is thought to have peaked between 1985 and 1990 at about 87 million per year."[39]

There is even the possibility that world population overall may reach a maximum and then decline:

- "the United Nations Population Division's biennial compendium, World Population Prospects... will include a "low variant" projection that anticipates zero population growth for the world as a whole by the year 2040, and negative growth--that is to say, depopulation--thereafter."[40]

What about energy? Is our use of fossil fuels and nuclear power inevitable? Could renewable energy sources (wind, solar, water, wave energy, etc) produce all of humanity's requirements? Yes, certainly: the technologies are now very well established and are being used more and more. The amount of renewable energy available would be ample on current projections. But the total of humanity's requirements in the future depends upon how our societies are organised. All of humanity could live materially comfort-able lives with much lower overall energy use than at present. The principal obstacles to increased use of renewal energy are economic and social, not technical or physical. We are very fixed in our present social patterns.

Is hunger inevitable, given the size of the Earth's population? It doesn't seem so:

- "Food is not in short supply. In fact, food products have never been so abundant. There is enough available to provide each of the Earth's inhabitants with at least 2,700 calories a day. But production alone is not enough. ..."[41]

- "...some scientists calculate reassuringly that, with present-day technology put to work on all potentially arable lands, planet earth could feed fifteen, twenty or even forty billion inhabitants. But rarely does the real world intrude upon theoretical computations wearing such a gaunt face as it does in the case of food."[42]

Hunger is caused by the social patterns that exclude people from the food that is produced and from the land they need to grow their own, not by biological constraints. We certainly don't need another 'Green revolution' in food, using for example, genetically modified plants.

What about other aspects of serious poverty? Are they beyond the scale of what is possible to provide? Not at all.

- "The UN calculates that the whole of the world population's basic needs for food, drinking water, education and medical care could be covered by a levy of less than 4% on the accumulated wealth of the 225 largest fortunes. To satisfy all the world's sanitation and food requirements would cost only $13 billion, hardly as much as the people of the United States and the European Union spend each year on perfume."[43]

What is at issue is who gets what and who doesn't, not whether it is physically possible to eliminate poverty. The present system, with people locked into the pressures of financial flows, simply doesn't address the problems of serious poverty.

And then there is disease. There is a statement earlier in this chapter about the large number of illnesses and deaths that are a by-product of environmental degradation, particularly in poorer countries. Similarly, it is well known that the improvements of the health of populations in the more developed countries in the early 20th century were largely due to better hygiene and living conditions rather than advances in medical science. So again, here is a major problem rooted in social patterns, and certainly not inevitable.

What about wars, and especially the genocides and ethnic cleansings which so marred the 20th century? It is not that the Germans, Serbs, Rwandans, (and now the Israelis) have some gene that makes them particularly bloodthirsty or evil. Rather, when the conditions are right for it, groups of people get caught up in destructive ideas that become self-regenerating within that group, locked in place by powerful emotions. Often it is fears and insecurities arising from difficult economic conditions, which are then turned against some other group of people by demagogic leaders.

These large-scale ethnic conflicts can be seen as diseases of the human spirit. As with physical diseases, it is the underlying social patterns that create the susceptibility – not something innate and inevitable in human nature. The same arguments apply to all aspects of the global cancer. The conditions under which they are likely are widespread, and so they happen. There is no inevitability about them.

To the extent that societies are organised to do anything about it, the symptoms are usually tackled – often too late to do any good – rather than the conditions that give rise to them. The conditions come from the particular and largely accidental way human societies have developed. They are mostly taken for granted as, for example, our assumption that exchange must be through money.

If we have any hopes of living in a world without the global cancer, we need to be aware and organised to avoid those conditions, but also have strategies for catching them early should they arise. That is the purpose of eGaia.

eGaian principles

eGaia is the answer to the 'miracle question' described in the Preface when applied to the problems of the global cancer. It is an unashamedly Utopian vision of the future, designed to help clarify our problems and design sensible ways to resolve them. The miracle question goes something like this:

"Imagine yourself a modern day Rip Van Winkel who goes to sleep one day and doesn't wake up for two or three generations. While you are asleep a miracle occurs, and all the problems you see around you now are solved. What would life be like then? What does it mean to be a sustainable world and to be a peaceful world? What might you find when you woke up in several generations time after the miracle occurred? What would be different?"

The purpose of asking this is to help separate out the question of what we would like from that of how might we get there. Suspend negativity and cynicism at least until the book explores first steps and considers how far they could go.

You Yes, but in your own mind you surely believe that it will happen.

Me Not necessarily, but I do think it is a possibility. My concern is that if we don't at least look at the whole picture we will try solutions that don't actually address the problems they are meant to solve.

Three basic principles

This chapter suggests three overall principles, which follow directly from the analysis of the global cancer in the last chapter, and which characterise the world that our modern-day Rip Van Winkel awakes to.

1   *Peace* People have come to see all humanity as part of their extended family, accepting and appreciating the differences between cultures. They have added to their sense of identity a strong sense of being part of humanity and a concern for its overall well-being. Human activities are organised to take into account the needs of other groups and co-ordinate with them, rather than compete with them. To make this possible, the basic human communication skills of seeing from another's perspective, appreciating human differences, coming to agreement, and especially handling conflict would be seen as the most basic and fundamental parts of human culture. Thus handling competition and conflict has become a well-understood process. Conflict resolution would be as natural a social technology as growing food.

2   *Sustainability* Looking after the health of the natural world – the whole of the living Earth – has become a primary value for all of humanity. So human activities are organised with that in mind.

3   *The right goals* In the miracle scenario, the direct pursuit of peace, human well-being and sustainability have replaced our current goals of

pursuit of profit and financial survival (with human well-being as its supposed side-benefit). It transforms much of the economic and political structure of the world. The basic social organising principle is to be aware of the core goals and to act to correct errors, or deviations from them. What could be more simple or direct? In engineers' terms, it means society is organised as an error-correcting, feedback control system with its goals the well-being of the whole.

You So that's it? These three principles are all we need to create a Utopian world?

Me Only at the most abstract level. They may seem like platitudes when looked at in isolation, but I don't think it is obvious how they might all be satisfied at once. That, in practical terms, is what this book is all about.

You Well an error-correcting feedback control system certainly does sound rather abstract. What are you on about?

Me Here's a simple example. Imagine a farm in which the farmer's goals are to keep his land in a natural state of fertility, his livestock leading reasonably natural healthy lives, while doing his best to satisfy the food needs of the local population and to give himself and other farmworkers satisfying work. Imagine that farming is organised so that these goals become the farmer's motivation and not the needs of an industrial farming system or the prospect of a higher income.

The Earth becoming an organism

If humanity with its current huge population and dominance takes on this role of caring for the Earth-as-a-whole, the result is that it would come to have a coherence and a wholeness it has never had. In that respect it would become like a gigantic organism.[1]

Gaia is the name of the ancient Greek Earth goddess. Gaia theory has been popularised by James Lovelock and others as "a theory of the Earth as a living organism – where the evolution of the species and their material environment are tightly coupled but still evolve by natural selection"[2]. The Gaia theorists show how the effect of life as a whole on the physical Earth is to maintain the general conditions it needs to continue. Because of the presence of life, the Earth has become a loosely self-regulating system that keeps the composition of the atmosphere, the surface temperature, the presence of liquid water far from chemical equilibrium, as needed for life's survival. Similarly, a mammal or a bird keeps its internal temperature constant, regardless of the outside temperature.

However, to call the Earth an organism now is going too far. The Earth is now more properly thought of as an ecosystem. In an ecosystem like a forest or a seashore, the different creatures live together in a mixture of competition and mutual support or symbiosis for self-regulation. The work of the Gaia theorists shows the importance of mutual support even in an ecosystem, in contrast to popular views of nature which see competition as predominant. This idea is developed much further in Chapter 4.

The Earth now lacks the wholeness and coherence which characterise those things we currently call organisms. The coherence of an organism goes along with a greatly reduced role for competition between its parts and much more mutual support. When an itchy scalp results in a hand scratching it, that is a highly co-ordinated co-operative response by billions of cells. No ecosystem has that kind of co-ordination. However, a large-scale global effort to relieve a famine or earthquake damage in one country has something of the same character.

The point of the three fundamental eGaian changes above is to spread that kind of support and co-ordination to all aspects of human life, and beyond – to the natural world. Such a change would mark a major step in the evolution of life on Earth. Through its evolutionary history, the scale of the coherence of life has increased from that of the first microbes, to complex cells, to multi-cellular forms, to organisms like plants and animals. Extending that coherence to the whole planet, creating a planetary-scale organism, could be the next step in that progression. That is the full significance of the miracle.

Humanity as a global nervous system

This book suggests that the mechanism for the social process that changes the Earth into an organism is communication and information processing. The function of humanity within that organism would be analogous to a nervous system. An animal with a nervous system is an error-correcting feedback control system with the nervous system as its communication and information processing system. A nervous system is as much controlled by its body as vice versa. It is part of the body and responds to its needs. Thus when you scratch that itch, the nervous system first has to notice the discomfort and send signals about that to the brain (feedback). Comparing the signal (itching) to the desired state (no itching) shows there is an error. The nervous system then determines the action required and sends signals through the nerves in the arm and muscles to activate the movements needed (the error-correcting control).

Similarly, transforming the Earth into an organism involves humanity becoming integrated within it. Humanity responds to the needs of the Earth rather than trying to control it for its own purposes. For humanity to look after the health of the natural world, it has to monitor its state, work out where action is needed and act accordingly. For humanity to look after its own health, it has to monitor and understand that, going beyond the differences in perspective of different groups, and act accordingly.

This emphasis on communication and information processing is the reason for the e in eGaia. In this miraculous eGaian future, electronic communication will be the key technology that connects us to each other. A nervous system-like culture will need rich communication to form locally and globally self-organising and self-regulating social structures. Moreover, as described in the final part of this book, it is also the key to the kinds of practical first steps leading in that direction.

> **You** Surely you're not saying that the development of the Internet is leading us to a peaceful, harmonious future? As far as I can see, apart from the convenience of email, it is mostly another way of selling things, making the world still more commercial.
>
> **Me** In fact, the early development of the Internet was along co-

operative lines but I agree that since it has come to mass popularity it is becoming part of the commercial juggernaut as you say. However, as it links a substantial part of the world's population, it opens opportunities that weren't there just a few years ago. There are now opportunities for new groups of people to co-ordinate their activities with eGaian aims in mind, and for the use of information beyond the control of the mass media empires to highlight and counteract some of the damage we are now doing. It is human communication that will make the difference. Electronic media simply provide the infrastructure for that communication.

Underpinning the basic principles

The growing popularity of the Internet is just one of the changes that underpins an eGaian future. The three principles that opened this chapter all have echoes in recent history.

It is only during the past century – through films, radio and TV – that people have seen into each other's cultures on a mass scale. People everywhere now identify with the victims of famine and war anywhere. An eGaian culture would require us to move beyond the culture-bound blindnesses of our past. We are only now reaching the point where we can build a sense of identity as part of the global human species rather than as part of one culture competing with the rest.

In the past few decades we have been able to see the Earth from space, to give us a sense of the Earth as home to us all. Now the living Earth and the threats to it are becoming understood. At the same time as our population has burgeoned and our technology has increased its impact, our scientists have become able to monitor the damage we are doing. Global warming, holes in the ozone layer, loss of habitats and species, air and water pollution are now routinely taught in schools. Children are many of our most committed environmentalists.

During the last century we developed an understanding of feedback, stability, control and their use in self-regulating systems. These ideas inform our understanding of how organisms and ecosystems maintain their form and health. As we have developed machines that communicate, the theory of communication has grown with it. Studies of human psychology have teased out important principles of how we make sense of the world and how we form our sense of self. It is only through the conscious application of these ideas that we can replace our destructive expansion with a stable, self-regulating culture.

This powerful cocktail of ideas, together with the technical means of communication, gives us the opportunity to create self-aware, stable, self-organising social structures based upon co-operation and community. The image of eGaia can provide pointers in the direction of that future. It can generate guidelines for ways to behave, ways to live sustainably and in harmony with each other. This can provide the 'shoulds' and 'oughts' which science, as we know it now, cannot. These turn out to be the same at a deep level as some of the teachings of the ancient religions, but without the need to appeal to ancient authority.

The image of eGaia builds upon the earliest spiritual imagery of humanity: Gaia, the Mother Earth goddess. It can provide a sense of being part of a larger whole and also a sense of purpose. Many people share large parts of this vision. Huge numbers are seeking ways of living more sustainably. Many are looking for co-operative, community-based ways of living. The æther is thick with new forms of spirituality, many based on a regained harmony with nature.

CHAPTER three

A TASTE OF
AN eGAIAN FUTURE

This chapter moves beyond the abstraction of the previous one to give some idea of how an eGaian future might work in practice. What might life be like with humanity functioning as a global nervous system? As this is still an imagined answer to the miracle question, it must resort to fiction.

> **Yes** So now you are a Utopian novelist.
>
> **Me** Not even a short story writer I'm afraid, so apologies if my characters are two-dimensional. The story is there to bring alive the social principles. Nevertheless, it inevitably embodies my fantasies and tastes: as you read it, you may find that you like the social principles, but would prefer a different tale.

The point of the story is to show some possible mechanisms for implementing the three basic eGaian principles:

- peace – how could a community handle the conflicts and problems which arise between people while maintaining a sense of mutual concern and understanding?

- sustainability – how could a community organise itself in such a way as to take into account the needs of the natural world – but without leading an extremely basic, ascetic life?

- the right goals – how could a community use communications to organise itself economically in a way which is directly determined by the needs of the natural world and humanity, rather than indirectly through monetary exchange? Can co-operative structures provide the choice supposedly offered by competitive markets?

This tale is set some time in the future, after the miracle, in a world which has moved a lot of the way towards an eGaian society. It is a tale of a day in the life of some of the members of 'Pinecone Network' which is a group of perhaps several hundred people in a provincial town in some western country. It is one of many such networks in the town, all loosely linked to each other and to larger networks of different kinds.

Merry

Merry is a young girl, recently turned 12, who is just joining Pinecone Network in her own right. She has been using it through her parents' accounts since she was small, so she knows a lot of its members already. She has just completed a short introductory course and has been given her membership.

Merry accesses Pinecone Network through her computer and opens her new account. She starts by setting up the identity she wants the Network to know her by. She puts in an icon she has been working on in preparation for this, a nickname, and a short description of herself.

She opens her Account Book and finds that her parents have transferred all her favourite clothes and things from their accounts to hers. So now she has her own footprint (from Chapter 1: environmental footprint accounts for the area of land needed to support a person at a given level of technology). As she looks through each item she can see that it includes two ratings, one for its impact on the Earth, and one for the number of hours of human effort it took to create. Her footprint is the total of the footprints of all the things in her account.

Merry has grown up with the idea that a sensible person tries to get what they want while keeping their footprint at a reasonable level for their age. She looks at the public parts of the accounts of various other people in Pinecone Network that she knows, to see what their footprints are. They all seem quite different. Some are well above their age average and others are well below it.

Merry opens the contributions section of her account. It is completely empty. Is that fair, she thinks? All those chores she has done, all those errands she has run, all the help she has given to the old people at Water-melon House? Why shouldn't children's early contributions be there when they join, like in her friend's network up north. At least they will be in there from now on. She looks at the public parts of the accounts of various children who are already members. A lot of them seem to put in very few hours a week, but some put in so much time she isn't sure she believes it.

She looks at her cousin's account: Bertha has a public rating of 9. She's been doing things for almost a year for which she has asked for public ratings. Merry thinks about the sort of things she might do now and when she is older that might be rated. Perhaps she can join a group picking strawberries at Elderberry Farm. That might be a tasty beginning for a main skill as a biologist, which she has been thinking about.

41

You Let's see if I've got the points here. You have an economy where people have accounts for buying from the Network, but they use 'footprints' not money. Footprints include, somehow, the effect on the Earth and the number of hours it took to make the thing?

Me Yes, that's about right. Cost has those two main components – effect on the Earth and on other people, expressed directly, rather than (as now) hidden or ignored within monetary cost.

You And people also have contributions, in hours, which is what they do for the Network? But how is that connected to what they get? Is it sort of like having credit?

Me No, it's quite different from credit. Now you can't consume without having money or credit. Therefore, having money has become a goal in its own right. In Pinecone Network what a person gives to the community and gets from it are separate and reflect human variety. However, their totals are public. Serious or professional contributions are rated and so are subject to public opinion from within the community. That becomes the principal control over behaviour, not the possession or lack of money.

Albert

Albert is 49 and manages Apple Transport, a small firm that was once a car showroom and garage. He is still its legal owner, but for all practical purposes it is a co-operative 'owned' by the community it serves, including both its customers and its employees, who are intensely loyal to it. Apple Transport takes full responsibility for all aspects of its customers' vehicles. It gets them, services and updates them and disposes of them.

Apple Transport

This month's customer satisfaction rating 92%

We look after all vehicles, new and old.
Updating and renewing our speciality
Our vehicles all have very low ecological footprints

For a worry-free life, let us look after your group's vehicles.

Short-term and back-up vehicles always available

Links
Who's working this week?
Bookings for parts, service, up-dating
Vehicles available/wanted

Albert spends about three days each week working for Apple Transport, which is considered to be a lot. A couple of his employees share his managerial responsibilities and stand in for him when needed. Albert often spends another day or two working at other small jobs which interest him. He also helps out at the market garden/farm and at the town hospital.

He starts each day at his computer, looking at Apple Transport's sign-up sheets on Pinecone Network. First he checks that enough people have signed up to work for him over the next few days. He has a workforce of about 5-10 each week, most of whom work for him a few days each week. They are drawn from a much larger pool who work for him from time to time. He always has enough in reserve to cover absences or peak workloads.

The workforce is variable but well organised and reliable. Many of them work at more than one transport vehicle co-operative locally.

He notices that Conan will be in this week. That is probably because one of Conan's best friends has also returned. Albert has noticed that his workforce has settled down recently into two overlapping groups, each containing a few people who don't get along with one or two in the other group.

Albert then checks the customer lists. For urgent jobs, Albert can always fit people in. He may sometimes have to call in extra people or consult with the customer's regular repairer, but his workforce has the needed flexibility. He often sends someone out for minor breakdowns.

There is a rating system on-line which most of the customers use after every visit. Albert prides himself that his garage and his employees almost always receive very high ratings. That is the basis of his very strong customer loyalty. He and his staff carefully check out each case of a low rating to see what they can learn from it. Can they improve their working practices? Does someone need more training? Was it a misunderstanding and if so, how can they avoid that in future?

Francoise has booked in for a service next week. She is a new customer who has changed to Apple Transport from another firm. He must find out why she has changed. Were there problems between her and someone at her old firm?

Albert sees that he could do with two more workers for Friday because a lot of customers have booked in. He sends a group email to all his regulars pointing this out. If this doesn't do the trick within the next day or so, he will make a few phone calls and sort it out. And then next Monday almost no-one has booked in. So he emails two of the staff due to work then and tells them not to come in. He hopes they will be happy to have the day off.

He looks through the messages in the Regional Transport Network, which links all the firms like his as well as the researchers in the university and other related trade networks. As a senior person in his industry locally, he has also qualified as an inspector, and he signs up to inspect two firms in the area. He also puts Apple Transport down for inspection. With the inspections, customer ratings, and research information he gets, his firm is kept on its toes and is far more up-to-date and efficient than it ever was in the old days of competition.

And now the day starts properly with the first customers, all of whom he knows, mostly for several years. He chats with them, discussing whether any of their vehicles need updating or modifying. It is relatively unusual now for people to have entirely new vehicles. There has been a fashion recently for changing the body shells of the smaller cars, made of tough, lightweight but re-cycleable plastics. They can be made in some wild custom colours and designs to order. Albert can search on the network for suitable vehicles, and modify them as needed.

He has a group of customers who enjoy having older vehicles, and with his help, can usually keep them going indefinitely. All his vehicles use fuel very efficiently, and with all the recycling of parts and the sharing of vehicles, they add very little to each customer's footprint.

It is quite a light day for Apple Transport. There are only two mechanics around, so Albert helps them out. He has farmed out a couple of jobs to another firm that had a few cancellations.

> **You** The main thing that strikes me is flexibility. People seem to work when it suits them.
>
> **Me** Yes, it's important that people are motivated to work because they like the work and because of the respect it gives them. That flexibility is made much easier by the on-line sign-up

sheets. The workload can be adjusted either up or down to follow demand. Albert has neither need nor desire to try to influence demand. The relationship with customers is important, also the use of on-line feedback to support it. Socially, it has some of the qualities of an extended family. Quality is maintained by feedback and peer inspection, not fear of loss of customers. That makes it function as an error-correcting control system

Elvis

Elvis is the manager of Elderberry Farm. Now 60, he has been a farmer all of his life. He often reflects on the complete transformation of farming within his lifetime. The word farm doesn't really do it justice anymore. In a way it is a modern high-tech version of what medieval estates used to provide.

Elderberry Farm is one of the principal sources of food for Pinecone Network and other local networks. But it does much more. Its woodlands provide fuel for the community and wood for furniture and building materials. The wood is also used as the raw material for the chemicals which Pinecone Plastics needs, replacing the oil an earlier generation would have used. The farm is a re-cycling centre for organic wastes which are converted to fertilisers and which also produce gas and alcohol as fuels. Up on Pinecone Ridge is a row of large wind turbines producing electricity. Elderberry Farm is a major supplier of fuel and electricity to homes, factories and workshops in the area. The result of all this is that Elderberry Farm helps the people of Pinecone Network keep their ecological footprint very low.

The farming methods have changed radically too. The woodlands have been extended to include fruit, nuts, berries and many other perennial edible plants. They are the home to deer, pigs, and various other animals that live wild and are culled for food by the farm. Organic agro-forestry has become the norm, with even the remaining fields looking more like mixed grassland than earlier single crop farming. The farm now requires a lot more labour than it did in the 20th century. However, this has not proved to be a problem, as Elvis supplements his small core of skilled staff with large numbers of casual workers.

The farm has been planted with an eye to aesthetics as well as food efficiency. It is now considered very beautiful and is a popular place for Pinecone people, who come to work there, just hang out, or participate in various events.

Elvis used to enjoy pop festivals and camps in his youth. He has turned Elderberry Farm into a place where people come to work during the day and to be entertained and party in the evenings. He regularly books entertainment and theatre workshops, catering for different interests on different dates. In between, people come and entertain themselves. Elderberry Farm has become as popular with performers as with its farm labourers. Then often wander amongst the labourers, with songs and street theatre.

He gets on his computer to check on the bookings for the next week. He sees that Bertha and her friends have booked again. Mostly, people book in groups of friends who camp together. He sees that Delilah, the dance teacher, is running a workshop and guesses that was one of the main attractions for Bertha and friends. He looks at the list of tasks coming up and selects a few he thinks would appeal to Bertha's gang. There is a tremendous variety due to the rich nature of the farm.

47

Elvis would not be able to manage without the help of the farm management software that has been developed for the new type of farm. It helps him keep track of what is becoming ripe and where so he can arrange for it to be picked, and can prepare notices for the community and the supermarket. It monitors the state of the energy sources on the farm, so he can advise all his customers. His skill, as a good modern farm manager, is to keep the farm as near as he can to a natural ecosystem while intervening just enough to make most of its produce of value to people.

48

> **You** This farm is an environmentalist's dream. It's organic, feeds local people, looks good, supplies energy. I'm not sure quite what is the point of turning it into a festival, though.
>
> **Me** Well, it's absolutely in line with the principle of fitting in with the health of the natural world. The point of the festival atmosphere is to create motivation to work. Farm labour is made attractive by spreading it widely among the people the farm feeds and making the work fun. Isn't that better than forcing it upon the poor? It's a different kind of relationship than you usually get between a farm, its customers and workers. That way the issue of competition with other farms nearby or across the world doesn't arise.

Henrietta

Henrietta is 76 and lives in Watermelon House, a large co-operative hostel owned by Pinecone Network. It caters largely for single people and couples without children. It was converted into a hostel from a redundant hospital. It has sections that are adapted to the needs of the elderly and those with disabilities.

Henrietta is partially disabled, as a result of a stroke a few years ago, but her mind is sharp. She likes making an active contribution to the community. Pinecone Network has opened opportunities for this in ways that would have been impossible for older and disabled people in earlier times. She likes living in a mixed community with people of all ages. She often works in the kitchen in Watermelon House, as she has always loved cooking. Often when there is cooked food left over, she puts it in small containers, freezes it and sends it to the supermarket.

Henrietta spends much of her time organising the Transport Users Co-op. It functions as a self-organising taxi and delivery service for Pinecone Network. It is heavily used by children and people with limited mobility, saving huge effort for parents and carers. They like and trust it because they generally know the drivers. Henrietta and the drivers take their user ratings very seriously and try to learn from any low ones.

Organising the Co-op is relatively easy for Henrietta because of its on-line software. Henrietta has become quite good at using it, but she does need regular help from Delilah, who is her personal computer consultant. She is very excited about getting a new computer to run the new version of the software. Some of its parts will be taken from her old one, and the whole machine won't add much to her ecological footprint. She has asked for a bright pink case that she thinks will go with her curtains.

Much of the signing up for shifts, rides and deliveries is done directly by people on line. However, there are still plenty of people who don't want to do that. Mostly they telephone Henrietta. The co-op owns a small fleet of cars, mini-buses and vans, which are supplied and cared for by Apple Transport.

Today she will be getting a visit from Delilah's son, who she often looks after. He helps her clean her room, and enjoys the stories she tells him about the bad old days before Pinecone Network. She tells him about her

49

own mother, and how difficult things were when she was old and infirm. In those days, old people had to rely on help from the government, from strangers. Now the community looked after its own. Henrietta had been a political activist, and remembers how difficult it was to get anything changed. It is so much better with these new networks: everything is done on a personal basis.

> **You** Interesting...this is a clear mixture of the environmental and the social. You've got a responsive, friendly, semi-public transport system which must save a lot of fuel. If it worked well, some people wouldn't want their own cars.
>
> **Me** Yes, there is concern for the Earth and a co-operative social structure. And the way the Transport Co-op is organised illustrates the error-correcting feedback system working to the right goals.

Francoise

Francoise is 33 and lives with her partner, Gerry and their two children. Both Francoise and Gerry lead busier lives than are fashionable these days. This puts pressure on their family lives in a way that would be more familiar in the early 21st century. Fortunately, the community support provided by Pinecone Network removes much of the problem.

Their older son, who is 12, often spends afternoons at Watermelon House, where he has several adopted grandparents among the elderly residents, including Henrietta. He runs errands and does odd jobs for them. They help look after him, teach him and feed him. Both children have busy social lives. Francoise frequently uses her computer to arrange for them to be taken and collected by the Transport Users Co-op organised by

Henrietta. But more often they walk or cycle. These days traffic is so much lighter and there is so much less street crime that Francoise thinks that is quite safe.

Francoise and Gerry both devote much time to sports. Francoise co-ordinates sporting events using the latest Community Sports Planning software. Everyone can access it through the network. Through it she can identify groups who are interested in different sports at various levels. She uses it to match interests with venues and coaching. Software used in this way, to match supply and demand for all sorts of purposes – for goods, services, events, facilities – has become the foundation of social organisation.

Francoise usually works for several days each week in the Pinecone Plastics factory. It is still legally a part of an old-style multi-national and has close links with their other factories and research labs. At the same time, it has become a co-operative, integrated within Pinecone Network. It has recently been upgraded with the most modern automated equipment and serves a wide range of needs for Pinecone people.

The factory is a large modern building – like many others, roofed with solar panels. Some panels are photovoltaic and produce electricity; others are thermal to heat water. Most of its additional needs for fuel and electricity are supplied by Elderberry Farm. It tends to adjust its workload seasonally, increasing its output when the wind or the solar energy are greater, and reducing output when they are lower.

Most of the raw materials needed by Pinecone Plastics come from recycled plastic from components it has made in the past. Most of its output is designed for this. Additional raw materials are made by chemically digesting wood and other vegetable matter from Elderberry Farm, but some comes from farther afield. All of this helps keep the

---

Pinecone Plastics

This month's customer satisfaction rating 85%

Spare and replacement parts for almost anything

Custom colours and designs our speciality

Our advanced, automated equipment
means *fast* service

Links

Standard items: household items, knobs, connectors, you name
it, we have it

Custom design: large library of designs, easy to use design
software

---

ecological footprint of its products very low. One of Francoise's regular tasks is to find sources for specialised materials from collaborating factories and farms in the region.

Today she is working on some new car body panels that Albert's Apple Transport has ordered. She doesn't have the design for that model in her library, so sends a message to the other plastics factories in the region asking for help. In her inbox there is a short article from the regional research labs describing an easier way to clean out used moulds. That will save her and all the other plastics factories hours. In the old days, one firm would use information like that to gain competitive advantage over the others.

She finds a request for dustbins from a factory in the next county, (its machine has broken down) and offers to produce them. Also, she finds an order for a bright pink case for Henrietta's new computer.

You Another environmentalist's dream! It uses renewable energy and local raw materials.

Me Yes, and re-use and re-cycling means it provides its customers with a good material living standard at low environmental cost. Also, notice that it responds to the requests from its customers. It doesn't need to go out looking for customers. Its workload varies with the seasons, with the weather, with demand. That, plus the rating system, is what makes it a control system responding directly to needs and its environment. The communication networks are what make it practical.

53

Gerry

Gerry is one of those energetic people who can't stop doing things. He spends several days working in the supermarket, but then invariably signs up for several shifts around the community. He often drives the minibuses and vans for Henrietta's Travel Co-op, he and his rugby mates take shifts together working on the roads and parks (always a good laugh), and he occasionally shows off his newly developed cooking skills in the hospital kitchen. And on top of that are his sports.

To help at mealtimes, Gerry often brings back frozen meals from the supermarket. These are not the old-fashioned, highly processed kind but are usually locally made by enthusiastic cooks in Pinecone Network.

The supermarket work provides him with his major challenges. It is very different from the supermarkets of old. Although it is still legally part of one of the big three from the early 21st century, in practice it is more like

---

Pinecone Supermarket

Customer satisfaction rating 96%

Everything you need under one roof and garden.
The best of local food, goods, crafts …
If we don't have it, we'll find it for you.

Links
Regular orders for collection or delivery
This week's special items

---

a medieval marketplace, serving its local community. It is a distribution place for most of what is produced by Pinecone Plastics, Elderberry Farm and other local organisations: food, clothing, goods, everything. Most are locally produced, but a significant proportion are not, and may come from anywhere in the world. It has strong links with distributors and other supermarkets.

Parts of the supermarket and its garden are full of small stalls from local workshops and other enterprises. This includes furniture, craft items, refurbished and re-designed clothing, renewed appliances. Anything that can be repaired, recycled or improved passes through it. It is also a main collection place for re-cycling. The food is mostly fresh, organic and local, but there are plenty of cooked meals, made by those Pinecone people who love cooking. The result is that it helps the people of Pinecone Network live well while keeping their ecological footprint low. As markets have always been, it is an important meeting place. It has been beautifully decorated, with sculptures and other artwork. There is always entertainment of some sort, and lots of stalls.

The challenge for Gerry is to provide the best match he can of supply and demand. Through the on-line networks he keeps careful track of what people want and what is available. He often puts out polls and questionnaires asking about what people want in the future. People routinely rate what they have received so he has feedback on quality and satisfaction.

The bulk of what the supermarket provides is routine and in plentiful supply. That includes the basic food staples, household goods and appliances. Much of this is ordered through people's computers. They either collect it in person or the supermarket delivers it, helped by the Transport Users Co-op. When people order something the supermarket doesn't usually carry, Gerry searches through the trade networks to find it. For luxury items, he and the other markets have developed a number of strategies. That batch of a special new ice cream flavour was offered on a first-come, first-served basis. Jewellery, art and other rare items sometimes circulate, with people holding onto them for a few months, or even just for a special occasion. Sometimes there are prize draws for special items.

You OK, so most things are local. That reduces transport which is good for the environment. But why do you need prize draws? Don't people simply buy what they want? In fact, you haven't said anything about prices, salaries or anything about how money is organised.

Me Being local, it isn't much affected by economic conditions across the county, much less across the world. I haven't said anything about money because I am assuming that money isn't used. Gerry tries to match supply and demand as best he can. He doesn't need to influence demand to improve his cash flow. Within Pinecone Network people make their contributions and receive what is on offer. Their total contributions are public knowledge as is their total footprint – so giving and receiving are subject to social approval, but are not linked on an item by item basis. Work is motivated by people enjoying it, by the prestige and approval they get for doing it, and because it is needed. Everything that we use money for is done through information: real costs (footprint), finding out what people want, organising who will do what work, knowing what is available, all made convenient by the on-line networks. People do what they want and get what they want. Unpleasant work isn't forced upon the poor, and scarce goods aren't rationed to the rich.

Conan

Conan is 25. He lives with his girlfriend, Delilah, in Watermelon House. Conan and Delilah eat most of their meals in the hostel's large dining room, which caters not only for residents, but also often for their guests or visitors to the community. The dining room walls are an ever-changing art gallery. It is also frequently used for musical and community events. It is a social focus for its residents.

Conan is more interested in doing things with his hands than with his computer, in contrast to many of his contemporaries. He likes working with machines and tools. He sees himself as a craftsman and an artist. His work is mostly around the hostel, but he is also a regular worker at Apple Transport. He loves the challenge of taking old cars that no-one wants anymore and updating, repairing and customising them so they will once again be someone's pride and joy.

He starts his day by checking his shifts at Apple Garage, and signs up for the date when his mate Sasha is on. Conan then looks through the list of jobs people have asked for in the hostel. There is that tricky plumbing job with the awkwardly sized pipe. He fills in an order form to have it custom made at Pinecone Plastics factory. A few seconds later a receipt comes back saying it has been booked and will be ready in two days. He then selects two jobs to get on with for the morning, but decides he will spend the afternoon working on his new mural for the dining room.

Conan is troubled by quite dramatic mood swings. Sometimes his temper is easily triggered, and he has a history of violence both to people and to things. People are aware of his difficulties and help him to handle them, partly by helping him avoid situations in which his anger will be triggered. There have been times when his mood has become so dark that he has been put into a secure community for the duration. When he has injured someone, he has been helped to understand fully what he has done, has had to make peace with the victim, and do something agreed to attempt to make up for the injury.

You You have some communal living for those not in families, which makes environmental sense. But the interesting thing is that we now have a villain. Not everyone here is perfect.

Me Conan is not a villain. He is more difficult than most but he lives in a community which has learned to handle him with sympathy and in a way which repairs the emotional and physical damage as best it can. In our world he would probably have been put into a prison which would have turned him into a bitter but well-trained criminal.

You This strategy must rely upon there being relatively few such people around.

Me Yes it does. They aren't grown and hardened as they are today.

Conan didn't grow up with peers who respected and glorified his violence. He always had opportunities to make positive contributions to his community that gave him approval and respect. That is what made his problems manageable. This is an example of society as an error-correcting control system in the social realm. The understanding that is shown to him and that he had to show to his victims is an example of using communication to solve social problems.

Delilah

Delilah has lived in Watermelon House with Conan for several years. She loves his playfulness and his practical talents. She has had special training to help him handle his darker moods. Like many young people nowadays, she splits her time between various passionate interests. For her, it is dancing and computers. Delilah has had dance training since she was a child. She is very popular in the region, getting bookings for solo performances and as a choreographer running classes and workshops. She gets consistently high ratings. With the current revival of the arts, the opportunities are much greater than in earlier generations.

She sits down for a short session at her computer. A video clip of her last performance has arrived by email. She edits it, adds some graphics, and puts it in her web site CV. Most of her bookings are by word of mouth and reputation, but the web site has got her occasional parts in distant shows. She agrees to a request to run a dance workshop on Elderberry farm soon.

Delilah loves her computer work because it challenges her in so many ways. She has a computer consultancy with a large group of regular clients. She gets them their computers, maintains and upgrades them, and recycles them when needed. She gets them new software when they need it and teaches them how to use it. Mostly though, she helps her clients when they get stuck. That can tax her social skills hugely. She enjoys visiting them, and several have become good friends. She has learned to tease out exactly where they have misunderstood and then puts them right in a way which doesn't makes them feel stupid. She is constantly amazed that after all these years when computers have become a vital part of the culture people still have such difficulty with them. And that despite the fact that they have become so much more reliable and simple to use since the industry became non-competitive.

59

Today Delilah will spend some time at the Pinecone Communications Workshop, where most of Pinecone Networks computers and other communications devices are assembled and recycled. They are assembled to customer order from standard parts made elsewhere. However, the cases are made locally at Pinecone Plastics in colours and designs reflecting local fashions. With all the recycling and re-use, they have a very low ecological footprint. Delilah has to put together a new computer for Henrietta. She collects a few designs for cases that she thinks Henrietta will like and emails them to her.

Before going to the Workshop, Delilah spends some time on-line catching up with local software developments. She notes with satisfaction that some programming she did last week to make the Accommodation Booking software easier to use has been accepted. Within a few weeks it is likely that most accommodation co-ops will be using it. That will enhance her reputation.

> **You** I'm not really sure if there is anything major that is new here. What is all this about her dancing?
>
> **Me** This story reinforces the the close relationship between client

and provider, through customised production and personal service. People dealing with areas they don't easily understand do it through a personal agent. It also demonstrates the flexibility of people's lives. They are free to express their creativity if they want to. This is good for artists of all sorts. Artistic creativity has taken over from conspicuous consumption. One of the signs of a happy culture is living in a beautiful environment, both in its natural and man-made aspects.

Bertha

Bertha is 17 and lives with her family. This morning she looks on the network for confirmation of her booking for the coming weekend at Elderberry Farm. She and her friends go there often to work on the farm while enjoying the music and dance that is laid on for them in the evenings. She loved the last dance workshop she did there with Delilah and knows there will be another one this weekend.

Pinecone Network has been a major support for her education, especially in her teenage years. Much of her education has been based around project work, some developed herself. Other projects are devised and set up by her teachers. Many have been collaborative projects, usually including some of her friends, but often with young people in other parts of the country or the world. Through the network she can find other young people to work with her, share information, co-ordinate work, and do background research.

Bertha looks on the network for replies to her application for a trip to an Eastern European country where there are still vestiges of ethnic conflict. This is part of her training in cultural conflict resolution, which she hopes will become one of her main career areas.

From early childhood Bertha (along with all the other children) has been taught the communication skills which people have learned to see as the foundation of social education. Through games and little plays they have learned how to listen, how to put yourself in another's shoes, how to check that you have been understood or understand another. Her current ambitions build on that basic education.

On her trip she will be a trainee in a large team made up of locals and people from around the world. They were assembled in response to reports of the growing popularity of some demagogues who were stirring up hatred of an ethnic minority. The team has several main strategies. They look at the discontents among the people who are receptive to the demagogues. They acknowledge those discontents and help seek resolution for them. They also use a combination of media events and local community activities to help both groups in conflict to see the others as full people rather than as shadowy hate figures. They create opportunities for both communities to meet and work together socially. The leaders of this team are highly trained and experienced. They know how important it is to get into an area where trouble is brewing early enough, and with enough support and resources from outside. Then they can usually defuse the conflict before the hatred becomes too great on both sides. Bertha hopes she might eventually become that kind of team leader.

Bertha has planned to travel slowly, visiting various places on the way. Through the Accommodation Co-op in Pinecone Network she has found the names of people in all the places she plans to visit. They are all friends of people in Pinecone Network who offer temporary room and board to friends of friends, as do many people in Pinecone Network. Several have replied offering her rooms. Similarly, she finds messages from the Ridesharing Co-op offering her lifts for about half of the journeys she will need to make. For the remainder, she books seats on-line for the buses and trains she will be taking.

> **You** A new tack. You seem to think childhood education about communication is crucial and that really big social problems can be headed off if they are caught early. You must be assuming that the local government and society around the troubled area allow the team in and support it. That wouldn't happen today.

> **Me** The answer to the miracle question leaps across the question of how we get there and looks for what we would like. This future society is geared up to resolve conflicts, which it accepts as arising regularly. It uses communication to acknowledge people's concerns and promote mutual understanding, rather than imposing solutions by force. Teaching communications skills is crucial so that people simply don't get caught up in conflicts and difficult relationships as easily as they do today. I cannot over-emphasize this.

Joline

Joline is a single woman aged 50 with two grown children. She has had long-term relationships, but is not in one now (although she has some possibilities). Her great passions are music and dance. She plays the flute, and frequently is seen wandering the fields and woodlands at Elderberry Farm entertaining the farm workers.

Joline is known throughout the area for her skills as a counsellor and mediator. She works with individuals, couples, families and work groups.

Joline J – counsellor, mediator, arbitrator

Difficult relationships?
Problems with your children?
Conflict at work? Depression?

*Would you like help to clarify your goals,
purposes and life path?*

Very discrete service.
Very experienced and well-trained

Link
On-line self-help groups
Sign up for relationship training
Frequently asked questions on relationships and conflict
Advice on personal growth and development

She has a reputation as the person to call when conflicts begin to appear in a workplace. With her help, a solution can usually be found before the conflict gets too serious. She also runs a lot of training courses, to help spread basic skills of communications and well-functioning relationships more widely through the population.

She has seen the Network grow in influence through her lifetime. She reflects on the parallel growth of communications skills in the community. They are now the foundation of every child's education. Without these skills, she doubts whether the new co-operative structures could ever have reached their present state of development.

She sometimes works with people she knows well, but most often it is by referral from people she knows. That way she retains the personal connection and also some detachment. Lately she has had to deal with several cases of people who had a lot of violence in their families when they were children. These are much rarer than when she first started this type of work. Now it is often dealt with early, and treatment given to both victim and violent parent. This has helped to break the cycle in which most violent parents had themselves been victims of violence as children, and so the pattern continued through the generations.

Another of Joline's interests is helping to facilitate community-wide decision-making in Pinecone Network. Most decision-making is the

WOULD YOU LIKE
COUNSELLING?
OR LEGAL
ADVICE?

64

business of the co-ops and other organisations, but issues like land use require the agreement of everyone. There was a proposal to expand the gardens of Watermelon House into what had been a small park. Such decisions are normally made by consensus, rather than majority vote, so that majorities cannot impose their will upon minorities.

Joline's skill is in helping groups with different views to understand each other's point of view, and then in finding solutions that are acceptable to everyone. The respect in which she is held means people are usually willing to accept her solutions. It sometimes amuses her to think that she is the modern equivalent of a politician. Yet in many ways she is the opposite of old-time politicians, who used to make a point of disagreeing with their rivals.

Much of this decision-making work is done on-line through discussions and repeated polls until a consensus emerges. Joline does very little of her counselling work on-line, but she does use her website to help her keep organised. It is useful to provide long-term support to former clients. And there are a few people who like the complete discretion of anonymous, on-line counselling.

Most of Joline's use of her computer is for organising her social life, getting routine food orders and maintaining her home and possessions. But its most special use is to keep in touch with her children. She loves the emails, photos and videos she gets from them both, and exchanges clips of music with both of them.

> **You** This is meant to show more of how the community solves its social problems.
>
> **Me** Yes, it is about the second fundamental quality, people as an extended family. This requires continuous attention and skill. Just as our society now has well-understood skills of building

roads and repairing them when needed, an eGaian society would need well-understood skills of building and maintaining relationships that work between groups and individuals. That's why I've again emphasized communications skills in schools. This is at least as important as concern for the natural world. It underpins the kind of collaborative society needed to solve our environmental problems.

Keith

Keith is pushing 60, with grown children and no partner – but a definite interest in Joline. For most of his earlier life he was a full-time academic, working at the local university as an environmental scientist. Now his life is much more varied. He enjoys being able to spend time on more physical pursuits, which keeps him feeling alive and healthy. He often spends time at Elderberry Farm, especially when they have jazz performances or when he knows that Joline will be there.

Some of Keith's work at Elderberry Farm is physical labouring, for the fun of it and to keep him healthy, but he also works as a scientific adviser. He regularly comes in to talk to the core staff to discuss the overall health of the farm and how well it is meeting the needs of its customers. Do any species need to be culled or protected? Do they need to introduce new predators to limit something? While mostly the farm grows quite naturally, the staff frequently make minor interventions to steer it in directions they think are needed. One of Keith's main contributions to Elderberry Farm is to keep in touch through the networks with the scientific community that specialises in agro-forestry farms of that sort. He gets advice when they have problems and learns of new approaches.

Keith is very content these days, enjoying his life. (And it might get better still if things work out with Joline.) As an environmental activist for most of his life, he has been involved in the major transitions of the last few decades. As a young man he was sure that humanity was on track to destroy the planet. Now, human impact on the Earth is very much less, with less transport, local production, more recycling, less pollution, renewable energy sources. Much effort has gone into restoring and rebuilding wilderness areas and sea habitats.

He has seen the major changes in people's attitudes towards consumption. Nowadays, when people consume anything, the effect on their ecological footprint is automatically calculated. It has become a matter of pride to live well while keeping your ecological footprint low.

But far more important for people's everyday lives have been the social changes. The community focus and the communications skills have reduced crime, alienation and have improved family life. Economic uncertainty is rarely a problem and most people do work they enjoy. Perhaps most important of all is the sense of connection to each other and to the Earth. The idea that people make up the nervous system of the Living Earth has taken on an almost religious character, adding to the love and joy in all the Earth's peoples.

> **You** Isn't that last bit a little over the top?
>
> **Me** Sure, this is an over the top story. It's the answer to the miracle question. Do you want to settle for less in your hopes and dreams? This is a picture of a joyous future, not a let's-be-miserable-to-save-the-Earth future. I've tried to show how interconnected the environmental and social aspects are, and that solutions to the environmental problems come out of major social changes. Faced with the need for major changes

because of the global cancer, surely there is no point in going for some partial solution which still leaves the world full of misery? The answer to the miracle question is the change from humanity as a global cancer to humanity as a global nervous system.

PART two

THE
FIVE
BILLION
YEAR
STORY

CHAPTER four

SYMBIOSIS AND COMPETITION:
THE STORY OF LIFE ON EARTH

"We are symbionts on a symbiotic planet, and if we care to, we can find symbiosis everywhere." *Lynn Margulies*[1]

All animals (including people) continually re-form ourselves from the food we eat (which comes from other animals and plants) plus water and oxygen from the air. The plants re-form themselves from water, air and trace minerals from the soil. We complex living forms are composed of organs and tissues, which in turn are composed of cells, in turn of molecules, in turn atoms, and so on. Each level of organisation can form and re-form itself only when the conditions are right for it. Each organ has its symbiotic place in the organism, each species has its niche in the web of life. It is all one great co-operative dance. The Hindus call it the dance of Shiva. In the Middle Ages in Europe it was seen as the harmony of life. The story of life and its evolution is a mixture of symbiosis – living together – and competition.

The Whirlpool metaphor

Picture a swirl of water, perhaps in a river near an outcrop of rock. The form of the whirlpool is clear, as it dances about, changing slightly about a general shape. Take a snapshot of the whirlpool and you will see the drops of water which make it up at that instant. Perhaps a small twig or leaf will mark some drops. Another snapshot, a few seconds later, will show a similar form, some of the same drops of water but in different places, and many new drops of water. The drops become part of the whirlpool and then leave it. Through its lifetime, the whirlpool is continually re-formed from the water of the river..

This image of a form that appears constant but is actually continually re-forming from the forces in which it is embedded will be very useful to us. It applies to organisms, to ecosystems, to organisations and also to ideas and belief systems, both constructive and destructive, and thus to social and individual behaviour patterns.

With the rise of the competitive market economy and later the Darwinian theory of evolution, the competitive side of the story of life came to be emphasised out of all proportion to its contribution. Our image of nature is 'red in tooth and claw' with only the fittest surviving at the expense of the others. This image is consistent with our view of the economy. Companies compete to survive, with the weak going out of business. Similarly, in politics, parties compete in a parliamentary democracy. The strongest, the majority parties, get to impose their views on the minority.

This consistency across our views of nature, economics and politics adds to a sense that it is all for the best and inevitable. Of course we should have a competitive economy and a competitive political system. That is the most natural way, the way of nature.

But this belief is one of the keys to humanity's global cancer. It is part of the pattern by which the global cancer regenerates itself. To show that the global cancer is not actually a law of nature requires a different view of nature. The prospect of a genuinely co-operative economy, based upon symbiosis and niche-filling is not on many people's agenda. Neither is a politics where differences are respected and a consensus sought which best satisfies those different views. But these are consistent with the view of nature that is described in this chapter. The story of life is about the interplay of symbiosis and competition. Competition does have a role to play, but it is only part of the story. In a multi-cellular organism, competition between the cells is actively suppressed in favour of symbiosis. In a co-operative society, competition between ideas remains very important, but not the kinds of competition which today lead to poverty and the suppression of minorities.

In order to build a co-operative society we will need new metaphors for what is natural. This chapter builds on the metaphors of recycling and of co-ordination of parts in an organism. A second important message that will come out of this evolutionary story is the warning lesson from the major extinctions of the past – several in the past few billion years: each time a large percentage of the Earth's living creatures died and many species went extinct. These were associated with changes in climate, very much of the sort which humanity is now triggering as one of the side effects of the global cancer.

Before life: the Hadean age

The Earth formed out of a spinning cloud of dust about 5 billion years ago. Most of that dust settled at the centre of the cloud and formed the Sun. The material of the Sun – mostly hydrogen – contracted and became hotter until the Sun ignited in a thermonuclear reaction that continues today. The remainder of the cloud (only a fraction of a per cent of the total), dispersed over hundreds of millions of miles, settled into a disk, and then into clumps. The largest of these clumps formed the nine major planets – Mercury, Venus, Earth, Mars, Jupiter, Saturn, Uranus, Neptune, and Pluto, spinning around the Sun in elliptical orbits.

The Sun is far too hot for anything solid to form. The planets are too small to burn like the Sun. For the complex molecules that make up life to form, the right materials had to be present, under the right conditions. The outer planets were always far too cold. The innermost planets – Mercury and Venus – were probably always too hot. Earth and Mars were the only two which ever came close.

The five billion year story

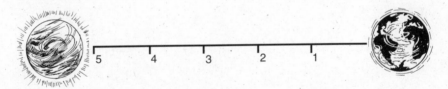

Billion years ago...

The conditions on the early Earth were totally unlike the present. Much of the surface was volcanic and the surface was too hot to allow any oceans. Any rain that hit the surface boiled away immediately. The atmosphere was largely carbon dioxide, like Mars and Venus today. Oxygen, so vital to life

The Hadean age[2]

now, wasn't there. The present conditions on Earth co-evolved with life over the billions of years since. Life has not been a passive passenger on Earth, but has been a major shaper and maintainer of the conditions it needed.

This period[3] before life is called the Hadean Age and fits well with the classical images of Hell. Eventually, the Earth cooled until its surface temperature dropped below the boiling point of water. The rains fell for millions of years and the seas were formed. The earliest sedimentary rocks date from this time.

The first part of the Five Billion Year Story was the Hadean age

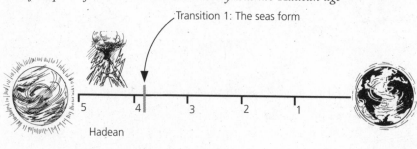

Transition 1: The seas form

5   4   3   2   1

Hadean

Billion years ago.....

First life: the Archaen age

When the seas had formed and the Earth was cool enough, conditions soon became suitable for the formation of the earliest forms of life. And life did form almost as soon as it became possible – within a few hundred million years.

> **You** You call a few hundred million years soon?
>
> **Me** On these time scales, yes.

Those early seas are what we call the primordial soup. The seas and the atmosphere contained molecules that were simple combinations of hydrogen, oxygen, nitrogen and sulphur that later came to make up most of the components of life. Local micro-environments formed where conditions were more stable and in which larger molecules could form. Simpler molecules were continually forming more complex molecules and breaking up again to form simpler molecules, their links forged and destroyed by the energy of the Sun. For example, molecules of hydrogen cyanide (one hydrogen atom, one carbon atom and one nitrogen atom – HCN) could form a chain by connecting to itself five times. The result is adenine ($H_5C_5N_5$), one of the main components of the genetic material, DNA.

Some of these molecules turned out to be catalysts: they acted as templates on which other molecules assembled to form larger, more complex molecules. In effect, the template formed a map of the structure of the molecule it helped to form With a template, the molecule could assemble much more readily.

Chains of reactions began, where the results of some reactions were the starting materials for other reactions, whose results were the starting materials for still other reactions, and so on. Eventually, some chains of

75

reactions appeared which were closed: the results of the last reaction were the starting materials needed for the first one, so the chain could start again. By this point, life was not far away. The other necessary component for life was the membrane: a molecular net with holes that allowed some materials through and blocked others. The earliest of these were simple repeated assemblies of molecules, formed by chains of molecules sticking to each other.

Molecules, closed chain reactions and membranes are the elements of a rudimentary cell. This was the forerunner of today's bacteria, and the basis of all later life. Those first cells can be seen as the beginnings of symbiosis on a molecular level. Each component was needed for the continuation of the others.

There is much more to the story before a bacteria-like cell appeared, but that is the start of it. The membrane had to allow in any raw materials not created by the cycle of reactions and allow out any by-products not used in them. The templates had to be able to re-form not only themselves but also the membrane. The whole had to be sufficiently robust so as to be able to re-form itself against damage caused by the continually changing micro-environment.

> **You** So that's the secret of life! Are you sure about all this?
>
> **Me** No, but it's the best we have. Almost none of it is based on direct evidence. It comes from a combination of laboratory experiments, mathematical and computer simulations, and a lot of theoretical speculation. It is all other people's work, and the details of it are way beyond my understanding. There are great gaps in it, but it seems plausible. More important, the patterns and processes I've been describing here are similar to others which will appear later in the book. I'm hoping to

show you a grand pattern, whose consistency on many levels will add to its overall plausibility.

These primitive cells show a whirlpool-like pattern – a form that is continually re-formed from a surrounding sea of its parts. With a cell, however, there is an important extra – the templates: the genetic material, the RNA and DNA, which appears in every cell in all living creatures. They provide a description of the essentials of the structure of the cell. It is that description that gives the cell the coherence that maintains its wholeness. The information in that description is crucial to the maintenance of the form of the cell. As we will see later in the book, it is similar to the use of information and communications to maintain the form of a co-operative eGaian society.

The symbiotic bacterial lifestyle

The earliest forms of life developed from primitive proto-bacteria to full bacteria over an extended period following the formation of the seas, and it was still longer before any more complex life evolved. This period, when bacteria were the only form of life, is called the Archaen, meaning ancient or beginning.

The first life appeared in the Archaen period

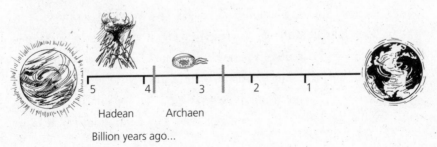

Hadean   Archaen

Billion years ago...

Bacteria are very simple cells; plant and animal cells are much more complex, with a separate nucleus where most of the genetic material is contained, internal membranes, and numerous small internal structures called organelles. Plant and animal cells also reproduce differently from bacteria. To understand the development of these more complex cells, we first have to look more closely at the life of bacteria.

You Just a minute. Surely bacteria are either plants or animals? Are you saying they are something different?

Me Yes. The old idea that life falls into two kingdoms – plants and animals – is now obsolete. There are many creatures that do not fit comfortably into those two categories. The modern division is between cells with and without a nucleus. Those without are the bacteria. They evolved first, in the Archaen, nearly 4 billion years ago. Plants, animals and fungi came very much later, less than 500 million years ago.

A bacterium contains a minimal set of genetic material, barely more than needed to re-form itself and reproduce. Yet bacteria are extremely adaptable. They can survive an amazing range of environments – nearly boiling waters, airless conditions, and environments that would be poisonous to any other creatures. They adapt rapidly to changes in their environment, as is clear from the way they have developed resistance to many antibiotics. How does this happen? Margulies and Sagan give a vivid description[4]:

> "Its minimal number of genes leaving it deficient in metabolic abilities, a bacterium is necessarily a team player. A bacterium never functions as a single individual in nature. Instead, in any given ecological niche, teams of several kinds of bacteria live together, responding to and reforming the environment, aiding each other

with complementary enzymes. The various kinds of bacteria in the team, each present in enormous numbers of copies, co-ordinate the release of their enzymes according to the stages in a task. Their life cycles interlock, the waste products of one kind becoming the food sources of the next. In huge and changing numbers, they perform tasks of which individually they are incapable."

So bacteria can be seen as inherently symbiotic creatures. Living together is an essential part of their lifestyle. This resembles the complementary nature of the reactions within each bacterium, with different reactions contributing materials needed by others and using the results of others.

79

In bacteria, reproduction and sex are completely separate. A bacterium reproduces by growing to twice its normal size, when its single strand of DNA duplicates itself and the cell splits into two identical cells. The daughter cells are genetically identical to the single parent (which no longer exists).

Sex is the exchange of genetic material. Many mechanisms are available for this. Two bacteria may combine into one, which ends up with all the genetic material. Or bacteria may exchange genetic material through a small tube that forms temporarily to join them (called conjugation). Also, small bits of genetic material may get packaged up in various ways and travel between bacteria. These packages include plasmids, phages and viruses. Viruses, which can be so deadly to creatures with complex nucleated cells like us, are not a separate form of life, but a normal part of the sexual repertoire of bacteria.

In plants and animals, the genetic material in one generation is very much like that in the previous generation. The form of successive generations changes very little within any species. Bacteria are much more fluid. They are continually changing their form and their genetic material, often very radically. This is how resistance to drugs can develop so rapidly.

You Why this prurient interest in the sex lives of bacteria?

Me You may joke, but this is a crucial point. One of the aims of this chapter is to squash the idea that competition is the basic organising principle of nature. It's clear already that to explain the behaviour of bacteria in terms of competition is to leave out most of what is significant.

The lives of bacteria are totally interconnected and interdependent. Their response to changing conditions is that of a group. By modifying the mixture of metabolisms available they adapt as needed. Because of their genetic fluidity, there is a sense in which all the bacteria on Earth can be viewed as a single species; because of their group interdependence, they can even be viewed as a single, global super-organism[5]. To see individual bacteria competing with each other is to misunderstand the nature of their lives. An individual bacterium's fitness to survive depends upon the adaptability of the local colony of bacteria around it.

The earliest bacterial colonies fed on the most readily available molecules in the primordial soup – carbohydrates and alcohols. This is the metabolism of a fermenter. These early forms of metabolism are still with us in the modern bacteria that make our cheese and wine and which live in the guts of most animals and form a vital part of the animals' digestive system. There were many different forms of fermenter, with different metabolisms. In any colony, one fermenter's waste was another's food, so that the basic materials were recycled. Recycling and re-use of materials has been a basic principle of life from the start.

As the early baterial colonies grew and spread, more and more of the available materials became incorporated into their bodies. Over time, many new metabolic pathways were developed enabling spreading life to eat up more and more of the primordial soup. There must have been many local crises, where no more soup was available and colonies died out. There must also have been many times when, under this pressure, a new metabolic pathway was discovered, and a new source of food allowed the colony to continue. Through the Archaen age, nearly all the metabolic pathways used by bacteria today evolved, and these are the building blocks of the metabolisms of all the more complex forms of life.

One particularly important metabolism was photosynthesis, in which sunlight was the energy source. The earliest photosynthetic bacteria were sulfur breathers. They gave off hydrogen sulfide (the gas which gives rotten eggs their smell). A later form of photosynthesizer used carbon dioxide gas, which was abundant in the air and dissolved in the surface of the early seas. Carbon dioxide and water itself provided most of the materials needed. These bacteria extracted carbon from carbon dioxide and hydrogen from water and used them to build the molecules they needed, giving off oxygen as their waste product. Thus the major metabolic pathway used by all modern plants had arrived.

This was a key breakthrough for life. It had resolved its first major crisis. Life had eaten up most of the primordial soup, but could now continue to grow with carbon dioxide as its food.

You Are you saying that photosynthetic bacteria replaced all the others?

Me Not at all. Remember interdependence, interconnectedness and recycling. All the others could continue too.

This was the beginning of the dramatic changes life was to make to the Earth. It had eaten up the soup, turning it into bacteria, and was now beginning to change the atmosphere. The long process of change had begun, from an atmosphere composed mostly of carbon dioxide to today's atmosphere which contains only 0.03% carbon dioxide. This time also marked the first great environmental crisis to hit life.

Today, we hear about carbon dioxide as a greenhouse gas; its increase leading to global warming. In the late Archaen age carbon dioxide levels fell and the world cooled, to give the first ice age. This event is a rough marker of the end of the Archaen age and the beginning of the Proterozoic.

The first ice ages roughly mark the end of the Archaen age

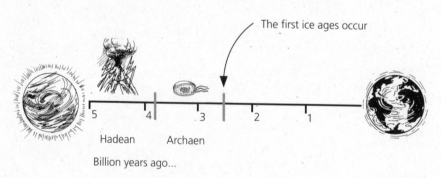

The first ice ages occur

5 4 3 2 1

Hadean   Archaen

Billion years ago...

Life in the late Archaen / early Proterozoic age

"To a casual observer, the early Proterozoic world would have looked largely flat and damp, an alien yet familiar landscape, with volcanoes smoking in the background and shallow, brilliantly colored pools abounding and mysterious greenish and brownish patches of scum floating on the waters, stuck to the banks of rivers, tinting the damp soils like fine molds. A ruddy sheen would coat the stench-filled waters.

Shrunk to microscopic perspective, a fantastic landscape of bobbing purple, aquamarine, red, and yellow spheres would come into view. Inside the violet spheres of Thiocapsa, suspended yellow globules of sulfur would emit bubbles of skunky gas. Colonies of ensheathed viscous organisms would stretch to the horizon. One end stuck to rocks, the other ends of some bacteria would insinuate themselves inside tiny cracks and begin to penetrate the rock itself. Long skinny filaments would leave the pack of their brethren, gliding by slowly, searching for a better place in the sun. Squiggling bacterial whips shaped like corkscrews or fusili pasta would dart by. Multicellular filaments and tacky, textilelike crowds of bacterial cells would wave with the currents, coating pebbles with brilliant shades of red, pink, yellow, and green. Showers of spores, blown by breezes, would splash and crash against the vast frontier of low-lying muds and waters."[6]

Complex cells: the Proterozoic age

Early photosynthetic bacteria gave off oxygen as well as taking in carbon dioxide. Oxygen was not present in significant quantities in the early atmosphere. It is too reactive: it combined so readily with many other substances that it did not persist as free oxygen. For a long time, rocks rapidly absorbed the oxygen produced by the early photosynthesizers. Some ancient banded iron rocks containing layers of iron oxide have been found, which are evidence for this process. Much of our present iron ore dates from this time.

Eventually, the oxygen given off by bacteria was more than could be absorbed, and it began to build up in the atmosphere. While to us oxygen is vital and a key to life, to the bacteria in the late Archaen it was a deadly poison. The reactivity of oxygen destroyed cells. The build-up of oxygen in the late Archaen was the greatest pollution crisis life on Earth has ever faced.

Major crises require radical solutions. The outcome of the oxygen crisis was the development of the eukaryotic cell – a new compound cell with a nucleus. Those cells now form the basis of all animals and plants. Their development marked the major division in life forms.

How did it happen? As oxygen began to accumulate in the Earth's atmosphere, and also dissolved in the sea waters, certain bacteria evolved which, rather than being killed by it, made good use of it. Some forms of *cyanobacteria*, one of the early photosynthesizers, learned the trick of using oxygen in a form of internal, controlled combustion as a source of energy. This was the beginning of respiration. These bacteria could take in oxygen and give off carbon dioxide. This trick not only protected *cyanobacteria* from the ravages of oxygen, it was also a very efficient form of metabolism compared with that of the earlier fermenters. *Cyanobacteria* thrived. Many new oxygen-using forms developed from them. They quickly replaced the oxygen-sensitive bacteria on the oxygen-rich surface, while other bacteria survived underneath them in the lower levels of mud and water.

The stage was also now set for the development of the compound cell. It is known that small bacteria can live independently yet symbiotically inside larger cells. The smaller bacteria find plentiful food inside the host, and their metabolism contributes to that of the host. In some cases, the invader might have started as a predator. Some hosts did not die, and developed not a resistance, but a need for their new partner. Margulies believes that the first step towards the complex cell was a merger between a swimming bacterium and a fermenting bacterium. This is the ancestral symbiotic cell, and makes up most of the modern cell. Next was a respiring bacteria, *paracocci*.[7]

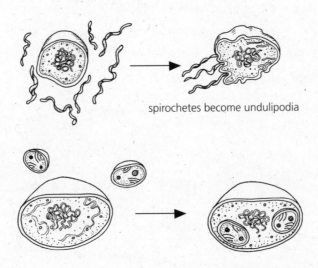

spirochetes become undulipodia

cyanobacterium and aerobic bacterium
combine in symbyotic relationship

In the midst of the oxygen crisis, this symbiotic arrangement, with oxygen-using bacteria inside, proved very attractive to some. It was the safe place to be in the new, oxygen-rich world. Symbiotic colonies of bacteria began to evolve which could use oxygen and which combined the strengths of their various members. In a modern eurkaryotic cell, the oxygen-using part is an organelle called a mitochondrian. Mitochondria today retain many of the characteristics of free-living bacteria. Their internal structure and chemistry is very similar to that of some bacteria.

Other cell structures are like this too. Plant cells contain choloroplasts, the sites of photosynthesis. They also have their own DNA, reproduce independently, and are nearly identical to a bacterium called *prochloron*.

The evolution of the eukaryotic cell starts as a colony of bacteria, living a symbiotic life for mutual benefit. Over time, the internal structure changed, with much of the genetic material coming together into a central nucleus. The process by which the DNA in the nucleus of a eukaryotic cell divides is much more complex than in a bacterium. The details of this division are aided by structures that also might have had bacterial origins.

Procaryotic and eukaryotic cells campared [9]

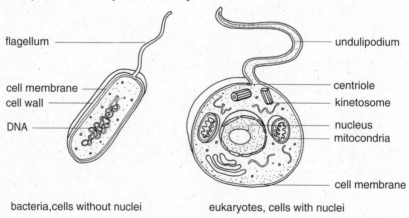

flagellum — undulipodium

cell membrane — centriole
cell wall — kinetosome

DNA — nucleus
mitocondria

cell membrane

bacteria,cells without nuclei   eukaryotes, cells with nuclei

The new large nucleus now contained most of the cell's genes. That is, it contained most of the templates needed to build the molecules from which the parts of the cell were made. Again, this provided a description of the cell that was the key to the maintenance of its wholeness.

This, perhaps, is the story of the greatest step in life's evolution. It is certainly clear that those new organisms that exploited oxygen survived much better than those that could not. The descendants of the latter now remain mostly in specialised environments, including our guts. But symbiosis was the key to the emergence of a new level of the organisation of life.

These new, more complex cells had some striking advantages over bacteria. Some were much more mobile. They contained undulating hair-like protrusions to propel them along. These are likely to have evolved from spirochaetes, whip-like bacteria with similar properties. This mobility and their larger size helped in gathering food. Their extra complexity enabled them to cope with a wider range of conditions.

These new creatures flourished. For about two billion years, until the animals, plants and fungi developed, they and the bacteria were the only forms of life. Those creatures that have cells with nuclei but are not animals, plants or fungi are called protists.

The Proterozoic age followed the Archaen age. Both bacteria and protists flourished

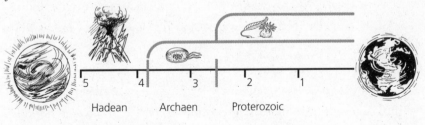

Hadean   Archaen   Proterozoic

Billion years ago.....

Many of the protists are single-celled creatures, like amoeba and paramecium. But some are also multi-cellular, like slime molds, seaweeds, kelp and sponges. (In fact there are multi-cellular forms of bacteria too.) These multi-cellular forms generally develop as clones of a single cell. There is very little specialisation of cells, unlike the plants and animals that were still to come.

> **You** And isn't a multi-cellular creature also a form of collaboration rather than competition?
>
> **Me** Exactly.

Multi-cellular forms, too, had many advantages, with their size contributing to the stability of their local environment. For a cell that is part of a multi-cellular form, much of importance in its local environment consists of its sibling cells. By enhancing the survival of its local environment, the cell enhances its own survival. It is an example of life co-evolving with its environment so that the life form and local environment become closely matched.

Complex creatures: the Phanerozoic age

The story moves on to the final part, the last 570 million years out of 5 billion, when most of the standard evolutionary story took place. It is the story of life as told mainly by the fossil record. Most of the earlier parts have been discovered only within the last few decades. That earlier life left no fossils, and its discovery awaited the development of more subtle techniques.

As the Proterozoic age drew to its close, oxygen began to build up towards modern levels. High in the stratosphere, ultraviolet radiation turned some of that oxygen into ozone. (Oxygen molecules normally consist of two oxygen atoms; ozone molecules are made up of three oxygen atoms.) This layer of ozone then absorbed most of the ultraviolet, creating a shield that protected life, and made possible its spread onto land.

As oxygen built up, carbon dioxide levels fell still further. The Earth cooled; another ice age followed. A major change in the geological record marks this point. After it, life proliferated as never before, now onto land as well as in the seas. Creatures with hard body parts evolved and so fossils began to appear. This is the Phanerozoic age.

The explosion of life began around 570 million years ago

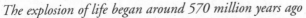
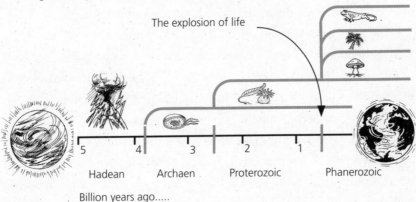

The explosion of life

| 5 | 4 | 3 | 2 | 1 |

Hadean   Archaen   Proterozoic   Phanerozoic

Billion years ago.....

Biologists now divide life into five kingdoms: bacteria, protists, fungi, plants and animals. By the beginning of the Phanerozoic, the first two of these were well established. In the Phanerozoic, multi-cellular forms of protists evolved into the fungi, plants and animals. All of them (and that includes all of us) are really symbiotic colonies of cells, which in turn are symbiotic colonies of bacteria. The three new kingdoms each developed as expressions of a new and specialised life strategy.

The fungi specialise in external digestion. They give off chemicals that transform some of what is around them into the chemicals they need as food, which they then absorb. They often live in a symbiotic relationship with plants, supplying the nitrogen and phosphorus the plants need. Plants use sunlight as an energy source to enable them to build themselves, mostly out of carbon dioxide and water. They give off oxygen as a by-product. Animals take in oxygen and use it in a controlled combustion process as an energy source, with carbon dioxide as a by-product. Animals generally need fairly complex chemicals (carbohydrates, proteins and fats) as the starting points for forming and re-forming themselves. To get these chemicals, they eat plants, animals or animal waste products. Their waste products and dead bodies also feed the plants, fungi, bacteria and protists.

The parts go round and round. Oxygen and carbon dioxide are cycled between plants and animals. Some creatures build up bigger bodies from simpler parts. Some creatures turn the bodies of other creatures back into their simpler parts. Bacteria, protists, fungi, plants and animals are all intricately enmeshed in this. It is a grand whirlpool pattern made up of smaller whirlpool patterns made up of still smaller whirlpool patterns.

Recycling is the essence of the pattern of life. It started at a local level with the bacteria. The possibilities expanded with new forms of bacteria and then protists. With the development of fungi, plants and animals, many new pathways opened along which the parts could be recycled. As a result, the total mass of life on Earth expanded tremendously – the explosion of life.

Early in their evolution, plants developed a form of sexual reproduction more familiar to us. Some of their cells divided in half without first doubling the genes within them, so that each of the new cells had only half the complement of genes. These then combined with similar cells from another individual. The result was a cell with the full amount of genetic material, half from one parent and half from the other.

This sexual reproduction from specialised cells was part of a general pattern, where plants came to be made up of parts whose cells were specialised for different functions – roots, stems, seeds, leaves and ultimately flowers. Each individual now was a symbiotic colony of parts, each of which supported the others in its own way. This specialisation allowed greater variety in life strategies: leaves could catch the light while roots absorbed water from under the ground.

Maintaining wholeness

The first cells, the bacteria, had a wholeness that was more than a whirlpool-like unity because they had genetic material that acted as templates for the molecules of which they were made. In the more complex eukaryotic cells, the templates, the genetic material, are mostly concentrated in the nucleus. Again, they provide the description that maintains the wholeness of the eukaryotic cell.

Multi-celled creatures with specialised cells involve another level of description. The specialised cells within one creature can be very different. In plants, the difference between pollen, petal, leaf, bark, and root is striking. Yet it is as nothing compared to the difference between cells in animals: white blood cells are similar to amoeba while bone cells are more like a tree trunk. Nerve cells, skin cells, muscle cells, light sensitive cells in the eye – all are so different that in isolation they might be thought totally unrelated.

All the cells in a multi-cellular creature contain

identical genetic material, but only some is used in each type of cell. Only the templates for the parts needed for that cell are active. It is as though the genes for many different creatures were combined in one place, but with only some of them switched on at any one time. The next level of description of a multi-cellular creature is that which determines which genes are switched on and off in a particular cell. The switching on and off of genes is an essential part of the functioning of an organism, beyond just the growth and specialisation of the cells. Switching on a gene means that the chemical for which it is a template gets produced. It is largely under the control of hormones, which are a set of chemicals which circulate through an organism, as a general control system.

At any of these levels of wholeness – bacteria, eukaryotic cell, or multi-cellular organism – co-ordination at an overall level replaces any competition between the parts. Where it fails you get disease, as cancer is growth out of control of the whole.

The earliest plants were the mosses and liverworts. Ferns with seeds followed them. These were the first land plants. They formed the first forests between 345 and 225 million years ago. Our modern coal fields are the remains of some of those early forests, showing that the recycling was not complete. By burning that coal today we are returning carbon dioxide to the atmosphere which was removed from it by those forests when they were alive.

The first conifers appeared about 225 million years ago. They relied on the weather to distribute their seeds. The first flowering plants appeared about 123 million years ago. They evolved together with the insects in a symbiosis in which flowers attract the insects to the nectar within, and in the process of travelling from plant to plant, the insects pollinate the plants.

Animals, like plants, are complex symbiotic colonies of specialised cells. The distinction that is now made between animal-like, multi-celled protists and what are now considered true animals was that the latter developed from an embryo. Another key feature of true animals is sophisticated communication between cells, particularly through a nervous system. The combination of nerve cells and muscle cells allowed synchronised contraction of the muscle cells to produce co-ordinated movement. The combination of nerve cells and cells that responded to light or to chemicals in the water or air gave sight, smell and taste.

These organisms provide useful metaphors for the kinds of co-operative societies dealt with later. They have a variety of parts, each working together in their own way for the better survival of the whole, with competition between the parts suppressed. Their common wholeness is described in the templates – the genetic material that is the same in each cell but expressed differently in different cells. They have a communication system to help them identify problems and solve them in a co-ordinated manner.

The earliest animals were some primitive worms, dating from about 700 million years ago, actually before the start of the Phanerozoic age. From these came the segmented worms, then the other segmented creatures, like those with external skeletons (trilobites, crabs, shrimp, insects and spiders). From some of the segmented worms developed creatures with a chord of nerves running through their length. When this became encased in bone it formed the first spinal chord, and from this came the fish (513 million years ago), then the amphibians (345 million years), the reptiles (245 million years) and finally the mammals and the birds (210 million years). Over time the mixture of creatures changed. The parts were rearranged in different ways. New pathways along which the parts were cycled arose while old ones disappeared.

Catastrophe and diversity

The changes in the mixture of life forms was not usually smooth. The pattern of the Archaen and Proterozoic ages – crises followed by the emergence of new forms – appears to be the normal pattern. The Phanerozoic, too, is marked by massive crises, sudden great extinctions when a large proportion of the life forms vanished, followed by the development of new forms.

About 250 million years ago there was a massive extinction which killed off 90% of all species of life.[10] Although the causes aren't too clear, it seems that there was a slow decline in species for a few million years before it, and then a sudden catastrophic event. There was slow climatic change caused by the coming together of some of the continents. This also resulted in a period of huge volcanic activity that released vast amounts of carbon dioxide. The carbon dioxide in the seas was a direct killer, but it also led to a sudden temperature rise of 5–10°C. That was the catastrophe which did most of the killing.

> **You** Shades of today's fears of global warming.
> **Me** Exactly.

This catastrophe marks the start of the Triassic period in the geological record. It took millions of years to re-stock the land and the seas. Even the 10% of species that survived were severely depleted. The few survivors found themselves in a wide-open world with very little competition, so they flourished and diversified into the new niches. This was a good time for reptiles, and the first dinosaurs appeared. The first true mammals also appeared at this time, but mostly they were small insectivores and tree dwellers.

There was another mass extinction at the end of the Triassic, 200 million years ago. Although not as severe as the one which started it, it is still one of the big five extinctions. Again, it seems that a series of environmental problems, like big volcanic eruptions, led up to it. This time the final catastrophe seems to have been triggered by a four or five-mile-wide meteor colliding with the Earth, forming the 70-mile-wide Manicouagan Crater in Quebec.

This extinction event marks the end of the Triassic and the start of the Jurassic period. The aftermath was that the dinosaurs became the dominant land animals. It took the two major mass extinctions for this to come about. They weathered the extinction with only modest losses and were dominant for about 120 million years until the mass extinction event 65 million years ago.

The final cause of that extinction was a now notorious meteor or comet. It was at least six miles in diameter and hit the Earth in the sea near Yucatan, Mexico, creating a 180-mile-wide crater and massive tidal waves. More than half the Earth's vegetation burned in the weeks after the impact. Acid rain made the seas too acid for much life, and global warming resulted from the release of carbon dioxide. Even before this time, though, many species were already in decline or were going extinct. It seems that there were three separate causes: climate change from carbon dioxide emissions, sea level change and then the meteor.

The mass extinction event 65 million years ago killed off most of the dinosaurs, leaving as their only descendents the birds. A few mammals also survived and went on to become the dominant form of life. They went through a burst of evolution, starting with a load of very small mammals. Then, about 40 million years ago, the Earth cooled, leading to the spread of grasslands that favoured the evolution of large mammals. There were many giant mammals: many elephant species, mammoths and mastodons, giant camels and enormous ground sloths, giant dogs, cats and bears too. By about six million years ago, the world appeared nearly in the form that it was in when humanity evolved.

The final chapter in the story of life starts about 2.5 million years ago. Again, a variety of events led to more cooling, and the Earth entered a period of ice ages. Since then the climate has oscillated between longer ice ages and briefer inter-glacial periods. This cooling brought about a pulse of extinctions. The modern extinction started then. Again, it started with climate change a few million years before the major event that provided the *coup de grâce*. Thirty per cent of North American land mammals went extinct at the onset of the ice age. However, the knockout punch for the larger mammals was delivered about 11,000 years ago, when two-thirds of North and South America's larger mammals suddenly disappeared over a period of about 1,000 years. This coincided with the arrival of humans in the Americas. It was the first chapter in the story of humanity as a global cancer.

You Doesn't all this talk of extinctions and survivors mean that at a time of crisis the fittest survive? And you keep writing about symbiosis, but you barely mention competition and survival of the fittest. Surely you aren't just going to ignore them?

Me I think I've spelled out enough of the history so that I can tackle this issue of competition and fitness directly now. Just for starters, I'll answer your first question. At a time of crisis the meaning of fitness changes, so different creatures survive than survived before it.

Symbiosis and competition

By now the intricate interconnectedness of life is very clear. All creatures rely on many others to provide their food and shelter, decompose the accumulated rubbish all create, and generally provide the rest of all the cycles of which they are part. The environment for each is all of the rest. The life cycle of any creature cannot be understood without understanding its environment. All creatures are simultaneously separate individuals and parts of a larger whole.

From this perspective, fitness means fitting in the sense that a piece in a jigsaw puzzle fits into the hole left for it. That hole is the particular way of life, the niche, of that individual. Fitness certainly does not mean a general superiority of one creature over another. A niche can also be seen as an opportunity, a possible way of living for something. An organism evolves and finds its place in its conversation with its environment. The niche is the other side of that conversation.

Under normal conditions, when there is no crisis in progress, virtually all the niches available get filled. In natural grassland there will be a mixture of grazing animals, each with somewhat different teeth and digestive systems so they can eat different mixtures of the vegetation. There will be different birds, each with differently shaped beaks specialised to eating different sizes of insects, or those that live at different depths under the surface. There will be some animals specialised to feed on virtually every one of the plants and some predators and parasites that eat virtually all of the animals.

Of course, the jigsaw puzzle analogy is somewhat limited. The edges of the biological holes are not sharp as in the puzzle. There is a certain amount of overlap between the niches of one creature and another. It is in these areas of overlap that competition comes into play. It provides a jostling for position that clarifies this overlap and leaves the niches more distinct.

You You are giving competition a very marginal role then?

Me Well it's a very important role. The interconnections and symbiosis determine the overall shape of the pattern, the mixture of creatures and how they live. The clarity with which the parts of this pattern fit together; the closeness of the fit, comes from competition. That is what I understand by survival of the fittest.

Another limitation of the jigsaw puzzle analogy is that the shapes are fixed, while biological niches are continually changing. With no environmental crisis, the changes are small and slow. Creatures become highly specialised, very closely adapted to the conditions around them, their food species, symbiotic species, predators and so on. Then along comes a crisis: the primordial soup runs out, oxygen begins to appear, an ice age begins or ends, a mass extinction event occurs or maybe it is something much smaller and more local. Then the shape of all the holes changes. The niches are no longer what they were. The intricate web of support is rendered. It is no good being a mighty dinosaur, capable of killing any large animal around, and especially those puny little mammals. If the food of your food goes, you go too. In a crisis, the fitness of an individual animal or species is not relevant. It is the set of relationships in the whole ecosystem around it that counts.

After a crisis there is no longer as close a matching of life forms. New pathways become available. New strategies for living can emerge. A crisis favours generalists, creatures which can feed off a wide range of others or who can live in varied conditions. There is a rapid development of new forms of life.

> **You** Perhaps there is a lesson in there for us. If the global cancer triggers a major crisis, then generalist groups and individuals will have an advantage.
>
> **Me** Yes.

Under the new conditions, some creatures find they have some very useful abilities, perhaps developed for another purpose. Fish living in shallow shore waters who learned to breathe air a little and use their fins to push along the bottom might find they could survive on land a little. They are already adapted to the new conditions. At first the new forms don't have to be very well adapted to the conditions. The first land animals couldn't walk very well. The first birds couldn't fly very well. Competitive pressures soon sort out a new set of niches with specialised, well-adapted creatures. As walking or flying predators appeared, their prey learned to run and fly fast. As the new set of niches becomes filled, change slows down and a normal period arrives.

> **You** I think I'm beginning to get the idea. You aren't saying that competition isn't important, just that this symbiosis business and being part of the web of life is actually the major part of what counts.
>
> **Me** Yes, that's right. The image of nature as a war is a projection onto nature of a market economic system! It is very recent, only appearing since Darwin in the last century. It replaced a projection of feudalism onto nature, 'God's harmony' with everything in its hierarchical place.

You Aren't you trying to create a projection onto nature of your view of society? What is nature really like?

Me I suppose that is what I am doing (although it's not just my view). What is nature really like? I suppose a sage would say that nature 'just is'.

You I'm not completely satisfied yet. Can we go back to competition? What about the competition between male animals for dominance or access to females? Surely that is a major part of their life?

Me OK. Within one species the same principles apply, and we can sometimes even begin to glimpse another level of organisation.

Within one species the overlap between niches is especially strong. All the foxes in a wood eat the same prey. All the rabbits like the same plants. What generally happens is that the niches for creatures of the same species are geographic. Individuals or groups have their own territories within which there is sufficient to meet their needs. Competition again appears at the boundaries of the territories. Birds sing in large part to say "this is my territory."

For many animals, other members of their own species are of major importance in their environment. At the very least, they need them to mate. Thus it is not surprising that when competition arises between members of a species, it is usually minimised. Often there is a ritual or rule that determines which creature wins. With certain butterflies, the first one on a particular leaf has priority. With many animals threatening postures are enough to see off a rival.

The issue between two rival animals is to see which one gets to mate, or gets the territory. This is a matter of communication between creatures with very limited means of communication. If the appropriate criterion is the size and showiness of your tail feathers, then a display will settle the issue. If it is a matter of strength, then a fight is needed. However, animal fights rarely end in death or serious injury. They generally end when it is clear who will win.

It is striking how many different animals live in groups: flocks, herds, schools, prides, or whatever. For these animals, the benefits of being in a group clearly outweigh competitive pressures from sharing a niche. Being part of a group can give protection from predators (grazing animals), help with care of offspring (lions), co-operation in hunting (dogs). Some of the social insects have very specialised forms. An individual ant or termite is hardly a separate creature. It may be able to gather food, or produce eggs or defend the colony, but not any of the other tasks. It is more like a cell in the super-organism that is the colony.

101

Imagine you are watching a large flock of starlings, several hundred birds. You notice a main group and various smaller groups, constantly changing. A few birds circle high in the air watching for predators. One or two take off to the next field to search for food. A few more peel off from the main group to join them. If they are successful and settle onto that field, others will see them and join them and soon the bulk of the flock will leave its present location and join them. If the watchers signal danger (you perhaps), the whole lot will suddenly take off and fly away.

Birds are the ultimate symbol of freedom. None of those starlings tells any of the others what to do. They live in a flock, choosing their roles from moment to moment in support of the flock, synchronising their behaviour with each other, because that is what it is to be a starling. Freedom and collaboration are in no sense in conflict with one another.

CHAPTER five

THE CO-OPERATIVE APE:
THE EARLY HUMAN STORY

The last chapter set a context for humanity. Now it is time to look at what it means to be human. The last chapter dispelled the myth that the natural world is inherently competitive and warlike. This one does the same for humanity.

Today it is very common for people to find themselves in situations where the appropriate response seems competitive or warlike rather than co-operative. People have become very skilled at being competitive. Our most sophisticated technology is that of war. But human history suggests that this has been the case only since the advent of what we call civilisation – very recent in our evolutionary story. This chapter will trace this aspect of humanity's history. The story is of an animal whose niche, whose speciality, was working in co-operation within small social bands, sharing food which had been gathered and hunted, sharing child care, learning from their ancestors' experience, etc. Our big brains, languages and cultures evolved to make this possible. Our physiology and personalities evolved as animals who were co-ordinating their group actions well beyond that of any other mammals.

Origins

In the family tree of life, humans are on the mammalian branch, which appeared some 210 million years ago. We are part of the primate sub-branch, which includes monkeys, apes and others like lemurs, tarsiers and lorises. The first primates appeared about 70 million years ago. About 20 million years ago, out of Africa came the Oak Ape, *Dryopithecus*, the ancestor of all the modern apes, including the chimpanzees, gorillas, orang-utans and humans.

> **You** Don't you mean the apes and the humans?
>
> **Me** No, I think it is pure conceit to give us a group by ourselves. I'd rather make the continuity more explicit by including humans among the other apes.[1]

Our closest relatives here are the chimpanzees, which is probably why they are so appealing to us. In fact, our genetic makeup differs from that of the chimps by only 1%. It is an important 1%, but it is nonetheless clear that in terms of our physical makeup we are just a variation on the ape theme. Chimps are highly intelligent animals. They can do simple counting and fractions, and can recognise simple geometrical shapes. Someone has estimated that chimps have an IQ (in human terms) of 80[2], which is not bad at all.

There have been many experiments in which people have tried to teach chimps human language, with a certain amount of success. Chimps do not have the muscular control of their faces and vocal chords needed to produce words, but they can learn to use sign language, or to communicate using special keyboards and they can understand limited human speech. They tend to combine words with gestures. The Bonobo chimps seem to have the most advanced abilities. They can understand sentences of the complexity of:

"Get a Coke and give it to Rose. The Coke is on the table there."

"Get the ball that's outdoors." (another one was in view)

Their language ability is limited to objects and events in their direct experience, and is comparable to that of a child of two or so.

Chimps are very social animals with active and intricate social lives. They live in bands for mutual protection and companionship, spending much time grooming each other. They can spontaneously learn to use

104

objects around them as simple tools. They use twigs to fish ants from holes in wood. Groups of chimps hunt monkeys: some will chase the monkey into an ambush formed by several others. Fighting is common among chimps, but their social bonds are so important to them that fights usually end in reconciliation.. "Within a minute of a fight having ended the two former opponents may rush towards each other, kiss and embrace long and fervently and then proceed to groom each other."[3]

There is a dominance hierarchy of males and females in a chimp band. The most dominant male has the greatest sexual access to the females when they are in heat. His function is to protect them from attack or annoyance, especially by other males. To maintain his dominance he needs the active assistance of the females. In *Chimpanzee Politics*, Frans de Waal describes the intricate manoeuvres chimps get up to as one male, or perhaps a pair, will challenge another for dominance. "Whole passages of Machiavelli seem to be directly applicable to chimpanzee behaviour".[4] Deception is part of their normal repertoire of behaviour. This is significant in what it tells us about chimpanzee mental abilities: for a chimp to be able to deceive another, it must be able to imagine what it is like to be that other chimp.

Chimps have friendships, but do not form permanent sexual bonds. Female chimps do not normally mate except when they are in heat. When a female chimp is in heat, the other males pay special attention to her, and may bring her gifts of food. Otherwise, food is not generally given by one chimp to another, although a group will share eating an animal they have killed.

Humans and chimps parted company around four million years ago. The climate had changed somewhat; the forests were shrinking, but there were opportunities for apes to exploit on the edges of the forest. Perhaps it helped if you could run out of the forest into a nearby clump of vegetation,

105

grab some fruit or nuts and carry them back to the safety of the forest. To do this you had to use your hands and walk on your feet only. (Apes can walk on their legs and carry things with their hands if they want to, but normally they walk on all fours, putting some of their weight on their knuckles. Like most mammals, their backs are suited to supporting their body's weight at both ends.)

The apes that exploited this new way of living soon became adapted to it. The angle of their hips changed, their feet changed, the angle of their heads changed. Their backs – bone and muscle – adapted to standing on one end to support the entire weight of their bodies. These upright apes, *Australopithecus*, were our earliest direct ancestors. Other than their upright stance, they were like other apes. Their brain size was the same, and we can presume that they were as intelligent and social as the other apes.

There is another way in which humans differ from the other apes, one mentioned less often than our big brains and upright stance. We are by far the sexiest of the apes. Our women are sexually receptive even when they cannot conceive; they have lost the ape's distinguishing physical signs of being on heat. Women have sex when they are pregnant, during menstruation, and on into old age beyond the childbearing years. This increased sexuality probably dates from very early in human evolution, at the time of *Australopithecus*. For us, sex has taken on an additional function. It is not just to conceive children: it also promotes bonding between people, a first step towards increased sociability and culture.[5]

Standing upright might have had its advantages for food gathering, but it also created certain problems. The change in the angle of the pelvis disrupted the easy passage of the infant through the birth canal. The difficulty humans have in giving birth started at this early point, and was compounded much later when human brain sizes increased. The solution was that babies were born slightly earlier, and thus smaller, than other ape babies. These less mature babies needed more care than earlier ape babies, so the friendly attention of the men was very welcome. The food sharing which was offered to a sexually receptive female previously would be of great benefit to a sexually receptive female with an infant. Any increased care and attention would promote the survival of mother and child. Thus was born what Helen Fisher calls 'the sex contract', a close tie between two people for mutual support based on sexual attraction, but not just to produce babies. It developed into our present sexiness and contributed to what we call falling in love.

Standing upright itself, with the new angle of the pelvis, might have promoted increased sexuality as the sexual organs were displayed more directly. Eye contact was enhanced and face-to-face sex, with its greater intimacy, became more favoured. Various physical differences between humans and the other apes are likely to have arisen at this time and would have increased human sexiness – loss of most body hair, skin that is more sensitive to touch, enlarged breasts (as a reminder of the sensuality of nursing?), larger penises, and prolonged sex. (For chimps it lasts just 15 seconds.)

From this early stage, becoming more like what we would call human was to do with increased sociability. The early bonds between men and women were a step towards human culture: one could even speculate that face-to-face sex, close eye contact and more kissing meant that the muscles of the face and mouth became more flexible, allowing subtler movements. As the couple had more to do with each other, communication between them would become much more important.

You So it was the *Australopithecus* women who first started saying to their men, "We need to communicate more!"

107

Me Probably yes! My speculation is that the physical changes for increased sexiness pre-adapted people for better communication and speech.

Mary Leakey discovered a famous set of fossilised footprints of a small group of *Australopithicus* in Tanzania. As Helen Fisher interprets it:

"The time was the beginning of the wet season some 3.6 million years ago... On this afternoon a large adult hominid, about four feet eight inches tall, was strolling through the damp volcanic ash. Beside him was his companion, a smaller (probably female) hominid about four feet tall. They strode through the muck together, almost rubbing shoulders. Behind the larger individual, another smaller one followed, carefully stepping in the footsteps of the leader. ...Mary Leakey thinks that the two adults who walked side by side almost four million years ago were holding hands; that all three were playing."[6]

So now we have an upright ape, with hands free to carry, manipulate, and use tools, and with an increased sexuality to promote bonds between individuals. These bonds created collaborations that would have been to the benefit of the individuals and the whole band: more efficient gathering of food, protection and child care.

Me As I've stuck my neck out this far, I might as well stick it out still further.

With this heightened sexuality, no longer linked only to procreation, and with the advantages that sexual bonds brought, sexual bonds may have developed between two men or two women. These, too, would have been beneficial to survival. Two men might become a more efficient hunting team. Two women might share the care of children conceived with their male lovers. As no offspring are produced, homosexual bonds would have been relatively infrequent, as they are now. Nonetheless, it is consistent with this pattern to see homosexuality appearing very early. It seems to be a small part of the normal human sexual repertoire, just as red hair is a small part of the normal variation of human hair colourings.

Towards modern humans

Australopithecus may have been an upright-walking, sexy, social ape, but was still a long way from the big-brained, talking, cultured people of today. The next major change occurred about 1.6 million years ago, probably triggered again by climate change. The Earth entered another phase of ice ages which continues today, so far as we know. Because these ice ages are so much more recent than the ice ages 2.5 billion and 570 million years ago, there is much more evidence.

> **You** Another period of ice ages? I don't understand. If the Earth cools down so that conditions are right for an ice age why does it heat up again so the ice ages end only to be followed by another period of ice ages much later?
>
> **Me** The best sense I can make of it is that over the longest time scales, billions of years, the Sun is getting hotter, and so if it weren't for life, the Earth would now be very much hotter than it was in the early Archaen age. In fact, it might now have been much too hot for life as we know it. However, life has gradually been reducing the carbon dioxide in the atmosphere, so keeping the temperature more or less the same. At times it gets a little cooler and the Earth slips into

ice ages. The difference in average temperature between ice age and no ice age is only a few degrees.

A few million years ago, a new type of plant evolved which could live more efficiently on lower levels of carbon dioxide, and carbon dioxide levels fell still lower. Various other conditions were significant too: the continents had shifted to suitable positions, with Antarctica over the South Pole where it could support an ice cap, and a ring of land around the North Pole on which an ice cap could form. The result was that the climate became unstable and could easily be triggered into or out of an ice age about 1.6 million years ago. Since then the Earth has oscillated into and out of ice ages regularly – triggered partly by wobbles in the Earth's orbit.

Between 1.6 million and about 730,000 years ago there have been about 20 short cycles, lasting about 40,000 years each, of ice ages followed by inter-glacial periods. In the past 730,000 years there have been about eight more cycles, with the earlier cycles lasting about 70,000 years and the later ones about 100,000 years. We are presently in an inter-glacial period that began roughly 10,000 years ago. The one before was about 130,000-115,000 years ago.

The next stage on from *Australopithecus* – with much larger brains – started to appear at the beginning of this ice age period, 1.6 million years ago. But it wasn't until the beginning of the last interglacial, 130,000 years ago, that fully modern people appeared with bodies more or less the same as ours. So most of the time since big-brained humans appeared, the Earth has been in an ice age.

The dramatically changing climate of the past 1.6 million years created crisis after crisis to which all life on Earth, including developing humanity, had to adapt. During the inter-glacial periods, huge parts of the land were covered in forest – temperate in cooler areas and rainforest in the tropics.

During the ice ages, ice sheets covered large parts of Europe, Asia and North America. Below this was largely tundra. The rainforests shrank and fragmented into small, separate areas. When the next inter-glacial arrived the forests and rainforests rapidly re-grew and joined. This repeated fragmentation and re-joining is probably responsible for the enormous variety of species found in rainforests, which are now fragmented by us. Crisis after crisis also favoured the evolution of more generalist animals, like humans.

Like chimpanzees and gorillas, *Australopithecus* had a brain size of about 450cc. The earliest of our bigger brained ancestors, *Homo habilis*, had a brain twice that size (and we have brains about three times that size.). Their hands were almost as dextrous as ours. With their remains have been found simple stone tools, probably used for crushing nuts, breaking open bones to expose the marrow, other food preparation, scraping, cutting and hammering. They did only a little shaping of the natural stone, choosing stones with a useful shape to start with.

Later, and somewhat bigger-brained, *Homo erectus* first appeared in Africa about 1.6 million years ago. By 730,000 years ago they had spread to the Middle East and southern Europe. By 250,000 years ago they had spread throughout Europe and Asia.

They used quite a variety of stone tools, carefully shaped. They made hand axes, choppers, chisels, scrapers, cleavers, awls, anvils and hammerstones. To do this they had developed quite elaborate techniques for breaking and shaping stones. They also built dwellings and used fire. With this level of sophistication, they were likely to have used animal bladders to carry water and use animal skins for clothing in the cold ice age winters.

This is a long way from the lifestyle of the oak ape, ancestor to all the apes. This is culture: people learning detailed ways of doing things from each other. It wasn't only the bodies (including brains) of our ancestors that were evolving, their ideas were evolving too. The technologies of making tools and the lifestyles associated with them were passed from person to person and from generation to generation. For these early humans the intricate web of life in which all creatures are enmeshed now included their ancestors. Human culture – relationships with other humans – came to be more and more important as part of the environment of an individual human.

The evolution of bigger brains and early human cultures were two aspects of the same process. Bigger brains allowed the understanding needed for the developing culture, which in turn created the pressure for the elaboration of the brain.

Part of this process must have been the development of language. Early language would have been very close to direct experience and memory, a few steps beyond what a chimpanzee can learn today. It was a language of objects, and manipulating objects, simple stories of how to do this, and what happens when you do that. What can you eat and how do you prepare it? Where and when are these plants found? How do you catch and kill these animals? This made a major difference in the life experience of early people. Along with their direct experiences of food, other creatures and the weather, they had experiences shaped by language. There were associations between certain stones and the tools they could make, names that linked whole classes of objects. Thinking, as we know it, was born.

Modern humans

Homo sapiens seems to have evolved in Africa too, descended from *Homo erectus* populations there. They first appeared around 130,000 years ago, and they too spread widely. They had arrived in the Middle East about

112

90,000 years ago, had spread throughout Europe and even reached Australia by 40,000 years ago, but did not get to Japan or Siberia until about 30,000 years ago. They reached North America some 10-15,000 years ago. In the middle of the ice age, with so much water locked up in the ice sheets, the sea level was much lower. There were land bridges between Siberia and Alaska, and only a short distance by sea to Australia.

By about 60,000-40,000 years ago, in the middle of the last ice age, came fully modern humans, *Homo sapiens sapiens*. At around this time a new level of culture appears in human remains. This was the time of cave paintings of animals and people, which appear beautiful even by modern artistic standards. Tools with great aesthetic appeal appear. This was a time of ritual burial – bodies carefully laid out with a variety of objects. Beautiful carved statues have been found, in the form of abstractions of a pregnant woman. These are generally interpreted as symbols of a fertility goddess. Abstract thought, symbolism and religion had arrived. This is quite recent on the time scale of human evolution. There appears to have been very little further development of human bodies and brains since. If an infant from that time were raised in a modern western city, it would probably be indistinguishable from the rest of its new family. Its speech would be fully fluent and with a modern accent. It might grow up to be a nuclear physicist or a politician.

113

> **You** More likely unemployed. You say a politician, but didn't you also say that chimpanzees were good politicians?
>
> **Me** I said that chimpanzees' social manipulations were Machiavellian, but they are not capable of giving a speech showing that their actions are for the public good!

The point is that the level of complexity of human culture that had evolved by the time *Homo sapiens sapiens* appeared was fully modern. Brains capable of handling the level of abstraction their cultures required are also capable of handling the abstractions of modern science. Languages subtle enough for their purposes were subtle enough for the careful shadings of truth of modern politicians. What continued to evolve were the ideas, technologies and forms of social organisation.

The early *Homo sapiens sapiens* lived in small bands, of perhaps 30 to 50 people. They were wandering gatherers and hunters. This has been the principal way of life of humans from the very beginning. It began to be displaced with the beginnings of agriculture about 10,000 years ago, and then still more with the advent of cities and large scale social organisation, about 5,000 years ago. Substantial populations lived in this way as late as the 19th century, but only small isolated pockets of these cultures are left today.

The gathering/hunting way of life required a very detailed and sophisticated understanding of the life cycles of plants and animals. Which parts are good to eat? Which have medicinal properties or can be used as poisons to hunt others? How do you make tools for carrying, hunting or shelter out of stone, bone, wood, or animal parts? Where are the game animals or the ripe edible plants this week?

All of this was wrapped in a rich social life in which people collaborated in finding and preparing food, and caring for their children and their old people. Talk around the campfires might be of the availability of food, but also gossip about the doings and mis-doings of the people in their own and neighbouring bands. Our complex brains and languages evolved with and were formed by the need to cope with this rich knowledge of the natural and social environment. Most adults knew most of what was needed to thrive. By contrast, in modern cultures the cumulative and stored knowledge is much greater, but any individual knows very little of that total.

A major function of culture has always been the maintenance of the bonds between people, because interactions with other people make up a very large part of the environment in which people live. Many cultural devices evolved to support this: rituals, music, dance and ceremonies.

> **You** Let me get this clear: are you saying that the purpose of music and dance is to maintain bonds between people?
>
> **Me** Yes, I imagine that they evolved fairly soon after abstract thought evolved, and for exactly that reason. Any aspect of developing culture that supported group coherence would aid group survival and would be likely to continue. That is also why music and dance have such a strong emotional impact.

115

The development of abstract thought meant that human minds could add extra layers of association to their experience. Not only could they distinguish tigers but could recognise that many different animals had the same cat-like qualities. They could even associate aspects of cat-like behaviour with aspects of human behaviour. This is metaphor, the mapping of the qualities of one set of experiences onto another. With this ability to use metaphor, many mysterious patterns which people experienced could be explained in terms of familiar social experiences. So the essential nature of the deer might have been given a separate existence, with human-like qualities: a deer-spirit. If there were few deer around to hunt perhaps this deer-spirit had been offended. This is animism, the explanation of natural patterns in terms of spirits or souls.

Early modern humans would have had a very clear intuitive sense of the picture painted in the last chapter – of the inter-connectedness of all living creatures, of the inherently supportive quality of nature; and also of almost constant chaotic and disruptive change. They would have expressed it in the only vocabulary and images they had available: metaphors expressing natural patterns as human-like spirits. They were clear about their part in this interconnectedness, and treated nature with respect.

> "...for hunter-gatherers themselves, a central concern has been their relationship with the creatures they harvest. In this form of management, people trust that if they do the right things, the world will stay as it should; the creatures and plants they eat will feel welcome and know they are respected, and will therefore continue to make themselves available."[7]

This respect generally applied to other people as well, and reflected the nature of gather-hunter social organisation.

> "The egalitarian individualism of hunter-gatherer societies, arguably their greatest achievement and their most compelling lesson for other peoples, relies on many kinds of respect."[8]

This was the time of the goddess cultures. Lovely statues and images of a pregnant woman, somewhat abstracted with no details of face or hands, are found associated with many ancient cultures. They are likely to have symbolised nature, what the ancient Greeks called Gaia, the Earth goddess.

> **You** You seem to be romanticising these cultures. Weren't these also woman-bashing cavemen? Do you really imagine a nature-worshipping, peace-loving, hippy paradise?
>
> **Me** No, I'm simply trying to counter the view that before civilisations started, humans were ignorant, aggressive savages, struggling against the odds for survival. That is why I am emphasising the collaboration, intelligence and intuitive wisdom of early cultures. But I haven't finished with the issue of aggression.

116

It seems clear that one side of being human is an animal that has taken sociability and collaboration far beyond that of any other animal. We are adapted to it physically, with the language abilities of our brains, faces and vocal chords. With our extended sexuality, and our generalised ability to feel love, we are adapted to it emotionally. Another side of being human is an animal that has taken aggression and conflict far beyond that of any other. These two sides clearly both co-exist in modern cultures. The question is whether the extremes of aggression and conflict exist in all human cultures? Are they – like music, dance, language and our sexiness – a mark of being human or do they only apear under certain conditions?

They do seem to be universal in so-called civilised cultures. And since civilised cultures are a boundary beyond which people rarely look when considering human nature, the myth that they are universal has flourished. To set this straight it is worth considering the range of human cultures that has existed since the appearance of *Homo sopiens sapiens*, some 40-60,000 years ago. From the artifacts left by a prehistoric culture it is very difficult to determining how agressive the people were. Speculations about this probably say more about the preconceptions of the investigator than of the culture. It is better to consider studies of similar cultures which have existed recently. Some certainly are fierce and warlike, others gentle and peaceful. Here are some examples of the latter.

The people of Tahiti

"The people in general are of the common size of Europeans... their gait easy and genteel and their countenance free, open and lively, never sullied by a sullen or suspicious look — their motions are vigorous, active and graceful and their behaviour to strangers is such as declare at first sight their humane disposition, which is as candid as their countenances seem to indicate, and their courteous, affable and friendly behaviour to each other shows that they have no tincture of barbarity, cruelty, suspicion or revenge. They are ever of an even unruffled temper, so they ought not to be suspected, and an hour's acquaintance is sufficient to repose an entire confidence in them."[9]

"Tahiti in the early 1960's when I began my field work there seemed in regard to gentleness little different than the reports of the late 18th and early 19th century had suggested. ...my own observations during a period of more than two years...indicated in comparison with Western experience and in comparison with reports of many other non-Western societies an extreme lack of angry, hostile, destructive behaviour."[10]

The Yequana of Venezuela

"[There] is a respect for each individual as his own proprietor. ...Deciding what another person should do, no matter what his age, is outside the Yequana vocabulary of behaviours. There is great interest in what everyone does, but no impulse to influence — let alone coerce anyone. A child's will is his motive force. ...The Yequana do not feel that a child's inferior physical strength and dependence upon them imply that they should treat him or her with less respect than an adult. No orders are given a child which run counter to his own inclinations as to how to play, how much to eat, when to sleep, and so on. But where his help is required, he is expected to comply instantly. Commands like 'Bring some water!', 'Chop some wood!', 'Hand me that!', or 'Give the baby a banana!' are given on the same assumption of innate sociality, in the firm knowledge that a child wants to be of service and to join in the work of his people. No one watches to see whether the child obeys — there is no doubt of his will to co-operate. As the social animal he is, he does as he is expected without hesitation and to the very best of his ability."[11]

"One of the most striking differences between the Yequana and any other children I have seen is that they neither fight nor argue among themselves. There is no competitiveness and leadership is established on the initiative of the followers. In the years I spent with them, I never saw a child argue with another, much less fight. The only angry words I did hear were a very rare burst of impatience from an adult with a child who had done something undesirable."[12]

The Buddhist culture of Ladakh

"A concern not to offend or upset one another is deeply rooted in Ladakhi society; people avoid situations that might lead to friction or conflict. When someone transgresses this unwritten law, ...extreme tolerance is the response. And yet concern for community does not have the oppressive effect on the individual that one might have imagined.

In traditional Ladakh, agression of any sort is extremely rare: rare enough to say that it is virtually nonexistent. If you ask a Ladakhi to tell you about the last fight he can remember, you are likely to get mischievous answers like 'I'm always beating up my neighbor. Only yesterday I tied him to a tree and cut both his ears off.' Should you get a serious answer, you will be told that there has been no fighting in the village in living memory. Even arguments are rare.

I asked Sonam once, 'Don't you have arguments? We do in the West all the time.'

He thought for a minute. 'Not in the villages, no — well, very very seldom, anyway.'

'How do you manage it?' I asked.

He laughed. 'What a funny question. We just live with each other, that's all.'

'So what happens if two people disagree — say about the boundaries of their land?'

'They'll talk about it, of course, and discuss it. What would you expect them to do?'"[13]

The Fore of New Guinea

"The Fore protoagricultural communities were quite different from anything I had previously encountered. There were no chiefs, priests, medicine men, or the like. Moving about at will and being with whom they like, even the very young enjoyed a striking personal freedom.

Infants rarely cried, and they played confidently with knives, axes and fire. Older children typically enjoyed deferring to the interests and desires of the younger; sibling rivalry was virtually undetectable. A responsive 'sixth sense' seemed to attune the hamlet mates to each other's interests and needs. ...A spontaneous urge to share food, affection, work, trust and pleasure characterised the daily life. Aggression and conflict within communities was unusual and the subject of considerable comment when it occurred."[14]

> **You** That is quite amazing. I find it hard to believe. These descriptions don't sound like people as I know them.
>
> **Me** Yes indeed, it just shows how limited are most people's experience of the possibilities of human nature.

For these cultures, and many others in the anthropological literature, there is a natural, intuitive sociability and co-operation with coercion and aggression rare. The lesson of the starlings applies: they combine freedom and collaborative support. For these people, this is the obvious way people behave.

You But let me be clear. You are not saying that all cultures were like that before civilisation.

Me No. I've been describing the extreme peaceful end of a spectrum. It simply shows that that extreme is within the bounds of possibility of human nature. I'll take a first look at some of the reasons for the differences now. Unpicking those differences fully is one of the main theme of this book.

Two of the books quoted in this chapter express strong views about why some cultures are more aggressive than others. They point to child-rearing practices as a major factor. Ashley Montague says:

"Years ago Margaret Mead was the first anthropologist to inquire into the origins of aggressiveness in non-literate societies. In her book, *Sex and Temperament in Three Primitive Societies*,[15] she pointed to the existence of a strong association between child-rearing practices and later personality development. The child who received a great deal of attention, whose every need was promptly met, as among the New Guinea Mountain Arapesh, became a gentle, co-operative, unaggressive adult. On the other hand, the child who received perfunctory, intermittent attention, as among the New Guinea Mundugomor, became a selfish, unco-operative, aggressive adult. Later research among nonliterate and civilised peoples has substantially confirmed this relationship, and so do the studies presented in this volume."[16]

Jean Liedloff, in *The Continuum Concept*,[17] and Ashley Montague, in another of his books, *Touching, The Human Significance of the Skin*,[18] are even more specific. Jean Liedloff writes at length about "the in-arms experience", in which an infant in many pre-industrial cultures is continually carried in its mother's arms and is allowed to feed on demand.

Ashley Montague describes this same practice as an "external gestation". He says it is important because human babies are born relatively immature compared to other apes. The sense of security and being cared for in the womb is continued in the early experience of the infant. This provides the foundation for their later views of what the world is like.

> **You**   So we are back to permissive parenting. It is not so easy and can result in spoiled children rather than non-aggressive children.
>
> **Me**   There is much more to it than that. And 'permissiveness' does not capture the essence of it. The 'child as boss' approach can be as harmful as the 'parent as boss' approach. The key issue is the way the infant learns to see its environment. Is it being supported or is it being opposed?

Both Jean Liedloff and Ashley Montague are clear that child rearing is not the whole story. Ways of caring for infants and children cannot be taken out of the context of the whole culture. There needs to be a consistency between the supportive nature of child-rearing practices and the rest of the culture. This is what Jean Liedloff means by the 'continuum concept'.

The original affluent society

A quick look at the nature of economic systems in hunter-gatherer societies helps put our own economic system in perspective. Later chapters demonstrate that it is not the obvious best choice for our future.

There is a common view that life for hunter-gathers was very hard. "Our textbooks compete to convey a sense of impending doom, leaving one to wonder not only how hunters managed to live, but whether, after all, this was living."[19] For the most part, this is projection in order to justify the difficulties of life in civilised cultures. After all, if so many people are poor now, and we have the benefits of agriculture and civilisation, things must have been much worse before that. The reality was quite different. Early humans were a highly successful species, spreading throughout the world and becoming the top predator wherever they went. If they managed to survive those years when conditions were very difficult, they must have survived quite easily in the normal, good years. This easy life is the view of very many people who have studied modern hunter-gatherer cultures, and inspired Mashall Sahlins to call it "the original affluent society".[20] He cites various studies:

> "The most obvious, immediate conclusion is that the people do not work hard. The average length of time per person per day put into the appropriation and preparation of food was four or five hours. Moreover, they do not work continuously."[21]

> "The Bushman figures imply that one man's labor in hunting and gathering will support four or five people. Taken at face value, Bushman food collecting is more efficient than French farming in the period up to World War II. ... For each adult worker, this comes to about two and one-half days labor per week. ...A 'day's work' was about six hours."[22]

> "Reports suggest a mean of three to five hours per adult worker per day in food production. Hunters keep bankers' hours..."[23]

These days we have institutionalised hunger on an unprecedented scale, quite unlike the Old Stone Age. The industrial and commercial working week we have come to expect is not what humans faced through most of their evolutionary history. Production of food and many of the other goods of everyday life is a co-operative venture in hunter-gather societies. People do things with and for each other, exchange and give gifts. Sometimes this is casual and informal, sometimes highly organised, formal and even ritualised. The range of different forms of exchange is as varied as there are human cultures. Sometimes this exchange is local, within a family group, and other times it may be more distant, as trade. Here are a couple of examples.

The !Kung bushmen of the Kalahari Desert

Although they live in a desert, the bushmen consider their homeland abundant and beautiful. They hunt various animals and gather a wide range of plant food. Their staple is the mongongo nut, which is easy to gather, and highly nutritious. In discussions with anthropologists it is clear that they were capable of planting the nuts, if they chose to do so. But one commented: "Why should we plant when there are so many mongongo nuts in the world?"[24]

Hunting is more difficult and less reliable than gathering. When a hunter kills an animal, it is his responsibility to divide it up among the members of the band. This is a socially complex act, guided by relationships, past giving, and precedent. Often a young man will seek the advice of his elders on it to ensure he does not commit a *faux pas*. In contrast, gathering of plant food is easy and is done by everyone. The food gathered is shared widely and casually.

The Trobriand Islanders and the Kula ring[25]

For more settled groups, with simple agriculture, exchange is often more complex. The Trobriand Islands lie to the east of New Guinea. Much of the food of the islanders comes from shifting gardens, planted in different places in different years. There is a complex arrangement of ownership and use of these gardens. The *Towosi* (garden magician) supervises the clearing, planting and tending of the gardens. He initiates each stage of the gardening with a magical rite, which determines its timing. His expertise, expressed through the rituals he runs, thus ensures that everyone gets the best out of the land. Community members give ritual gifts to the *Towosi* as part of the ceremonies.

"There are different systems of communal work on various scales; sometimes the several village communities join together, sometimes the whole community, sometimes a few households. ...In the more extensive kinds of work it is the chief's duty to feed the workers."[26] There is a lot of redistribution of garden produce according to custom and ritual. This is a culture that is "enmeshed in a network of reciprocal obligations and dues, one constant flow of gift and counter-gift."

The chief is given ritual gifts of food on various occasions. He acts as a storehouse and redistributor. He can also transform food into objects of permanent wealth, through trade with other communities.

There was a trading system, called the Kula Ring, that included not just the Trobriand Islanders, but many other island communities to the east of New Guinea.[27] It was based on the exchange of two types of article of high value but of no real use – armshells and necklaces made of red shell-disks. Both were intended as ornaments but hardly used even for that purpose. Neither was kept for very long. Both travelled on a circular route, through trading partners with life-long relationships. An old chief might have a hundred trading partners, while a young commoner would have only a few. The necklaces travelled clockwise while the armshells travelled counter-clockwise along the trading routes. Thus in each trading pair one person would be giving the other armshells and receiving necklaces, while the other would give and receive the opposite.

The armshells and necklaces were in very limited supply. There was only a loose sense of the equivalence of the various valuables. The more valuable of them had individual names and histories and were known far and wide. The objective of the trade was to arrange to obtain the more prestigious ones from your trading partners. You in turn would soon pass them on to one of your other partners, thus obligating them to give you something prestigious in the future. To sweeten the trade, and to entice your partner to give the best objects to you, rather than to one of his other partners, all sorts of gifts were given as well. This included much more practical and useful items, such as pigs, yams and various other things. The trade enabled islands with agricultural surpluses to supply islands with less food, but other useful objects.

126

This trade had very great practical benefits to the people that participated in it. However, from their point of view, it was the prestige of receiving high value Kula items that mattered socially, not the practical uses of the side gifts. There is a similarity here with our modern economy. In both cases, the medium of exchange (money for us, armshells and necklaces in the Kula ring) takes on primary importance and appears to be the purpose of the trade.

The reciprocity spectrum

Sahlins classifies these forms of exchange along a spectrum, from what he calls generalised reciprocity, through balanced reciprocity, to negative reciprocity.[28]

- *'Generalised reciprocity'* includes the most altruistic forms – gifts, sharing, hospitality. However, generalised reciprocity is not simply a one-way transfer. There is an expectation of a return, but not on an immediate basis, or for a given item. So parents look after children who they expect to look after them when they are older. Such practices as 'kinship dues', 'chiefly dues' and 'noblesse oblige' are also examples of generalised reciprocity. Generalised reciprocity implies an on-going relationship between the people concerned. They are part of the same family, band or tribe.

- *'Balanced reciprocity'* is the mid-point of the spectrum. The return is immediate. This is the classic form of barter and includes much of what involves 'primitive money'. It is less personal than generalised reciprocity, and involves a looser relationship.

- *'Negative reciprocity'* is "the unsociable extreme, …the attempt to get something for nothing with impunity. …The participants confront each other as opposed interests, each looking to maximise utility at the other's expense."[29] The extreme end of negative reciprocity is theft, rape and pillage.

For the !Kung bushmen, and most hunter-gather societies, exchange tends to be at the generalised end of the spectrum. In the Trobriand Islands, exchange within a community was more generalised while the Kula ring tended more towards balance. In our modern economy, exchange tends to range between the balanced and negative ends of the spectrum. The eGaian image is of exchange that retains the complexity and richness of the technological world, but with the use of communication technology to support new social forms that allow a return to the generalised end of the spectrum.

CHAPTER six

Towards the global cancer: the late human story

The origins and early history of humanity is about the ape that specialised in co-operative behaviour, developing language and culture as a means of enhancing our survival. Early humans lived a life to which they had evolved and adapted over nearly two million years. Their impact upon the natural world was comparable to that of other medium-sized mammals. Then, over a time period which is an evolutionary blink of an eye, humanity came to dominate the world, to have an impact which can be seen as a global cancer. This chapter traces that stage-by-stage transition. Recent research into the mechanisms of cancer shows that it too starts gradually:

> "Cancer begins deep inside the molecular machinery of a cell: first one genetic mutation, then another, and so on until the gene products that provide the usual checks and balances to cell division go awry, and the cell careers down the path of uncontrolled, cancerous proliferation."[1]

The course of humanity's global cancer shows a similar progressive loss of connection from the natural world and the checks and balances of evolution.

- With the development of settled living and agriculture, humanity started to become disconnected from the natural constraints on obtaining food, so its population could begin to rise.

- With the beginnings of civilisation and with it the transition from oral cultures to writing, human thought and spiritual life began to lose its intimate connection with natural processes. Wars, conflict and environmental destruction took a great spurt forward.

- With industrialisation came the change from wood and wind for

energy to the use first of coal and later oil, gas and finally nuclear fuels. The natural constraints upon energy use began to be lost. The impacts of human technology could increase until they were large enough to change the climate.

- The final stage was reached in the late 20th century with the development of a globalised, commercially-dominated world economy. The constraints of local cultures were lost, and to a large extent those of national governments. Unending growth of production became the shrine and goal of public policy, with the preservation of the Earth an unpleasant side-issue that has to be coped with somehow.

130

Fortunately the possibility of a global eGaian culture was also established in that final stage. For the first time, there is the possibility of a new stage in evolution: self-awareness and co-ordination on a planetary scale.

> **You** Hang on. Don't get carried away. And your potted history of human culture sounds a bit simplistic.
>
> **Me** I'm sure it is hugely oversimplified. But let me spell the four stages out in a bit more detail.

Disconnection from food: settled agriculture

This final chapter of the human story starts about 10,000 years ago, at the end of the last ice age. At the time, the total human population of the world was about 4 million. Then, for reasons that are not very clear, people began to lead more settled lives. They began to replace hunting with the domestication of animals and to replace gathering with crops they planted.

At one time it was thought "that the advantages of agriculture were so obvious that it must have been adopted as soon as human genius and invention had progressed far enough. Now such easy answers seem less plausible."[2] The hunter-gather life seems generally to have been easier. There was no need to plant, harvest and store crops. Agriculture relies on fewer crops so that in a bad year shortages and famine are more likely. Wilkinson speculates that rising populations led to a loss of 'ecological equilibrium'.[3] Perhaps the rising population was an over-reaction to the warmer, lusher conditions that appeared when the ice age ended. So here again, it may have been the response to a crisis that led to a breakthrough.

Agriculture seems to have developed independently in different parts of the world using different crops and animals. "The key centres were south-west Asia, China, Mesoamerica, the Andes and the tropical areas of Africa and south-east Asia."[4] Within these past 10,000 years it has spread throughout the world. Now very few hunter-gatherer societies remain, mostly in very isolated areas, usually with extremely small populations.

Whatever the reasons for its origins, once it became more highly developed, agriculture began to produce food surpluses. This meant that human populations could increase beyond the limitations of the carrying capacity of the land for gatherer-hunter societies. Humans had made a major break from the natural constraints on population for animals in the wild. The parallels with a cancer are clear.

The change from gatherer-hunter cultures to agriculture was a major one in physical ways for our co-operative ape. The diet and way of life that had shaped human physiology and psychology had changed substantially. The flesh of wild animals and fish is much less fatty than that of domesticated animals. Dairy products and grains as staples were new additions to the human diet. Not surprisingly, even today they are harder for us to digest than fruit and vegetables. For example, it is thought that for a person to retain the ability to digest milk after they are weaned is an adaptation that evolved in early cattle herders.[5] Most of humanity, especially in southern Europe, Asia and Africa become intolerant to lactose after weaning.

> "Studies of today's few remaining traditional hunter-gather communities reveal a virtual absence of raised blood pressure, obesity, heart disease and diabetes in middle and late adulthood. This mismatch between our Pleistocene-attuned biology and our current way of life has been amplified over the past century as urban sedentariness, dietary excesses and various socialised addictive behaviours (alcohol consumption and tobacco smoking) have become prominent features of modern human ecology."[6]

Disconnection in thought and spirit: civilisation

Early human cultures had a sense of connection with the natural world around them which is not at all part of the life experience of most people today. That disconnection took a great leap forward with the transition from settled farming to civilisations. In many cases those early farming societies also became more hierarchical and unequal. Ponting takes up the story:

> "Chiefs and religious authorities controlled much of the surplus food and redistributed it mainly in accordance with their priorities. As they did so they exercised more control over the people in their community. ...Societies at this level of development existed everywhere across the world for thousands of years..."

> "In a handful of areas some societies... went much further and became coercive states and created the organisations, institutions and culture which we call civilisation. This process occurred at most six times in human history – in Mesopotamia, the Indus valley, China, Mesoamerica and the central Andes."

"These societies were distinguished by a number of features – they supported an elite of thousands of non-producers (priests, rulers, bureaucrats, craftsmen and warriors) who lived mainly in cities and who exercised power over the rest of the population through forms of taxation and tribute. …Most developed some form of written script for various forms of record keeping."[7]

"The evolution of writing was central to the development of civilisation…it was fundamental to the functioning of the state in most early civilisations. Its purpose was not to represent a language but to store and transmit information. At first this was mainly about trade and administration…"

133

"Writing was central to the power of the state and the ability of it and the elite to control and exploit the majority of people."[8]

It was in these newly invented states, with their controlling elites, that the disconnection of thought and spirit began. David Abram, in *The Spell of the Sensuous*[9], presents a persuasive picture of its origins. His thesis is that the change from oral cultures to cultures with writing (and especially alphabetic writing) was the key point of change.

Oral cultures perpetuate themselves through continually telling stories about their surroundings. Stories about specific locations and about plants and animals are crucial to their understanding of how to live. 'Spirits', as we call them, were not abstract, disembodied essences, in some other non-material realm, but aspects of the natural world around them. In their use of language, oral cultures participate in the world. "Here words do not speak *about* the world; rather they speak *to* the world, and to the expressive presences that, with us, inhabit the world." This is in contrast to "the character of linguistic discourse in the 'developed' or 'civilised' world, where language functions largely to deny reciprocity with nature–by defining the rest of nature as inert, mechanical, and determinate..."[10].

As writing progressed beyond record keeping to literature and philosophy, particularly in ancient Greece, this disconnection intensified. Oral culture, with its constantly repeated stories preserving cultural wisdom, became less and less important. People could look back at the written word, reflect on it and comment on it. This became the dominant way in which the culture was passed on. The evolution of human cultures had taken on a life of its own, no longer intimately tied to direct experience of the natural world.

People live in an environment shaped at least as much by ideas as by their direct experiences. These collections of ideas can regenerate and maintain themselves as they are passed from person to person. Once freed from the constraining bonds of nature, it was perhaps inevitable that all the features of the global cancer would eventually appear.

The practicalities of living in the early cities created a major disconnection from the natural world. Those who were not directly engaged with producing food were much less connected to it. Those who were, found that their activities and demands were increasingly determined by their relationships with the others who controlled them. People began to rely on other people to provide much of what they needed. It was no longer the case that most people knew most of what there was to know in the culture. Most still worked on the land, but others specialised in producing implements, cloth, or in building or trade. This meant that people were no longer dealing directly with people they knew well.

Trade and barter became more important and money appeared. Money in the form of coins was said by Herodotus to have been first used in the 8th century BC. "They are the first people on record who coined gold and silver into money, and traded in retail."[11] The close coupling of producer and consumer had begun to loosen. Exchange had begun to move farther from the generalised end of Sahlins' reciprocity spectrum.

The sense of intimate support in the gathering-hunting band was no longer there. The earliest reports of widespread crime, corruption and dissolute youth come from the early civilisations. Professional fighters and standing armies appeared. Now there were groups of men whose principal function was to enforce the will of some groups on others. Wars on a much larger scale appeared. The technology of war took a huge leap forward in weaponry, military tactics and training. There were wars between gathering-hunting groups too, but they were conducted by men whose usual role in the culture was hunting and gathering. Those earlier wars were often highly ritualised, like much animal conflict. A war might end when the first blood was spilled.

135

Environmental problems appeared. Fertile land was farmed too intensively in places, creating deserts. Parts of northern Africa, now desert, were the granaries of the Roman Empire.

With all the social and political change came a new set of mythologies and world views. Authoritarian male gods and hierarchies of gods appeared, reflecting and justifying the political hierarchies in the early civilisations. The Earth mother goddess (the original incarnations of Gaia) and all the spirits of natural forces had lost their central place.

You So our global cancer really started with the beginning of civilisation? Are you saying it would it be better for the Earth if we all returned to that early hunter-gatherer lifestyle?

Me The size of the human population is far too great for the Earth to support us as gatherer-hunters. It is now about 1,500 times as large as it was at the end of the ice age, one measure of the extent of humanity as a global cancer. Moreover, I don't think it is remotely desirable from humanity's perspective. What I do think is possible is that we could regain the social intimacy and supportiveness of the most peaceful gatherer-hunter cultures while retaining a sophisticated technology, perhaps something like I described in the Pinecone Network story.

Disconnected energy and technology: industrialisation

The start of industrialisation in the 18th century marked another substantial increase in the impact of the global cancer, and of the disconnection between human cultures and the environment. The key to this increased impact was the development of new energy sources that enabled a huge growth and development of technology. In the 1750s agriculture occupied about 90% of the population. The relatively low productivity of agriculture limited the population overall and the proportion of the population that could be supported outside of agriculture. By the end of the 20th century, less than 5% of the population of the industrialised countries worked in agriculture.

The principal source of energy for agriculture up to the 18th century was human labour. Animals were used too, but humans ate less food. Supporting a horse required 4 or 5 acres of land. Oxen needed slightly less and so were the main draught animals. In 18th-century Europe there were about 24 million oxen and about 12 million horses.

"As late as 1806 one French agricultural writer could still advocate abandoning the plough and returning to digging fields by hand which although slower, was cheaper and more thorough."[12]

According to Ponting, industrialisation started first in England, not because it had increased its agricultural productivity but because it was able to import large quantities of food from its nearest colony – Ireland.[13] This, combined with the forcible eviction of peasants from their land by the big landlords, provided a workforce for the new industrial economy. Once started, the expansion of income from trade and increased imports from the colonies created a spiral of growth.

Waterpower was the main energy source for much early industry, with textile industries and other factories strung out along suitable rivers. In areas like the Netherlands, where waterpower was limited, wind was exploited. Wood was the main fuel until the 19th century. In the form of charcoal it was the primary industrial fuel for iron smelting, brewing, and glass making. It took a lot of woodland to fuel the early industrial revolution. An average small iron furnace used up about 250 acres of woodland every year. So industrial output was limited by the availability of what we now call renewable energy sources: human and animal power plus water, wind and wood.

Wood was also used for things like the construction of buildings, ships or furniture – so intensively that it became scarce. People had to make do with coal, considered a much inferior fuel at the time because it had to be mined and because it smelled bad when it burned.

> "There is so great a scarcity of wood throughout the whole kingdom... the inhabitants in general are constrained to make their fires of sea-coal or pit-coal, even in the chambers of honourable personages."[14]

Once again, a change was adopted not because it was seen as an advance but because of a crisis in the older system. Once adopted, the new fuel opened new horizons. The growth of human industry was no longer constrained by the available energy from renewable sources. All of those were obtained indirectly from current sunlight falling on the Earth. Now energy was obtained from ancient sunlight, from forests that grew about 300 million years ago. This was the beginning of human ability to pollute the Earth on a grand scale. As coal was followed by oil and then gas as major fuels, more and more ancient forests were burned. Ancient carbon that had been removed from the atmosphere was returned as carbon dioxide. This was the beginning of global warming. The global cancer was getting large enough to change the Earth's climate.

In the early stages of industrialisation, the pollution from released carbon dioxide was insignificant compared to the more obvious pollution of the newly expanded industry.

> "By the nineteenth century across Europe and North America there were areas of concentrated pollution and environmental degradation – ruined landscapes of chimneys belching smoke and poisonous gases, huge slag heaps of waste materials, rivers full of a cocktail of industrial wastes and surrounding areas where the vegetation was destroyed."[15]

There were many other changes as well. The modern world was taking shape. Cities became much more important, What had been trading centres and a focus for the rich and their courts were now centres of industrial production.. Transport and communications improved, first with the development of canals and then, once the steam engine arrived, the railways. Governments took on new functions. Before that their main function was military. Now, with the new urban cultures, with a new class of industrial poor, and all the new industries, they added policing and prisons, regulation of industries (especially the strategically important railways) provision of water and sanitation in the new cities.

There were major changes in political control too. Between 1750 and 1900 Europe came to dominate the rest of the world. In 1800 Europe controlled about a third of the world's land surface, in 1900 over four-fifths. The stage was now set for the final chapter in this story – globalisation.

The disconnected economy: globalisation

The human story in the 20th century – especially in its second half – is of the cancer reaching its limits. With globalisation, human intervention on the natural world lost its remaining constraints, those of local cultures and governments. The driving force for most human enterprise has become the pursuit of monetary flows, an abstraction quite free from physical and biological requirements. Our impact on the natural world became so large that changes in weather patterns and climate became noticeable, and not just a scientific prediction, while the undermining of wilderness areas, fisheries and soil fertility is catastrophic.

The state of food production illustrates the situation. At the beginning of the 20th century, most agriculture worldwide was for local consumption. Local food was adapted to local conditions, so that every region had its specialities, season by season. Soil fertility depended almost entirely on manures and composts produced on the farm. But in the second half of the 20th century, food and farming became just one more industry, now using industrial techniques to improve the money flows through the industry. Through the use of farm machinery, the number of people required in agriculture dropped drastically. The use of larger machines led to larger fields and increasing dependence upon single crops, which were more susceptible to diseases and pests, and so were kept in check by chemical herbicides and pesticides. Productivity was increased by the use of chemical fertilisers. "The soil was treated less as a living organism and more as a medium to hold crops in position as more and more chemicals were poured on to them."[16]

As an eminently marketable product, food developed in ways that enhanced its profitability rather than its effect on the health of people or the land. So highly processed foods appeared, with additives to prolong their shelf life. Fruit and vegetables lost their seasonal round. Limited numbers of standardised varieties are now shipped all over the world, replacing local varieties. Freshness, flavour and nutritional value take a poor second place to pristine appearance and suitability to industrial farming and distribution. High margin junk foods are the most heavily promoted. When did you last see a TV advertisement for fresh vegetables? Supermarket layout and design is a highly developed science; you can get PhDs in it. Atmosphere, lighting and smells are all carefully designed to put you in a receptive mood. Go into a supermarket in most industrial countries and you will find yourself in familiar territory.

Of course food is marketable only to people who have money. So land in Asia, Africa and South America came to be used to grow crops for export, leaving only the worst land for the poorer local populations. The result is a world in which billions go hungry while food is in plentiful supply. A domestic cat in the United States eats more meat than the average inhabitant of Africa and Latin America.

And it's not just food that has become globalised. During the early part of the industrial revolution wealthy individuals and families owned the new factories, mills and then the big retail outlets. They were still part of the local culture. The middle of the 20th century saw the rise of multi-national corporations which changed that completely. Professional managers began to run the corporations, and financial institutions — banks, insurance companies and pension funds — owned their stock. As global transport and communications improved, it became possible and desirable (financially) to run a company that was distributed throughout the world. In the 1960s the Ford Motor Company in Britain made the Cortina for British use. In the 1980s its replacement, the Escort was designed for the European market and assembled in three plants incorporating parts made in 15 countries.

Large companies are now many of the largest economic organisations, dwarfing the economies of all but the largest nations. National governments have a very limited ability to influence them, as large companies threaten to move their production elsewhere. On the contrary, governments woo companies, offering financial inducements and freedom from social and environmental restrictions to locate in their territories.

Perhaps the clearest sign of how disconnected the human economy has become is what has happened to the financial markets. Before globalisation, the buying and selling of currencies was a necessary service to the rest of the economy. Now currency trading totally dominates world trade. With the abandonment of the gold standard by the US in 1970 and then the deregulation of currency transactions in the 1980s, all limits were removed. As late as the 1970s, the typical daily volume of foreign currency transactions was in the range of $10-20 billion. On a normal day in 2000 that had risen to $2,000 billion. This amounts to over 150 times the total daily international trade of all commodities and services worldwide.[17] This is speculative trading, whose purpose is to make a profit from the changes in value of the currency. As John Maynard Keynes said:

> "Speculators may do no harm as bubbles on a steady stream of enterprise. But the position is serious when enterprise becomes the bubble on a whirlpool of speculation. When the capital development of a country becomes a by-product of the activities of a casino, the job is likely to be ill-done."[18]

With a cancer, unlimited expansion is all that matters. From the point of view of the growing cancer cells, it might seem great, "Our empire is expanding!" But from the point of view of the body, it means death and, ultimately, death to the cancer cells as well. All of humanity is currently caught up in the out-of-control, unlimited expansion that is our global cancer. Much of the problem is an unwillingness to look deeply enough and question the nature of our society.

The possibility of eGaia

Fortunately, as the cancer has reached its global limits it has also brought with it the possibilities of overcoming it. Several of the changes that made globalisation possible are also essential to a re-connection.

The late 20th century forced upon us a global view: a growth in environmental awareness, an awareness of humanity-as-a-whole through multi-culturalism and global television, some halting attempts at a framework for global peace, and most recently, a communications infrastructure which can enable humanity to function as a global nervous system, should it choose to do so. These possibilities form the contents of parts 3 and 4. Can we re-connect:

- with food, restoring our physiological link to the natural world

- in energy, so that we allow the Earth's climate to recover or at least stabilise

- in our economy, so that we act to promote the health of humanity and the natural world

- in thought and spirituality, so that we begin to form a single, global organism that could be eGaia?

PART three

AN eGAIAN GUIDE: PHILOSOPHY AND PRINCIPLES

eGAIAN RELATIONSHIPS

The starting point for eGaia is developing co-operative rather than competitive relationships with others. This is necessary if we are to see ourselves as part of a larger whole, the living Earth. This requires an understanding of the communications principles necessary for co-operation. This chapter explores these ideas by going back to first principles: how we construct the personal worlds in which we each live.

Further chapters of Part 3 apply that kind of relationship in wider contexts – to conflict resolution, to a co-operative economy and to a sustainable Earth.

The relationship spectrum

What does it mean for 'the Earth to function as an organism' and for 'humanity to function as the nervous system of that organism'? The primary characteristic of an organism is its wholeness: its parts do not act independently; they act in support of the whole and thus in support of each other. At a personal level, this implies a shift in relationships from competition towards mutual support and collaboration. That change of relationship is a shift along a spectrum, as in the diagram below.

145

A spectrum of relationships

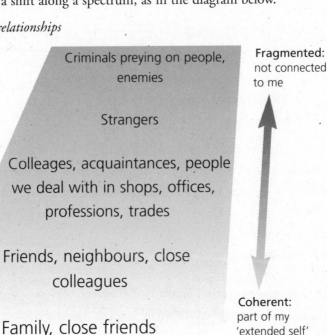

Criminals preying on people, enemies

Fragmented: not connected to me

Strangers

Colleages, acquaintances, people we deal with in shops, offices, professions, trades

Friends, neighbours, close colleagues

Family, close friends

Coherent: part of my 'extended self'

Relationships at the near end of this spectrum are 'coherent' in contrast to 'fragmented'. Relationships at the coherent end are close, loving and supportive, those at the fragmented end are distant, coercive and difficult. At the coherent end are people who are like an extension of oneself. At the fragmented end, people are disconnected, part of Earth as ecosystem, not organism.

> **You** But I know lots of people who hate other members of their families.
>
> **Me** Sure, but it is the qualities of relationship in this spectrum that I'm trying to clarify. The fact that there are many exceptions is not relevant to the argument.

146

What is it that changes along this spectrum?

- the degree to which people identify with each other, as part of a sort of 'extended self'

- the degree to which people understand each other, from the other's point of view, and the way this leads to acceptance and tolerance of differences.

As will become clear later in the chapter, to maintain a relationship at the coherent end of the spectrum, it helps to have communication strategies that can resolve or at least diffuse the conflicts that inevitably arise.

To begin to clarify this relationship spectrum, here is a fairly extended set of examples, which later sections will draw on. It starts at the fragmented end.

Professional burglars, thieves and muggers   Crime is one of the world's largest industries. When someone snatches your bag, chances are they don't think of you as a person like themselves, any more than a lion feels compassion for the gazelle it kills. You are 'other', something that doesn't matter to them. They don't hate you, and aren't angry with you. You, the person, simply don't come into their awareness. They can sustain this as a way of life, largely because they are part of a sub-culture in which it is acceptable, regardless of what the rest of society says.

Cultures at war The Arab-Israeli conflict is one of many similar examples of cultures at war at present. The next chapter, on conflict resolution, uses it as an example, but the essence of the argument. between the two sides is depressingly familiar to all. Outsiders may see a spiral of violence – the actions of both sides are taken by the other side as justifying their own violence and even making it necessary – but each side takes a more limited view. Their own anger and pain blinds them to the suffering they are inflicting on the other side, who they demonise. They see themselves as victims of the other side, not as part of a process in which both sides are the cause of the other side's violence.

147

Strangers meeting casually *Fear*: you walk past a strange-looking group of people in the evening on an empty street in a large town. You think to yourself, "Am I about to be attacked?" You walk on past. There is no eye contact, no exchange of greetings. You continue to walk in fear for quite a while.

Casual friendship You walk in a wild, hilly place with a group of friends, and you encounter another group of walkers. You pass, you say "Hello!" and "What a beautiful day!" and walk on, never to see each other again. The entire relationship is brief but pleasant. The words and the body language say "I am not a threat, my intentions are friendly. You and I are people who like the same kinds of things."

Hospitality to strangers Many cultures have had very strong traditions of hospitality to strangers. "When in 1568 a European missionary arrived out of the blue at Nagasaki, he was given a Buddhist temple to stay in, and banquets three nights running... The Lithuanian word for guest is clansman (svetjas), because by eating and sleeping in another's house, a guest became a member of his host's clan. In Albania, a host who gave hospitality to a stranger was obliged to take revenge on anyone who harmed him before he reached his next destination."[1]

The people in the shops There's a shop selling electrical and electronic goods, staffed by bright young men wearing the shop's shirt and tie. They don't know anything about you and they don't ask. They show you several models and sing the praises of one of the more expensive ones. Do they get more commission on that one, or is it really better? Can you trust them? Are they serving you or themselves? There's another shop where several of your friends work. Whenever you walk in you get a nice greeting but sometimes have to forestall long conversations if you are busy. You know their advice is, at the worst, their view of your best interests.

Creative arts camp[2] This example of ordinary Western people meeting under circumstances which bring out the best and most co-operative within them is used as an extended example in Chapter 9, but is introduced here.

There may be as many as several hundred people, a lot of them children, at the camp. People come expecting to camp in a circle around a common campfire with some friends. Each camping circle usually unites more than one group of friends and some newcomers and become instant communities. They are memorable social units. People will say, "You remember so and so. They were in such and such's circle, over by the grove,

148

two years ago." People come from various backgrounds and income levels, but share a love of music and of these camps. The setting is conducive to creating friendships. There are many tasks to share – cooking, tending the fire, looking after the children – and activities to go to together. Most of the routine tasks of looking after the camp as a whole are spread out among the campers, working half a day each, in a fairly organised way. Crews of campers keep the toilets clean, work in the café and the children's area. The camp would be much more expensive if people had to be paid to do that.

Over the years, a culture and tradition of the camps has grown up which is passed on to newcomers – so they find a sense of instant community, created effortlessly. Many people find the camps very powerful experiences, and want more like that in their lives.

149

The happy couple Despite all the broken families and dysfunctional relationships, there are still many relationships that do work well, and they form a fitting end to the relationship spectrum. The happy couple know that the other's mood can make a difference to their own mood, so it is self-interest as well as love which leads them to act to support the other's happiness. They are very aware of the practical and emotional benefits of having someone to share their lives with.

They spend a fair proportion of their time together, but also have quite separate lives and interests. Both respect their partners' independent time and enjoy hearing about it. The differences between them lead them to have quite different views on some subjects. (This is sometimes to do with very personal aspects of their life, such as tidiness and hygiene, food, dress, etc.) They know that these differences are inevitable, and generally enjoy and accept them light-heartedly. They feel that this acceptance and tolerance is a major strength of their relationship.

When the differences between them begin to cause tension, (as it must from time to time) they have learned strategies for diffusing it. Lateral thinking is often a useful way out of conflict. They find some solution that satisfies both of them. Neither is shy about complaining, having found that the other generally listens with sympathy and tends to take the complaint on board. Their mutual acceptance and tolerance leads to low defensiveness.

They share some of their income, but not all. Their contributions to their joint expenses are roughly the same, but they don't worry about trying to keep careful records or about getting it exactly equal. It isn't worth the effort, and besides, they like doing things to please each other.

You So you think all relationships should aim to become like the happy couple? I don't want to spend my time hearing all about the personal lives of the people I meet in shops and doubt if I will ever come to love them.

Me No, I didn't say that. Everyone has relationships in many different parts of the spectrum. All I am suggesting is a shift along it. I am trying to tease out what the crucial differences are along the spectrum so we can create the conditions for coherent rather than fragmented relationships.

Selves and extended selves

"A human being is part of the whole, called by us 'Universe', a part limited in time and space. He experiences himself, his thoughts and feelings as something separated from the rest – a kind of optical delusion of his consciousness. This delusion is a kind of prison for us, restricting us to our personal desires and to affection for a few

persons nearest to us. Our task must be to free ourselves from this prison by widening our circle of compassion to embrace all living creatures and the whole nature in its beauty."
Albert Einstein[3]

A good starting point for looking more deeply at this relationship spectrum is to look at our sense of self and how we create it. Our bodies are the most obvious first look at who we are. Peter Russell calls this "the skin-encapsulated ego."[4] We learn to see ourselves as our bodies in infancy as we become aware of our separateness from our mothers and our surroundings. A baby gradually comes to be able to control its body. It learns to control its limbs. It learns to give signs that result in its being fed, so satisfying internal needs. The sense of what is 'me' grows by contrast with what is 'not me'. I can bang my fist, but that table resists my banging. It is 'not me'. Thus begins a sense of 'me' as 'that which I am able to control and look after'.

This early psychological sense of self closely parallels the physical organisation of the body as a control system.[5] Our bodies control their internal temperature to within a fraction of a degree. They control and preserve the chemical composition of the blood and tissues very accurately. To enable the internal, unconscious parts of us to do this, our overall conscious part must behave in suitable ways. It must control the limbs to put clothes on and off to help maintain its temperature. It must act in ever more complex ways to ensure a suitable supply of food, shelter and other physical needs.

Peter Russell contrasts 'the skin-encapsulated ego' with a broader sense of self as "unbounded, part of a greater wholeness, united with the rest of the Universe."[6] This book proposes a related but more limited sense of

151

extended self as a starting point while keeping Peter's vision around philosophically.

My study as my shell

As I sit at my desk in my study, an environment that has been mostly shaped by me surrounds me. The books, messy desk, ornaments, pictures on the wall all give anyone entering the room a strong sense of me, my interests and personality. Just as I eat, exercise, dress, etc to keep my body healthy, I act to keep my study as it suits me. It is part of what I care about and look after. Even in the animal kingdom, 'the organism' may mean more than 'the physical body'. Is the shell of a snail part of the snail or part of its environment? What about a bee hive? Scott Turner, in *The Extended Organism*[7] makes the case that the structures animals build should be properly considered to be external organs of physiology.

We can use the term 'extended self' to reflect this internal, psychological sense of self, as 'that which you care about and look after'. So in this sense, your immediate family and close friends are generally part of your extended self. You may do a lot for your children, at great personal cost, because they are part of what you care about. Similarly, your personal possessions and home are part of your extended self. (People feel violated when their home or car is broken into, even though they haven't been physically harmed themselves.)

There are wider, but perhaps less intense aspects of the extended self, like your values and those aspects of your community, your culture or the world which you care about. When you give money to relieve a famine on the other side of the world you are seeing the people there as a part of your extended self in a small way. If you are upset when you read of a genocidal war or the destruction of a rainforest, those people and that forest are, at least momentarily, part of your extended self.

Going back to the relationship spectrum, it is clear that the Arabs and Israelis are not part of each other's extended selves. Nor are the burglar's victims. With friendly and hospitable strangers a little extended self begins to creep in, as it certainly does in the friendly shop. The creative arts camp is set up in such a way as to encourage people to see each other as parts of their extended selves, as it is expected that they will be looking after each other. And of course, the lives of the happy couple are so intertwined that the old cliché 'my other (better?) half' certainly applies.

153

Thus anything which encourages people to see each other (and also the natural world) as part of their extended self is a step towards an eGaian world. This includes much of the environmental movements and peace movements, and many of the experiments with new forms of community (*kibbutzim*, communes and co-operatives) of the past century. The message from the creative arts camp is that it is possible to set up new structures in which people naturally find themselves seeing each other as part of their extended self. Social structures that do that will form the basis of the steps towards an eGaian world.

The View from inside: constructing one's world

To fully understand the sense of self we need to understand how an individual 'constructs their world', from the inside. For example...

Sitting in my garden...

I sit in my garden writing this book. If I reflect superficially as to what my world is at the moment, I might say it is what I see and hear around me: the house, the garden and beyond, shapes I recognise as flowers, bushes, walls and windows. I hear birds, wind, traffic and other people in the distance.

But looking a little closer, there is much more to it than that. I experience a mixture of emotions: excitement, a little fear and impatience with myself for being so slow. Thoughts are tumbling through my mind, some related to the book, others to various other aspects of my life: chores I have to do, my next meal, my partner. I live in an almost incessant stream of 'words-in-my-head' that flits about from one sub-stream to the next. My primary reality, my personal 'View' is that continuous and subjective jumble of thoughts, feelings and perceptions. My physical surroundings and body are just a part of it. They are secondary, something I sometimes pay attention to.

I take a sip of tea from my favourite mug and experience the familiar taste and feelings of relaxation I associate with cups of tea. My experience of drinking tea includes elements of all previous cups of tea I have drunk and the social situations in which I have had them. My enjoyment of the design of the mug is there too. The present-moment physical sensations are only a small part of the experience.

154

So our starting point is this fundamental experience that it is our private and subjective 'View' of the world which is our primary reality. Our experience of the physical world is secondary. It is constructed out of that View. [8]

The construction of a person's View is an active process. It is not simply the mixture of thought and perception that determines experience. Your View seems like a detailed, seamless world, as though it were being recorded by a video camera. Actually, your perception is very limited. The full information you would need to receive all the shapes, movement and sounds around you to really experience that detailed, seamless world is vastly beyond the capacity of your senses. Moreover, your brain would need a lot more information processing power than it has to make sense of it all. Instead, what happens is that you continually guess what is going to happen next. Your mind anticipates what will happen from its past experiences. It fills in most of the missing information from what it expects.

Sometimes that process of seamless construction breaks down and you become aware of it.

The time I shouted at my trousers

I went into the bedroom early one evening and spotted a shape on the bed. In the half-light I wasn't instantly sure what it was, but I suddenly thought, "The dog is on the bed!" The size was about right and I could just about recognise its head, ears and tail. I shouted "Get off!" as I had a long-standing policy that the dog was not allowed on the bed I slept in. I rushed forward to enforce my will, switched on the light, and broke out in laughter. On the bed were my trousers, jumbled up as I had left them earlier. In the light they looked nothing like the dog, but my memory is clear: In the half-light I 'saw' the head, ears and tail.

The step that wasn't there

I was leaving the home of good friends whom I had visited before. The outside light bulb had failed, but the path was familiar to me. There were several steps down, around a dark corner where I couldn't see. I walked down the first three steps confidently, but on the fourth 'step' I nearly fell. My memory had failed me. There were only three steps. My body movements, anticipating a fourth step that wasn't there, were completely inappropriate to level ground.

Misheard names on the telephone

Have you ever noticed that if someone answers the telephone with their own name as the first word ("Richard speaking..."), it is impossible to understand? It takes a few words for you to key into the characteristics of another person's voice. Only then can you anticipate the next words and thus recognise them. A name doesn't have enough context to allow you to do this. If you pay attention to what you actually can remember when you hear a new name on the phone then you will get a clue as to how much of your 'experience' is actually filled in by your anticipation.

156

Making a light switch vanish

Here is a party trick. You can make a light switch or any small object on a plain wall appear to vanish by using the blind spot in your eye. Locate a small object on a plain wall opposite you. Put your right hand over your right eye. Then extend your left hand and point to the object with your left forefinger. While concentrating on your finger, move your left hand to the right very slowly. After you have moved your hand about six inches to the right the object will seem to vanish. It will be in the blind spot of your left eye and you will see a continuous blank wall. For this to work you have to avoid the temptation to look directly at the object. Keep looking at your finger, but notice when the object disappears from view. Your mind does not allow you to experience a hole in your perception. It fills in the details from the clues it has available, in this case the surrounding wall.

Yes That seems like a clever trick, and I will try it, but what is the point you are getting at? What does this have to do with people trying to collaborate?

Me Much of what we think we are experiencing, that is, stuff coming from 'out there' is actually our minds filling in details from what we expect to experience. This can fool us when we are dealing with other people. Haven't you ever found that you thought you had an understanding with someone who later claimed to see it much differently than you? Often we think we agree with someone on the basis of brief comments.

157

We have filled in a lot of agreement that was never really there. A lot of careful checking of agreement is needed.

So you can't make sense of a person's View simply by looking at their external circumstances. From the outside, it might seem as though they should be happy, should believe certain things, should choose certain actions. From their internal perspective it could look completely different. It is perfectly reasonable for two people to have what an observer might think was the same experience and yet have a completely different understanding of it. Each is actually taking in different aspects and filling out their construction based upon their own past history and expectations.

158

> ***First principle of a coherent relationship*** Both people must attempt to understand each other from each other's perspective, from each others' View.

It follows from this is that you cannot make sense of another person's View without sufficient communication to know what that View is.

To summarise the argument so far, we live in our View, our private subjective reality that consists of a mixture of feelings, thoughts and perceptions. At any moment, memories of many similar events are evoked by our current perceptions. We use these to make sense of the present moment and to anticipate what will happen next. Without that anticipation, very little of our perceptions would be understandable. There is just too much coming in at any one time to make sense of it otherwise.

Convergent communication: knowing that you are in agreement

Everyone has had experiences where they thought they had an agreement with someone else and later found that wasn't the case. It may have been on some personal level such as an arrangement on where and when to meet. It may be an understanding with someone you work for, or with someone offering you a service. Sometimes you might be convinced that the other person has knowingly distorted the agreement, but sometimes it is clear that both genuinely saw it in different ways.

This is where the idea that our View is our primary reality becomes so powerful. Differences in View need not be seen as contradictory. They can be perfectly consistent within the context of each person's different experience and anticipation.

159

Here is a comical story that was circulating on the Internet. Ignore the dreadful gender stereotypes and enjoy the way two very different Views are formed out of a joint experience.

The differences between men and women

Let's say a guy named Roger is attracted to a woman named Elaine. He asks her out to a movie; she accepts; they have a pretty good time. A few nights later he asks her out to dinner, and again they enjoy themselves. They continue to see each other regularly, and after a while neither one of them is seeing anybody else.

And then, one evening when they're driving home, a thought occurs to Elaine, and without really thinking, she says it aloud: "Do you realize that, as of tonight, we've been seeing each other for exactly six months?" And then there is silence in the car. To Elaine, it seems like a very loud silence. She thinks to herself: "Geez, I wonder if it bothers him that I said that? Maybe he's feeling confined by our relationship; maybe he thinks I'm trying to push him into some kind of obligation that he doesn't want, or isn't sure of?" And Roger is thinking: "Gosh, six months."

Elaine is thinking: "But hey, I'm not so sure I want this kind of relationship either. Sometimes I wish I had a little more space, so I'd have time to think about whether I really want us to keep going the way we are, moving steadily towards… I mean, where are we going? Are we just going to keep seeing each other at this level of intimacy? Are we heading towards marriage? Toward children? Toward a lifetime together? Am I ready for that level of commitment? Do I really even know this person?" And Roger is thinking: "…so that means it was… let's see… February when we started going out, which was right after I had the car at the dealer's, which means… lemme check the odometer. …Whoa! I am way overdue for an oil change here."

Elaine is thinking: "He's upset. I can see it on his face. Maybe I'm reading this completely wrong. Maybe he wants more from our relationship, more intimacy, more commitment; maybe he has sensed—even before I sensed it—that I was feeling some reservations. Yes, I bet that's it. That's why he's so reluctant to say anything about his own feelings. He's afraid of being rejected." And Roger is thinking: "And I'm going to have them look at the transmission again. I don't care what those morons say, it's still not shifting right. And they better not try to blame it on the cold weather this time. What cold weather? It's 87 degrees out, and this thing is shifting like a goddamn garbage truck, and I paid those incompetent thieves $600."

Elaine is thinking: "He's angry. And I don't blame him. I'd be angry too. God, I feel so guilty, putting him through this, but I can't help the way I feel. I'm just not sure." And Roger is thinking: "They'll probably say it's only a 90-day warranty. That's exactly what they're gonna say, the scumballs."

Elaine is thinking: "Maybe I'm just too idealistic, waiting for a knight to come riding up on his white horse, while I'm sitting right next to a perfectly good person, a person I enjoy being with, a person I truly do care about, a person who seems to truly care for me. A person who is in pain because of my self-centered, schoolgirl romantic fantasy." And Roger is thinking: "Warranty? They want a warranty I'll give them a goddamn warranty. I'll take their warranty and stick it right up their…"

"Roger" Elaine says aloud. "What?" asks Roger, startled. "Please don't torture yourself like this," she says, her eyes beginning to brim with tears. "Maybe I should never have… Oh God, I feel so… " (She breaks down, sobbing.) "What?" says Roger.

"I'm such a fool," Elaine sobs. "I mean, I know there's no knight. I really know that. It's silly. There's no knight, and there's no horse." "There's no horse?" asks Roger.

"You think I'm a fool, don't you?" Elaine says. "No!" says Roger, glad to finally know the correct answer.

"It's just that... It's just that... I need some time." Elaine says. (There is a 15-second pause while Roger, thinking as fast as he can, tries to come up with a safe response. Finally he comes up with one that he thinks might work.) "Yes" he says.

(Elaine, deeply moved, touches his hand.) "Oh Roger, do you really feel that way?" "What way?" says Roger.

"That way about time." says Elaine. "Oh" says Roger, "Yes."

(Elaine turns to face him and gazes deeply into his eyes, causing him to become very nervous about what she might say next, especially if it involves a horse. At last she speaks.) "Thank you Roger." she says. "Thank you" says Roger.

Then he takes her home, and she lies on her bed, a conflicted, tortured soul and weeps until dawn, whereas when Roger gets back to his place, he opens a bag of Doritos, turns on the TV and immediately becomes deeply involved in a rerun of a tennis match between two Czechoslovakians he never heard of. A tiny voice in the far recesses of his mind tells him that something major was going on back there in the car, but he is pretty sure there is no way he would ever understand what, and so he figures

162

it's better if he doesn't think about it. (This is also Roger's policy regarding world hunger.)

The next day Elaine will call her closest friend, or perhaps two of them, and they will talk about this situation for six straight hours, never reaching any definite conclusions, but never getting bored with it either. Roger, while playing racquetball one day with a mutual friend of his and Elaine's, will pause just before serving, frown and ask: "Norm, did Elaine ever own a horse?"

This story illustrates how easily people's Views may become very different, even when they have what might appear to be a shared experience. Each is paying attention to different things. Both are dominated by their internal worlds, not the few actual words that pass between them. Even the words don't have the same meaning to both of them.

This potential for Views to diverge doesn't mean that communication and mutual understanding are impossible. It simply means that they cannot be taken for granted. Careful checking is needed to confirm agreement and to probe the limits of agreement.

During the last century, with the growth of new communications media, engineers had to develop means for machines to communicate reliably with each other. They were faced with the ever-present possibility that noise, interference and bad connections would corrupt messages. They developed principles for understanding the process of communication in the abstract, away from the messy emotional details of human communication.

So, how do computers 'know' they 'understand' each other? When computers connect to each other through the Internet they exchange data in discrete packets. Each packet is coded in such a way that errors can be detected. After each packet is sent, there is a 'handshake' to confirm that the packet has been accurately received. If not, the packet is re-sent and re-sent until the sending computer gets a message that confirms to it that the packet has been correctly received.

This continual checking for errors has been found necessary for machine communication to be reliable. People with good communications skills (not Elaine and Roger) often do the equivalent intuitively. Because language is so basic to being human we often take for granted that we are being understood. And we often find that we are wrong in that. As in the joke above, a conversation can simply be a series of exchanges of words, where neither side has any idea of whether the other has understood them. Fortunately, much human communication does a lot better than that. For example, one person may speak while the other listens and replies occasionally with nods, grunts or whatever. These may be a rough equivalent of the computer's checking of a packet.

> **You** Or they might just be pretence at listening.
>
> **Me** True, but someone who is skilled at communicating will make regular indications that they are following and understanding, and will ask questions when they aren't.

The telecommunications engineers' principles can be applied more explicitly to human discussions and can make it much more reliable too. The engineers have identified a basic communications cycle: sending some information and checking that it has been understood. We can take that as a basic unit of human communications too. Communication then becomes not just a series of statements but rather a series of: [statements plus checking that it is understood]. The illustration below shows the process.

The basic communications cycle

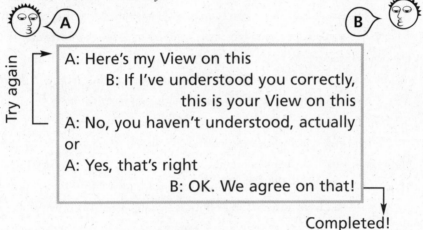

Try again

A: Here's my View on this
   B: If I've understood you correctly,
      this is your View on this
A: No, you haven't understood, actually
or
A: Yes, that's right
   B: OK. We agree on that!

Completed!

Let's unpick the various bits of this cycle:

- 'Here's my View of this.' is the statement A hopes B will understand. The rest is designed to check that it has been understood.

- In the second line, person B is reflecting back, from B's perspective, what B thinks A was saying (from A's perspective). This is quite different from either agreeing or disagreeing with A. The crucial point is that B is trying to see from A's perspective, to reflect back A's full View, not just A's words.

- In the third line, A isn't continuing the discussion. A is simply clarifying whether B has or has not understood. If not, A tries again, perhaps in somewhat different words.

- Finally, when A indicates agreement, B confirms it. Then both can be as confident as possible that they have reached agreement.

In a casual conversation, often nothing rides on the outcome. People may simply be passing time rather than looking for agreement. In that case, this cycle is not needed. The usual grunts etc will do to at least indicate that the listener is listening. In more serious circumstances, as when joint action is planned, a loose informal version of the communications cycle is a good idea. ("So long, see you at 5 tomorrow at the café", "I thought you said 5:30." "No, it was 5." "OK")

When the communication really counts, for example in tense emotional situations, a skilled communicator will use the communications cycle in full, repeatedly. They will make sure that they see the other person's perspective and have understood as fully as possible what the other intends and that the other knows that before moving on to the next point in the discussion.

Another important part of the telecommunications engineer's conceptual repertoire is to see the communications process in terms of layers or levels.

- At the lowest levels are the physical connections. What types of wires, plugs and sockets, voltage and current levels does a system use?

- At somewhat higher levels are the conventions and protocols used. How long are the packets and how are they put together? What codes should be used for checking and correcting errors?

- At still higher levels there is the content of the communication: your email messages, a picture you are downloading from the Web.

This concept of 'levels of communication' also applies to human communication. In the communications cycle described above there is the main statement which is the content of the discussion. The rest of the cycle has the function of checking that it has been understood. That checking process is part of the next level up. It is communication about the communication process.

In the story of Elaine and Roger, Elaine looks at Roger's face and body language to gauge his reaction. Again, this is the second level: monitoring the state of the discussion, this time using clues about emotional state. Elaine doesn't get it right because she doesn't check it, but at least she is using that level whereas Roger is not. Elaine gets upset because she thinks her remark has endangered the relationship. This concern about whether the relationship is converging or diverging is the third level. The third level is communication about the second level, whether it is succeeding or not.

To summarise these three levels:

- at the basic level is the content of the discussion. It consists of the main messages each person is trying to convey to the other

- the next level is communication about the discussion. It includes body language and tone of voice

- the third level is communication about the second level and is simply concerned about whether the conversation is converging (going well) or diverging (going badly).

Skilful communicators make good use of the three levels. They will remain aware of them at all times. If they think that there is misunderstanding at the level of the content they will move to the second level, checking that there is agreement. They may use the communications cycle explicitly, working to make sure the other person feels understood in terms of their own View. If a discussion seems to be going badly, they may appeal to the third level: "Hey, I thought we were friends! I really don't want this discussion to spoil that." "We seem to be continually talking across each other. I really want us to end up with a solution we can both agree upon."

Second principle of a coherent relationship A coherent relationship must be based on convergent communication. Both people must make an effort to be sure they are understood. They must regularly ensure that their views haven't diverged too much.

Coherent relationships, based upon convergent communication, are the basis of an eGaian world. In the fictional story of Pinecone Network, it was presumed that this was learned explicitly by everyone in childhood and was generally well understood by the population. It enabled people to resolve conflicts at an early stage. It made co-operation of all sorts much easier. People who are naturally good at it today are generally well liked and are considered to be 'nice'. There is no gene for niceness. It is a basic social skill that can be practised and learned.

CHAPTER eight

A PEACEFUL EARTH:
CONFLICT RESOLUTION

"Blessed are the peacemakers, for they shall be called the children of God." *Matthew 5:9*

"Nothing stands between us and disaster except ourselves. This principle applies to nuclear war as it does to resolving –peacefully, voluntarily, without guns or lawyers – a dispute between neighbors in suburbia over how early it's permissible for a lawnmower to break the morning silence. "[1]

This chapter addresses directly the first of the basic eGaian principles from Chapter 2 – Peace. It builds on the communication principles in the last chapter. The first and most fundamental question is whether Peace is possible. Is a well-policed truce the best we can hope for? Is peace even compatible with human nature? Chapter 5 gave examples of cultures in which serious conflict was rare by the standards of Western cultures: the Tahitians, the Yequana of Venezuela, Ladakh, the Fore of New Guinea. But are these exceptional, isolated communities, on the verge of extinction and irrelevant to the wider world?

We have no reason to believe that there has ever been a time when peaceful, collaborative societies were the norm for humanity. If the eGaian social vision does arrive, it will be unprecedented, pushed into existence by the need to overcome the effects of humanity as a global cancer before it is too late.

Conflict resolution

There there has been a lot of work on conflict resolution over the last few decades. Some universities give degrees in it and much research has been done on its roots and causes. Various organisations are now working to reduce tensions in troublespots around the world; others are working at the level of the community or the family.

There are some basic principles to be learned from all this work – first, from a few concrete examples.

Navajo peacemaking[2]

The Navajo Nation in the southwestern United States is a self-governing nation that operates within state legal systems, a 'nation within a nation'. It has a process of conflict resolution "taken directly from the traditional methods of dispute resolution used throughout the history of the Navajo people."

"The Navajo philosophy and system of justice focuses on healing both the wrongdoer and all the people that may have been affected – directly and indirectly. Navajo justice does not try to punish anyone. … The philosophy of Navajo *beehaz' aanii* teaches that everyone and everything is connected, so that the actions of one individual affect many others. Punishment of the individual not only does not help him or her – it also does nothing to help the community."

The Navajo have a formal process that is used whenever it it needed. "…the Peacemaker process transcends the notion of a method of resolving disputes and becomes a powerful tool for healing the inner processes of the individual and the group that contribute to the production of conflict."

The Peacemaker process is "based on the Navajo tradition of 'talking things out'. What Westerners would call a mediator is the "*Naat' aanii*" or "one who speaks wisely and well", who may come out of the Peacemaker Division or may be chosen by the parties involved. He/she is a member of the community, and may be related to the people in conflict or affected by the conflict.

The stages in the peacemaking process are:

- laying the groundwork

- the opening prayer

- defining the problem – includes allowing "as much time as it may take for the participants to express their anger, frustration, and pain." It also includes reminding them of their connection to the community. "A common admonishment on this theme is to tell an individual that he or she is "acting as if he/she had no relatives".

- creating problem-solving statements
- summarising the session
- commitment and solidarity
- the closing prayer.

Here's an example: *the case of the families who weren't fooled.*

"A young Navajo woman sued a man for paternity. When they got into court, the woman said, 'He's the father.' The man said, 'No, I'm not.' The judge sent the case to Navajo peacemaker court. The peacemaker sent notice to the man's and woman's families, and they went to the peacemaking. During the peacemaking, they stopped the 'He is/I'm not' talk. The families knew what had been going on all the time and said, 'We're going to talk about what to do about our child.

The young man didn't have a job, and couldn't afford to pay child support. The woman, who lived in a rural area, relied on firewood for heat and cooking fuel. The families agreed that the young man should supply firewood to the woman until he could pay child support.

By involving the child's family, the discussion turned from paternity to a practical discussion of how to solve a problem. There was no question about paternity – and no need for blood tests – because Navajo families know what their children are doing. They also know what is best for their grandchildren ."[3]

There are several important points to draw from this example.

The people involved in the conflict are part of a community that is important to them. They don't want to be thought badly of or to be excluded from the community. So those principally involved are motivated to try to work towards resolution and the others concerned have a strong influence upon them.

The principals and the peacemakers share a view that it is important to heal all concerned. The process of peacemaking is one of healing rather than of punishment, reducing the likelihood that an offender will simply withdraw into bitter isolation only to re-offend again later.

The peacemaking process is essentially a communication process. It allows all concerned to express their views and feelings. They recognise the importance of acknowledging the strong emotions which play a key part in maintaining conflict.

Conflict resolution in Ladakh[4]

"A concern not to offend or upset one another is deeply rooted in Ladakhi society; people avoid situations that might lead to friction or conflict. When someone transgresses this unwritten law, ...extreme tolerance is the response. And yet, concern for community doesn't have the oppressive effect on the individual that one might have imagined. On the contrary, I am now convinced that being a part of a close-knit community provides a profound sense of security.

In traditional Ladakh, aggression of any sort is exceptionally rare: rare enough to say that it is virtually non-existent."

"One means of ensuring a lack of friction in traditional Ladakh society is something I call the 'spontaneous intermediary'. As soon as any sort of difference arises between two parties, a third party is there to act as arbiter. Whatever the circumstances, whoever is involved, an intermediary always seems to be on hand. It happens automatically, without any prompting; the intermediary is not consciously sought and can be anyone who happens to be around; it might be an older sister or a neighbour, or just a passing stranger. I remember watching a five-year-old settling a squabble between two of his friends in this way. They listened to him willingly. The feeling that peace is better than conflict is so deeply ingrained that people turn automatically to a third party."

"Traditional Ladakhi villages are run democratically... disparities in wealth are minimal. ...Many activities that would otherwise require the whole village to sit down and draw up plans – like the painting of the village monastery or arrangements for Losar (New Year) – have been worked out many generations ago and are now done by rotation. Nonetheless, sometimes matters have to be decided on a village level. Larger villages are divided up into *chutsos*, or groups of ten houses, each of which has at least one representative on the village council. This body meets periodically throughout the year and is presided over by the *goba*, or village head.

The *goba* is usually appointed by rotation. If the whole village wants to keep him on, he may hold his position for many years, but otherwise after a year or so, the job will pass on to another householder. One of the *goba*'s jobs is to act as adjudicator. Though arguments are unusual, from time to time some differences of opinion arise that need settling."

"Before coming to Ladakh, I had always thought that the best judges were the ones who were in no way connected with the individuals they were judging...but having lived in Ladakh for many years, I have had to change my mind. ...when people settling disputes are intimately acquainted with the parties involved, their judgement is not prejudiced; on the contrary, this very closeness helps them to make fairer and sounder decisions."

"In the traditional Ladakhi village, people have much control over their own lives... rather than being at the mercy of faraway, inflexible bureaucracies and fluctuating markets. ...Ladakhis have been fortunate enough to inherit a society in which the good of the individual is not in conflict with that of the whole community; one person's gain is not another person's loss. Ladakhis are aware that helping others is in their own interest. ...Mutual aid rather than competition shapes the economy. It is, in other words, a synergistic society."

Again, a sense of community and an understanding of its importance are deeply ingrained in the culture, as are mechanisms for dealing with and avoiding conflict in its earliest stages. The 'spontaneous intermediaries' are a particularly important example of this.

The description of the fictional Pinecone Network in Chapter 3 included similar features. Everyone is part of various communities that are important to them and in which they see that their own good is not in conflict with that of others. Dealing with conflicts is seen as an essential part of society and is a basic part of every child's education. In terms of the concepts in the last chapter, conflict resolution works well where the people in conflict have a large shared View, and where part of that View is the importance of conflict resolution.

Conflict escalation among the Jalé of New Guinea[5]

This is a contrasting example – of a culture which doesn't have such extensive conflict resolving institutions. The Jalé people live in the Central Mountains of Western New Guinea (and are not to be confused with the Fore of New Guinea described in Chapter 5). They have a culture without the well-ordered, healing conflict resolution of the examples so far.

"In the absence of political and judicial offices, self-help – often in the form of violent retaliation – is an institutionalised method of conflict resolution when negotiation fails. ...[A] skirmish may mark the beginning of a round of battles and retaliatory raids lasting for weeks, months and even years."

Koch gives an example of a dispute between a father and son that started in 1959. The son returned from a trading trip bringing pandanus kernels that he shared with his father and brothers. The father thought he had been given the less delicious marginal parts of the fruit and an argument followed. The next day, the son was still angry and didn't invite his father to a meal of fruit from a tree the father had given him. The father was so angry at this that he cut down the tree and two others.

The next day the argument erupted again, with more people present. Several arrows were shot, and one hit the son in the thigh. Subsequently, the dispute spread to the villages of the two men and escalated into a war. On the third day of fighting a man was killed. In a later battle a second person was killed and one group of people was driven from their land by the other. An uneasy truce existed for a few years, but in 1964 more fighting broke out.

The Jalé have customs and views of justice which regularly lead to spirals of conflict escalation. When conflict arises there is no attempt by the parties involved or anyone else to help create a shared view. If we were to make a naive judgement of human nature by looking at the Jalé culture we would come to a very different conclusion than if we looked at the Navajo or Ladakhis. But by looking at the different ways in which conflict is handled in these cultures we can see that these result in a different way in which human nature appears to be expressed in different cultures. It is not the case that escalating conflict is a built-in feature of human nature.

Unfortunately, in our modern world, cultures in which conflict resolution is an intimate part of their way of living are quite rare. We are much more like the Jalé than the Ladakhis. We have a very ambiguous view of conflict. At some levels, conflict is institutionalised and encouraged.

An effective modern democracy is expected to have a strong opposition that has a reasonable chance of ousting the party in power. An effective politician is expected to disagree with the opposing party and find fault with them at every opportunity. It is considered reasonable that a law can be passed by a majority of as little as one, that a party with a very small majority should impose its views on a minority that may be nearly as large. Going for consensus, seeking solutions that genuinely satisfy all sides, is not part of the normal political vocabulary.

In economic terms, conflict in the form of competition is considered the hallmark of effective behaviour. Too little competition is considered undesirable, whether it is because a small number of firms dominate the market, or because a service is provided only by the government. The word 'competitive' is often used as a general-purpose virtue, where what is really meant is efficient and well organised. The underlying assumption is that competition is needed to overcome an inherent conflict of interests between an organisation and those it is meant to serve. Without competition, the organisation would favour its own interests over those of its customers or clients. To a large extent, this is an artefact of our money-based economic system, as the next chapter will show. The idea of a local organisation run jointly by its staff and customers/clients for the benefit of all is far from the normal reality.

What can we conclude from all of this for the prospects of a peaceful society? Mainly that a peaceful society is not just something which will or won't happen by itself. It can come out of an understanding of conflict, what causes it, and how it can be resolved before it gets out of hand. Conflict can be destructive or it can be extremely creative, depending upon how it is handled. Moreover, a peaceful society cannot be created by superficial action. Peace needs to have its roots deep within a society's political and economic structure.

178

Resolving major world conflicts

The examples of the Navajo and Ladakh in the previous section indicate some of the necessary conditions for effective conflict resolution:

- that the parties concerned need to be part of a larger community with influence over them and which seeks to keep conflict under control

- that there are always third parties available to help resolve conflict when it arises.

One of the world's most serious conflicts, between the Israelis and the Palestinians, demonstrates further lessons. This conflict is deeply entrenched and bitter, yet it has come a long way in the last 50 years or so. There are now the beginnings of an autonomous Palestinian state, and there is an official peace process, albeit very easily and often derailed. Some of the most difficult issues, such as the status of Jerusalem, are at least under discussion now whereas they were once beyond the pale.

179

The following includes extracts from a book by two people who have been involved at close quarters.[6] Bassam Abu-Sharif is a Palestinian who changed from being an active terrorist/freedom fighter (depending upon your perspective) to leading the internal Palestinian struggle to start the peace process. Uzi Mahnaimi is an Israeli who was an intelligence officer and became a journalist working for a peaceful settlement.

The Israeli-Palestinian conflict

From the Palestinian point of view, the Israelis have expelled most of them from their land, and through their settlements are continuing to do so. The Palestinian's violence is a reaction of despair, which, although arguably self-destructive, they see as desperately defensive.

Bassam: "Until the Zionists came, the Abu-Sharif family had lived in Jerusalem for the better part of 500 years."

From the Israeli point of view, the Arabs are living in land which was historically Jewish. This is the only place where they can be safe from the persecutions they suffered in the past. If the Arabs would only let them be, there would be no problems. But if not, they will show that they cannot just be slaughtered as in the Holocaust. The Israelis retaliate strongly to any attack on them. They see this as entirely defensive.

Uzi: "Gideon [Uzi's father] reached manhood with one very strong conviction: that to survive as a Jew meant learning how to defend yourself – to the death."

The two sides have entirely different world views, in which the other side is demonised. Many, perhaps most, members of each community have almost no contact with the other.

A Palestinian explains: "I grew up in Gaza hating all Jews, believing that they were bloodsuckers, that they had robbed me of my land, my rights and my freedom and that they killed my fellow men. That was before I met my first Jew."[7]

Uzi: "I knew nothing of the Arabs except that they were all demons. ...Like all Israelis, I had been brought up in the Arab-entirely-wrong/Israeli-entirely-right school of history. ... The dislike and distrust imparted by this teaching was compounded by the almost total lack of contact between the two communities. ...Most people in Israel know nothing about Arab people, and care less. They have no Arab friends. ...They think themselves superior in every way to the Arabs."

In the January, 2001 election, "The despair and anxiety that possessed the Israeli public – and the total lack of awareness of Palestinian pain and suffering – are what has put Sharon in power".[8] Neither side has any sense of the other as 'ordinary people just trying to get on with their lives', the way they see themselves.

From the point of view of someone sympathetic to both sides, they seem like cousins who have much in common, but have fallen out. There is an ongoing cycle whereby violence on one side creates a violent reaction on the other side that creates another violent reaction, and so on. They react with shock at each new 'outrage' from the other side as more evidence to confirm that the others are truly demons. Yet neither side sees what they are doing as connected to what the other is doing to them. Both sides believe that the other side will respond only to force.

Both sides are traumatised and drained of resources by the war effort and the destruction. The chairman of the Gaza Community Mental Health Programme says that 'martyrs' ('suicide bombers' to the Israelis) almost without exception had suffered severe trauma as children–watched their parents killed or humiliated or their homes destroyed–and felt they had to combat their sense of helplessness and victimisation on behalf of their nation.[9]

Very few on either side can really envisage the prospects of true peace. Yet a unified Middle East, with its oil wealth added to Israeli technical and industrial ability could be a world power to reckon with.

Bassam: "Peace should not mean only the end of war. At the same time it must mean the development of joint economic, social and political programmes. Israel could never fully become a part of the Middle East unless and until it made peace with the Palestinians. ...It is through a self-governing Palestinian state... that Israelis will eventually drive to shop in the Souq al-Hamadiyyeh, the magical ancient central market in Damascus."

182

There is a lot to be learned from this example, which applies to very many other human conflicts. First, there are two communities which are at the same time intimately connected and yet with very limited understanding of each other. Thus each can build up a view of the other's motivations which the other would totally reject. Each community, within itself, is continually regenerating that false view of the other community. Strong emotions stop both sides from even considering the View of the other side.

What of the larger community that (as in the Najaho or Ladakh examples) might have helped resolve the conflict? The world community was polarised by the Cold War until the 1990s and so its efforts at peace-making were largely seen as biased. It is not surprising that what progress has been made has come since the Cold War ended. However, most of the efforts in the peace process seem to be aimed at looking for compromises and then putting intense pressure on both sides to accept them.

From an eGaian perspective, the way to resolve the conflict is not simply to look for some compromise formula. Rather it is to start by breaking down the two communities' false views of each other. Some large-scale cultural equivalent of the basic communications cycle described in the last chapter is needed to help people to come to understand each others' Views (ie from each other's perspective). As Uzi Mahnaimi said: "Encountering the Arabs as human beings, I felt my entrenched antipathy to them waning slightly. It was the first stirring of a different kind of consciousness in me... ."[10] He subsequently used his position as a journalist to try to instil some understanding of the Palestinians through information he gained from Bassam Abu-Sharif.

There are various organisations that are taking just such an approach to conflict resolution on an international scale. For example, Search for Common Ground,[11] an NGO with "activities on four continents and offices in nine countries", functions "as social entrepreneurs who design and implement innovative ways to reframe issues and solve problems." Their activities include mediation and facilitation, dialogue workshops, inter-ethnic media projects, conflict-resolution training, arts projects, children's kindergartens, and reduction of stereotypes.

In the Middle East they published "simultaneously in nine newspapers from Istanbul to Tel Aviv to Tunis, with authors' interviews broadcast on BBC Arabic Service... a collection of articles by leading academics, intellectuals, and journalists from seven Arab countries, Israel, and Turkey, presenting a variety of visions of life in the Middle East in the year 2020... For probably the first time, mass audiences throughout the Middle East were exposed, in an uncensored fashion and in their own languages, to what other thinkers in the region envisage and aspire to for their collective future."

Search for Common Ground have done work in Sierra Leone, the US, South Africa and Macedonia, where they say "this collective effort was not sufficient to stop the latest violence. However, we strongly believe that our activities were one factor in preventing the recent fighting from deteriorating into outright civil war, and we remain encouraged that Macedonia has not broken apart."

One of the projects for Macedonia was a children's TV programme called *Nashe Maalo*, which features a cast of children representing each of the four ethnicities – ethnic Albanian, Macedonian, Roma (Gypsy) and Turkish. It "aims to bridge the cultural divide by offering children a window into each other's lives and by modelling positive strategies for coping with conflict. The program's stories seek to help children appreciate their differences as well as the values they share."

So this organisation's work is based on communication which enables people to understand each other and which explicitly develops skills at conflict resolution. They say, "All our tools are variations of one core method, as described by African National Congress leader Andrew Masondo: "Understand the differences; act on the commonalities."

Techniques for conflict resolution

> Conflict is an inescapable part of our daily lives. ... Learning how to deal with conflicts effectively is increasingly an essential life skill needed by every person and every group...[12].

Unlike the Navajo or the Ladakhis, most modern cultures do not have techniques and principles of conflict resolution at the heart of their culture. However, we do have many specialists with a great deal of skill and experience of handling conflict at many levels – in families and schools, in communities, in international relationships. A peaceful, sustainable eGaian culture will need to learn from these specialists and spread these skills much more widely. A number of these specialists have written popular, well-respected books.

Dudley Weeks has worked on peacemaking and civil rights around the world and in many communities. His book, *The Eight Essential Steps to Conflict Resolution*[13] is an excellent introduction to communication-based conflict resolution. His starting point is that conflict is a natural outgrowth of diversity among people, not something to be feared and avoided. It can be seen as an opportunity to strengthen a relationship and to learn something new. Of course conflict can be damaging and disruptive and can absorb all of the conflicting party's energies, to the cost of everything else they are trying to do, but that doesn't have to be the case.

Weeks is clear about approaches to conflict resolution that are ineffective. These include 'the conquest approach' in which one party tries to dominate and overcome the other, 'the avoidance approach' in which the parties pretend the conflict doesn't exist, and 'the bargaining approach' in which a temporary solution is found which doesn't satisfy anyone.

The origins of conflict come from diversity. "Diversity is a healthy aspect of human society. Diversity can open up possibilities, challenge us to consider alternatives, and keep us from allowing ourselves to stagnate. We need to celebrate diversity, not fear it or perceive it as a threat."[14] Diversity leads to differing needs, and "discord arises when one or both parties ignore needs... that [the other] define as essential". Sometimes, one party may be ignoring their own needs, which can also allow conflict to fester.

A crucial point here is that needs can be understood only as defined by each party for themselves. "People interpret reality differently. ...people can have different perceptions about how and why the event happened and what the event means. Some of these differing perceptions may actually be... misperceptions; but if the perceiver believes the misperceptions are true, in effect, they become reality to that person."

Power is another "essential ingredient of conflict", and Weeks presents ways to use power constructively. Other essential ingredients are the role of values and principles, and the feelings and emotions of those involved in the conflict.

The basis of Weeks' approach is what he calls 'the conflict partnership process'. It "establishes a foundation on which the people or groups involved in a conflict can transform the adversarial, combative I-versus-you pattern usually found in conflict into a healthy attitude, one in which the tone is: We are working together to improve our relationship and to deal with our differences."

This is consistent with the approach used by Search for Common Ground in the Middle East, or by Bassam and Uzi. They are not just seeking compromises that both sides can accept, but are trying to build mutual understanding, looking towards a vision of a relationship between Israelis and Palestinians in which both sides see the true benefits of peace.

> **You** A nice goal, but not an easy one.
>
> **Me** I don't think anyone involved in conflict resolution believes it is easy. People can be very attached to their conflicts. Strong emotions block their view of their opponents' needs, and of the possibility of positive outcomes. What is important is to understand what works. Conflict resolution might become easy if we ever get to stage where is has become deeply engrained in our culture, as in Ladakh. That should be our goal.

Weeks' Eight Essential Steps

1 *Create an effective atmosphere* – one that promotes partnership and problem solving.

2 *Clarify perceptions* – both sides need to understand the other's position, even if they don't agree with it. Emotions are legitimate and should be acknowledged. Use 'I – Statements' to tell the other how you feel, rather than 'You – Statements' that blame. Assert your needs without attacking the other.

3 *Focus on individual and shared needs* – Each side should acknowledge the legitimate needs of the other side, as well as those of their own, distinguish between real needs and secondary desires and identify the other's core goals they can support. Both should realise that they need one another to successfully resolve conflicts.

4 *Build shared positive power* – this promotes building together and strengthening partnerships, rather than imposing the will of one on the other.

5 *Look to the future, then learn from the past* – Images of a positive future relationship can provide motivation to move forward. The past is there to learn from. Forgiveness makes a large difference and may be the key to moving forward.

6 *Generate options* – Often, both sides will be set in entrenched positions, but with a little creativity, many more options will appear.

7 *Develop stepping stones to action* – "Do-ables are specific acts that stand a good chance of success, meet some individual and shared needs, and depend upon positive power, usually shared power, to be implemented".

8   *Make mutual benefit agreements.* Avoid win-lose solutions that damage the long-term relationship. Look for solutions that benefit both sides and that build the relationship.

Another good book is *Getting to Yes, Negotiating an agreement without giving in,* by Roger Fisher, William Ury and Bruce Patton.[15] The authors are directors of the Harvard Negotiation Project, with experience ranging from family settings, labour disputes, ethnic conflicts and international conflicts. Their approach has a similar feel to that of Weeks, but their emphasis is somewhat different. Their overall stance is to avoid bargaining over positions. Always look for the underlying needs of both parties.

The *Getting to Yes* method's four main parts:

1   *Separate the people from the problem.* Issues of personality and especially personality clashes often get intertwined with the problem and need to be separated. Often they result from people's misperceptions of each other, which need to be resolved.

2   *Focus on interests, not positions.* People often stand on entrenched positions that are irreconcilable. However, by looking at the interests they have that underlie their positions, it may be possible to find sympathy and common ground.

3   *Invent options for mutual gain* – very similar to Weeks' 'do-ables'.

4   *Insist on using objective criteria.* The main idea here is to find some criteria other than simply the will of one of the sides. Is there any external basis for deciding what to do that both sides could accept as objective?

You Both of these approaches assume that both sides are reasonable and want to reach a solution. What do you do if one side has much greater power and refuses to negotiate?

Me I don't think either book makes that assumption, although my simplified summaries may give that impression. Certainly it is very much easier if both parties genuinely want a solution. Here is where a larger community helps a lot. Nonetheless, both books suggest ways to help overcome entrenched resistance and power.

Summary on conflict resolution

Conflict is a natural part of life and arises from diversity and from differences in perspective. It can be seen as an opportunity to learn from those differences and to find ways of transcending them. The result can be a broader and more adaptive vision.

Conflict resolution is essentially a process of communication. Its essence is that the parties in conflict come to understand each other's positions and feel empathy for each other. This often includes an appreciation of each other's emotional states – anger, fear, pain or whatever. It may include apologies for harm done and forgiveness for injuries received.

Conflict resolution is a process of healing the damage done on all sides, with the result being a restoration of a constructive relationship or the creation of one. Positive steps to build that relationship are an essential part of the process.

When the parties in conflict are part of a larger community with influence upon them, conflicts are much more easily resolved. This is

189

especially so if the community can provide people to mediate and help with the healing process.

This approach to conflict resolution is very different to the mainstream attitudes of most modern societies. Conflict is more often approached through the imposition of force, so that the most powerful prevails, or through punishment and imprisonment. If we are to build a peaceful, sustainable Earth, we will need to let go of our current attitudes towards conflict. An appreciation of the creative power of conflict and a thorough grounding in ways of handling it constructively need to be built into our culture and our educational systems. Any group or organisation which is serious about building a more peaceful, sustainable lifestyle must take the process and techniques of conflict resolution very seriously.

CHAPTER nine

A CO-OPERATIVE ECONOMY

If there is to be any chance of creating a peaceful, sustainable world, its economy will have to be very different from at present. It will need to be a co-operative economy. Our money-based, globalised, competitive free-market economy is central to why modern human society is functioning as a global cancer. It is what enables us to live while disconnected from the natural world and from each other. This is not the conventional wisdom: you won't hear many politicians or business leaders saying that the basic structure of our economy is a problem – but very many people do agree. Many books have been written about this[1] and there are many initiatives involved.

This is possibly the biggest challenge facing humanity: Is a co-operative economy possible? What might it be like? Can we use our current understanding and our new communications technologies to create economic structures that support the health of the Earth and of humanity?

Recent initiatives in this direction include various forms of local or complementary currencies, community banks and micro-finance initiatives, ethical and fair traded products, ethical investment, social loan funds and co-operatives of all kinds. Earlier attempts to create a more co-operative economy include the Israeli *kibbutzim*, the British co-operative movement, and of course the 19th and 20th century socialist and communist movements.[2]

The popularity of these initiatives shows a great yearning for ways to get around the problems of a money-based, competitive economy. This chapter supports that yearning by using a communications-oriented perspective to clarify the problems of the present economy, to show some of the limitations of present initiatives, and to describe the principles of a genuinely co-operative economy.

It is very hard to see through our modern economy to the roots of its problems, because we are so immersed in it and it has grown to its present form over such a long period of time. Thus some of the more popular solutions do not get to those roots. For example, there are proposals for changing the tax system to include environmental costs.[3] Another alternative is government regulation: "It is regulation rather than taxation that more efficiently improves the market."[4] These proposals are unlikely to be implemented in a strong enough form to make much difference – witness the difficulties getting approval of the Kyoto agreement limiting carbon dioxide emissions. Moreover, if they were implemented, they wouldn't solve the problems to anything like the extent their proponents believe, as will be clear by the end of this chapter.

The fictional example of Pinecone Network (in Chapter 3) went well beyond tax changes or government regulation, with a co-operative, moneyless economy. The examples of co-operative economies of earlier

192

societies in Chapter 5 were also radically different. But the creative arts camps provide more immediate examples of the principles on which Pinecone Network was based

> **You** You mentioned these at the end of the Preface, where you gave your background, but I didn't realise that they were actually Utopian economies.
>
> **Me** They're not, but they do show how normal western people from a conventional competitive economy behave when they are in a setting that evokes co-operation.

Co-operation in the creative arts camp[5]

At the creative arts camp, about 500 people get together each year to camp in a field for 10 days to learn music, dance, and creative arts, and to live together while doing so. From the start, the organisers created an expectation of community, but this evolved over the years as the camps developed their own culture and ways of doing things. From the second year onwards, about a third of the people who came to each camp were new and absorbed the culture from old timers.

People arrived at the event bringing tents, teepees, yurts or other structures, expecting to camp with other people. When they arrived they found that the field was laid out with a series of large circles about 50 feet across, mown into the grass. At the centre of each circle was a firepit – a shallow depression where the sod was carefully removed and placed at the edge of the field to be replaced when the camp was finished. The assumption was that people would camp with their tents facing the fire and cook communally on it. (There was also a camp café, but mostly people ate in their circles.) Camping circles could accommodate between 20 and 40 people. (No-one was forced to camp in one of these circles. Most chose to, but once in a while people went off and camped on their own.) At various points around the field were piles of firewood, and also scrap wood of various sorts which people could use to build structures and furniture for their circle.

People tended to camp with friends and often tried to plan in advance whom they would camp with. But, since everyone wanted space for their friends, and each had an overlapping but slightly different group of friends, and there were always some newcomers, it never quite worked out as planned. Usually there were some circles where many people knew each other well and others where people were mostly strangers when they arrived.

Spontaneous co-operation As the culture grew over the years, people learned ways of making camp life comfortable for themselves. People would arrive bringing cooking equipment and food for the communal kitchen. Often people would arrive with prepared food for the whole circle – perhaps a large casserole or stew – so that people busy setting up on the first evening would have a meal. Some would gather and chop wood, then build the fire while others organised the meal.

Within the first day or two, people would gather bits of scrap wood and build rough benches for sitting around the fire, tables and shelves for storing food, and shelters from the sun and rain. Each circle was uniquely decorated, with flags, archways, candles, etc.

Normally, people would fend for themselves at breakfast and lunchtime (taking food from the communal kitchen) but have a communal meal in the evening. There were different ways of arranging who would cook each day. Sometimes a circle would work out a rota, but often people would volunteer one evening for the next day. Sometimes the cooks would go shopping during the day to buy the food for that night's meal, and pay for it themselves (on the assumption that if everyone cooked some time, it would more or less even itself out). Sometimes people would chip in to a common circle fund to pay for food.

All the campers, from teenagers up, were expected to put in a half day of work (in a 10-day camp) for the benefit of the camp as a whole. Some would help in the children's area, others would clean the toilets daily, some would work in the café, look after the shower and sauna area, or take out the recycling. This minimised the 'staff' needed, and people felt a strong sense of ownership of the camp and responsibility for its condition.

The camp as an economy As people at the camps were doing things for each other in quite a systematic and organised way, it is possible to think of the camps as a sort of economy. It's clearly very different from the normal, competitive economy.

Clearly the tasks people did – chopping wood, cooking, cleaning the toilets – were done because they were needed or desired and not for money. The pressure to work came from clear need and a desire to be seen as a useful part of the group. Each task was part of an ongoing relationship. You might cook one day and chop wood another day, and you would expect that everyone else would be doing something to contribute. The camp economy presumes a high degree of trust that you will receive in return for your contributions. (In the competitive economy no ongoing relationship is assumed. Each transaction is complete in itself. You receive something and you pay for it; you give something and get paid for it. As human societies became more complex, people began to deal more and more with people who were not part of their own community, with strangers whom they might not trust. Money made these dealings possible.)

As people's camp contributions were based on need and desire as part of a community, rather than money, they were naturally controlled. Chopping twice as much wood didn't get you twice as much food. The amount of wood you chopped was determined by the need for wood at the moment and your own inclination to chop it. If the evening was warm and there was less need for a fire, people chopped less wood. No one would dream of convincing people to build more and bigger fires so they could chop more and more wood.

The people who kept the toilets cleaned had no motivation to encourage people to use their toilets more. Their motivation was based on taking pride in their contribution, plus the knowledge that their friends would be annoyed with them if they didn't do a good job. A job that might seem unpleasant actually became fun when done only in small doses and with a group of friends.

In the conventional economy, most people need to work in order to be able to consume. (There are many exceptions: inherited wealth, income from investments, fees and royalties from earlier work, income from crime.) Working for money thus loses this natural control. Production becomes desirable and necessary for its own sake, so long as it can bring in money. There is no natural limit to the amount of money you can have, and thus no limit to the desirable amount of production.

In the conventional economy it is sensible for a producer to convince people to want their products, to distort needs and wants in their favour. If you can convince people to buy your product because it is fashionable or because you can prey on their insecurities, your business will do well. If you can convince people to buy shoddy goods without them realising it, you can become rich. In the camp economy such strategies would be an obvious nonsense.

This is the sense in which the competitive economy is upside-down. Doing things for money rather than directly to satisfy needs and desires distorts production and loses all natural controls. It means there is a built-in conflict between the needs of the producer and what is desirable from a larger viewpoint .

The camp economy is not a form of barter. People don't clean toilets in exchange for childcare or food. In barter, there is the sense that, for each transaction, what you get has the same value (or more) as what you give. You may bargain to try to make that happen. Barter is a form of balanced exchange. In the camps there is no fixed price for a job or a service, independent of who is giving or receiving, as in the competitive world. People don't try to get a better deal at the expense of others.

In the camp economy there is a more generalised sense of giving and receiving. People give as part of a contribution to a group of people who they have come to care about, and who are also giving to them. It makes sense to contribute because everyone receives so much from the group. There is a sense of balance, but it is much looser. Some people may like to build camp furniture, others may like to cook while some prefer to do the washing up. There is no attempt to force an equality to contributions which are not really comparable. The camp economy is based upon generalised exchange rather than balanced exchange.

It also became clear to many that trying to create a balance wasn't worth the effort and could create conflict. Formal cooking rotas to ensure all circle members did the same amount were difficult to arrange. People didn't know days in advance whether they would be free or would be at a workshop. Often people who weren't scheduled to cook but were around would help out anyway while some who were scheduled to cook wouldn't turn up. Collecting money in advance to pay for the day's food shopping

197

to make sure everyone paid the same amount was also difficult. How do you find everyone? Some were much poorer than others and would prefer to pay only for more basic meals. It was much easier and less contentious for the cooks to buy the food they cooked and just assume that it more or less worked out reasonably over the period of the camp.

No two contributions to a camping circle could be the same, just as no two people are the same. There is no way in which they could be 'equal'. Some people do a great deal more than others, and are appreciated for it. It was rare for adults to choose to do as little as they could, unless they were ill. Adults who appeared to be contributing too much might be gently encouraged to relax more. Giving and receiving in a context where people know each other and care about each other takes into account individual differences and appreciates them.

198

You So everybody was really well-behaved at the camps and no-one tried to get away with as little as they could?

Me These are just ordinary people. There was the usual sprinkling of difficult people and scandalous stories, but it's also true that the circumstances brought out the best in most people. Mostly, those people trying to get away with doing very little were teenagers, who were generally treated with amused tolerance (a little less so by their own parents). And, over the years of the camps, the teenage sub-culture changed too, affected by the camp culture, so that they did make some very useful contributions.

You But the modern competitive world isn't like the camps. There is no "ongoing relationship and community". That is why I think you are so idealistic.

Me That is just the point I am trying to make. Our challenge is not just to reform our current economic system, but to attempt to grow a new economy within the old, based upon ongoing relationship and community. It takes a big leap of imagination but now, at last, we have the technology and the ideas to do it. The personal benefits of being part of that kind of community are huge. People would weep at the end of the camps when they had to leave because there was so little of it in their everyday lives. And the dangers of not doing it are the inevitable outcomes of humanity as a global cancer. So why not go for it, far fetched as it may seem?

The example of the camp economy overcomes the most fundamental objections to our money-based, globalised competitive economy. They are the differences between an economy in which people's goals and interests are the same or consistent, and an economy in which their goals are set against one another, the difference between co-operation and competition. In the camp economy people come to feel that they are part of a larger group which is supporting and looking after them. They feel cared for and appreciated. That is why they are so sorry to leave.

199

Characteristics of a co-operative economy

Chapter 2 identified four key issues as the problems of a competitive, money-based economy:

- the wrong goals
- the problems with balanced exchange
- misused and misleading information
- inherent instability.

It is now possible to develop the basic principles of a co-operative economy that doesn't suffer from those problems – drawing on the example of the camp economy and the principles that were implicit in the description of the Pinecone Network in Chapter 3.

You Are you saying that the Pinecone Network should be a blueprint for your 'peaceful, sustainable Earth'?

Me Not really. I'm sure that, if humanity does move towards a peaceful, sustainable Earth, the solutions that come up will be as varied as there are human cultures. As co-operative solutions, they can co-exist comfortably. The Pinecone Network story is what I, with my particular background, think would be a desirable way of doing it. People with different backgrounds will surely find other ways that overlap with this vision, but may differ in many ways. My solutions are there to help people think through their own solutions.

To start with, there is very much in the modern economy that could continue. Any changeover will be easier and more successful if it is a rapid evolution rather than a revolution. Most production, distribution and services would be done largely on a professional, well-organised basis. This is not an 'everybody bakes their own bread, makes their own sandals, builds their own house' vision, although there might be more of people doing things for themselves and a higher proportion done on a craft basis rather than on a mass-production basis. The skill and efficiency that comes when things are done by people with training, experience and the right tools will be as vital in the future as it is now.

The modern economy is made up of organisations of different sizes, from local firms to large corporations with many branches, perhaps world wide. An eGaian co-operative economy would also have a diversity of organisations. But they would be co-operating, not competing.

The appeal of the free market is its freedom, the autonomy of its components. Individuals and organisations can operate as they see best, as understood from their own perspectives. The eGaian version retains that freedom. It does not impose a central control, but rather changes the relationship from competition to co-operation. It is a self-organising free market based upon individuals and organisations appreciating the advantages of co-operation and mutual support.

In the Pinecone Network there are several examples of organisations that have evolved from competitive origins to co-operative operation. Apple Transport was originally a conventional car showroom and garage. Pinecone Plastics was part of a multi-national corporation that had undergone a metamorphosis, like a caterpillar becoming a butterfly.

The right goals: a 'best match' economy

A change of relationship from competitive to co-operative is a change of goals. Being co-operative with someone simply means having goals that are consistent, mutually re-enforcing. It means doing things for each other's benefit, looking after each other, to at least some degree, and appreciating the benefits of that.

A co-operative economy can be a 'best match' economy, (rather than a 'most profit' economy) which means that players seek to provide a best match between supply and demand, taking into account the health of the environment. In the Pinecone Supermarket, the challenge for Gerry was to match the needs of his regular customers to what was available from his suppliers, based upon information he received from both sides, all of whom he knew reasonably well.

You But surely matching supply and demand is what most businesses do now, although perhaps without 'taking into account the health of the environment'.

Me To a certain extent, especially for those business people who take their jobs seriously and want to provide a good service. The problem is that financial pressures often get in the way. They need to encourage demand, not match it; push it in the direction which makes them the most money etc. The challenge for a co-operative economy is to find ways to organise exchange so that the best match principle is the main goal of businesses, without financial pressures to distort it. I am sure that most business people would prefer it that way, if they thought it possible.

Elderberry Farm in Pinecone Network was another example of 'best match principles. Elvis had to balance a whole range of considerations, starting

202

with the health and productivity of his land, the needs of his customers as passed to him through the supermarket and directly, and what his staff and workers were willing to do. In his case, he had to find ways of encouraging people to come and work on his land.

You So it looks like advertising comes back in a different form.

Me No. Pinecone Network isn't an upside-down economy where producers try to influence demand. It is the other way around. Given that people want things, it is up to those who are organising their production to convince people to do the necessary work. It may be necessary to find ways of making the less inviting types of work more attractive (in contrast to the present, when less inviting types of work are often forced upon the poor).

Without the distorting effect of financial pressures, all sorts of cultural activities can take their rightful place as a full part of social goals, part of the best match equation. Cultural activities function to keep people's goals aligned. They are vital parts of the social glue that keeps a community together and creates a sense of identity for its member. They shouldn't be extras, which need to be subsidised by 'real' economic activity as at present. There were several examples of this in Pinecone Network: Delilah put a lot of time into her dancing, Conan painted his mural for Watermelon House, Francoise and Gerry had their sport, and Joline played the flute at Elderberry Farm.

Organisation to enable generalised exchange

In a competitive economy, where people's goals are set against one another, trust is an early casualty. A co-operative economy needs that basis of trust. This can be achieved through a combination of social groupings where people know each other (like the creative arts camp) and public ratings.

203

Thus co-operatives and communities of many sorts are likely to be the basic social units in a co-operative economy. It is no coincidence that in the developing world co-operatives are becoming increasingly popular. The fictional Pinecone Network was one of several such in its area; it had links with many others.

If co-operatives and communities are the basic units of a co-operative economy, then networks of co-operatives would be its large scale structure. While it is impossible for any individual to have direct personal relationships with very large numbers of people, there is no limit to the number of indirect personal relationships. If there is no-one in your own network to provide something you want, you can look elsewhere, but find that there is always some linkage. In effect, a co-operative world would be linked by friends of friends of friends…

With a basis of trust and an ongoing relationship as part of a community, more generalised exchange becomes possible, as illustrated by the camp economy. People become willing to give for its own sake to people whom they know and whom they can see are contributing to their own welfare. Individual characteristics and needs become part of the equation. There is no longer the desire to get the most from another and offer as little as you can get away with.

From competition to co-operation: finding niches

In a competitive market, there are several or many companies making similar goods or providing similar services, with each trying to get the biggest market share at the expense of the others. In the co-operative alternative, the several companies making similar goods would seek to each be somewhat different than the others. Their goals would not be greatest market share, but rather to best serve a distinct market of stable customers who appreciate what they offer. Instead of competing, organisations would look for *stable niches*.

In many cases, this would be on a geographic basis. As in the natural world, where animals of the same species would be natural competitors, they tend to have distinct, well-understood territories.

> **You** But don't animals fight over those territories?
>
> **Me** Yes they do. They have very limited means of communication. But usually a fight over territory isn't a fight to the death, it is a fight until it is clear who will win and then the other submits. Often this can be determined through posturing or ritual rather than actual combat. We humans have much richer possibilities of communication. We can use the techniques described in the last two chapters to find the best solution for all concerned.

In Pinecone Network, Apple Transport served its regular customers, whose needs it came to know in depth. Mostly customers stayed with it because they appreciated the value of a relationship in which their needs were understood. They were free to change garages, and sometimes did for some reason or other. Apple Transport's job was then to learn whatever lesson they could from that change.

Once similar firms have distinct niches so that they are no longer in competition, it becomes possible and desirable for them to co-operate with each other. They can share their best ideas, as in the Free Software Movement, so that all can provide the highest standards. They can help each other during emergencies (such as staff illness) or when one has more work than it can cope with. All this was illustrated in the description of Apple Transport's operation.

In a co-operative economy, where the goal of production is to serve needs not to make money, the issue of a business cycle simply doesn't arise. In the camp economy, if there is less need to chop wood because the evening is warm, that is a benefit, not a problem. If the demand for a product is reduced, say because consumers start choosing something else, or because it can be made to last longer, that is beneficial all around. The producers don't have to work as hard and there is less manufacturing and distribution to affect the environment.

The information that is needed

The camp economy is a very simple one. All the information needed to organise the camp economy is public and shared by everyone. For the most part, it is clear to everyone what needs to be done (chopping wood, cooking, washing up, etc). The 'costs' of everything are clear too. If no-one builds a fire the cooks won't be able to cook. If no-one cooks, people will be hungry. If no-one clears up the camping circle, it will be a mess. Everyone understands how much effort is required to cook or to make a fire.

For a co-operative economy to develop with all the complexity of modern societies, the crucial ingredient will be its information systems. At a personal level, people need to know the effects of their consumption. In the Pinecone Network, Merry had her personal 'footprint' and a 'contributions' account. They showed her the social and environmental implications of her consumption and allowed her to compare the number of hours she contributed to the community with those she received in her consumption.

The idea of an 'environmental footprint' is a simplified version of the concept of 'real cost' which is the full implications of consuming something. . The concept of 'real cost' is much richer than monetary cost.

It can be divided into two parts:

- *The physical and biological impact of the object* What materials are required to create it and what is their impact upon the natural world (eg. mining, oil wells, forestry?) How much energy and how much water are required in its manufacturing and transport? What are the environmental effects of manufacturing and transporting it? What is required to dispose of it when its useful life is over (ie the results of a life-cycle analysis as will be described in the next chapter.)?

- *The human impact of producing the object* How many hours of effort did it take to produce and distribute it? Under what social conditions was it produced?

In the Pinecone Network story the first part of the real costs were approximated by the 'ecological footprint' of a product and the second by the hours it took to produce.

At present we have no clear understanding of how to present real costs so that consumers can make informed choices, but there are beginnings. Green consumer magazines such as *Ethical Consumer*[6] evaluate products on a range of issues, including environmental considerations, animal welfare, effects on people, and 'extras' such as political donations and genetic engineering. There is a rating for several sub-categories of each issue. The point is to enable consumers to decide to purchase or not on much richer information than monetary cost or the one-sided information the producer provides. In contrast to this, the monetary cost of a product leaves out much of what makes up the real cost, especially environmental impact and the social conditions of labour, and reduces the rest to a single number.

Another strand to the information systems is a detailed ratings system, so people know how others see them and how well they are doing. These information systems become the principal social controls, and enable money to be gradually phased out.

You Does a co-operative economy have to be a moneyless economy?

Me I think it does, eventually. Look back at the problems I've just described. A money-based economy is simply driven by the wrong signals. Things are done for the wrong reasons. Money is an abstraction disconnected from what matters. But a moneyless economy would be quite a late stage. In the early stages of a transition, I think it is sufficient that people understand the problems money causes and begin to find ways around them.

The efficiency of a co-operative economy

Finally, perhaps the biggest change in a co-operative economy would be an enormous increase in efficiency, in the sense of a reduced overall effort needed to satisfy people's wants and needs. We are so used to our producer-driven economy that we don't appreciate the huge amount of extra work that is generated by the need to compete.

A metaphor for competition versus co-operation

Imagine a large group of people trying to lift and move a huge object. If several different groups each push or pull in different directions while some spend their time trying to undermine those who want to go in a different direction from their own, very little will get done despite great efforts by everyone. Most of their effort will go into the conflict with each other. Now imagine that they all co-ordinate their efforts, lifting and pulling in synchrony. All the effort then goes into the job. That is the difference between a competitive world and a co-operative one.

In Pinecone Network, there is no need to spend effort on advertising to encourage people to consume. There is no need for insurance, banks, pensions, taxes, cash, cashiers or cash registers, accountants, stock markets, futures markets, money markets, no negotiations over prices and wages. By contrast, there is a lot of effort spent on finding out what people want and how satisfied they are with what they have received. There is a lot of effort spent on determining the real costs of consumption and informing people of it.

In a co-operative economy it makes sense for the lifetime of goods to be extended by recycling and re-use of parts. That simply leads to less work on the part of the makers, less need for energy, water, mining and raw materials. There is no conflict between efficiency and the producer's need to sell more. This was clear in the way computers and automobiles were handled in Pinecone Network. Far less has to be produced to satisfy people's desires directly than needs to be produced to fuel endless economic growth. It makes sense for different producers to share information on best practice and to cover for each other in times of difficulty.

In a co-operative economy the money-related motivations for crime and corruption are simply not there. Moreover, a social structure like that of a Pinecone Network inherently takes into account the diversity of people's Views, so much less conflict occurs. This leads to a much lower workload for police and social services.

A co-operative economy, driven directly by the needs of people and the environment, (the third basic eGaian principle) has the possibility of being a society that works in accordance with people's hopes and dreams. It has the possibility of being a healthy society, in which the Global Cancer has been cured.

CHAPTER ten

A SUSTAINABLE EARTH

This final chapter of the eGaian Guide looks at the second of the three basic eGaian principles – sustainability. What would it mean if humanity were organised so that looking after the health of the whole of the living Earth were one of its primary values? The chapter deals first with land use, particularly its use for food.

FOR SALE
LAST BIT OF WILDERNESS
NICE UNSPOILED HABITAT
PLANNING PERMISSION
FOR CAR/LORRY PARK

Food isn't just one more sector of the economy. It is fundamental to our survival as animals and to our connection with the rest of the living Earth. The chapter also looks at the sustainable manufacture and distribution of goods and at energy.

> **You** Didn't we know all that back in the 1970s?
>
> **Me** Largely, yes. At that time it was all new, and much of it now seems rather naive. We have the benefit of a generation of careful thought and research to turn what were just ideas into mature technologies. And much of the naivety was due to the assumption that sustainability could take place without the sort of fundamental changes in society and the economy described in the last few chapters.

The purpose of this chapter is to flesh out what ultimately makes for sustainability. It is pointing towards goals rather than looking at possible first steps, but will in so doing help explore and clarify first steps. Thus it is once again the answer to the 'miracle question'. The miracle question assumes away all the cultural obstacles to sustainability. So it looks at what is desirable for sustainability in physical and biological terms while ignoring constraints due to entrenched beliefs, our current economic system or the ravages of current wars and national or ethnic rivalries.

However, it will not ignore constraints due to the size of the human population. Our population is much too large for us to propose simply that humanity backs off and lets nature regenerate as it did, for example, after each of the last few ice ages. That is why humanity needs to function actively and consciously as a nervous system for the living Earth.

212

High-level principles for sustainability

There are many measures that are popularly thought of as leading towards sustainability: using less fossil fuels and more renewable energy sources to reduce carbon dioxide emissions; re-cycling glass, paper, cans and plastic; moving towards organic food production rather than intensive, chemical-based industrial agriculture; restricting the effluents which can be dumped into the atmosphere or watercourses. The list can be extended indefinitely, and every item on it is controversial in some circles, always on economic, but sometimes also on practical grounds.

To clarify the list, there are three high-level principles underpinning sustainability and based on the metaphor of the Earth becoming an organism.

- *Regeneration and recycling* The most fundamental characteristic of an organism is that throughout the cycle of its life it regenerates itself. It continuously builds and rebuilds, growing new cells as old ones die, using the nutrients it gets from its environment. Moreover, the wastes of an organism form the food of some other organism. And then, when it dies, when it can no longer regenerate itself, other organisms use it as food. The result is that the chemicals that make up organisms simply go round and round the biosphere.

213

- *Stability, resilience and self-repair* Organisms must face the challenges of environments which change and which sometimes damage them. All those which persist over many generations (ie are sustainable) can cope with change and repair themselves from injury up to a certain point.

- *Adaptability and creativity* This is simply the response to changing environments over a longer time scale. The organism may evolve to a new form; it may aquire new ways of behaving so that it is better adapted to the new conditions.

So what would it mean for humanity to have these principles applied to the Earth and to themselves as their principal social driving force rather than the pursuit of money?

Land use in an eGaian world

Preserving wilderness

There are parts of the Earth that we think of as natural, unspoiled, meaning they take their own form, rather than one which is determined by people. Some of these teem with life, like the remaining rainforests, temperate forests, grasslands, and parts of the seas. Others – like deserts, high mountains or the poles – have only scattered life.

The wild areas are biological reservoirs, places where life can live at its most diverse and most stable. These parts of the world can look after themselves and don't need our help, so long as they are big enough and so long as the climate doesn't change too much. They have the properties of regeneration, stability and adaptability described above.

If we suppress the usual assumption that they might offer good opportunities to make money, then the importance to the biological health of the Earth of preserving them becomes obvious and overwhelming. An eGaian world would preserve these as reservoirs, and make them as large as possible. Unfortunately, given the size and continued growth of human population, it is perhaps unlikely that they could be much larger than at present, even under an eGaian human culture.

> **You** When you say 'reservoirs' do you mean that no humans should live within them?
>
> **Me** No, and people do live in them now. I think it desirable that they have small, low-density human populations, living what is essentially a traditional gatherer-hunter lifestyle (but also in

communication with the rest of humanity). They would be the caretakers such communities always saw themselves to be. Some would be the continuation of existing indigenous cultures, but treated with a new respect by the rest of humanity. Some entirely new forms of gatherer-hunter cultures might also arise, which people from more settled cultures might move into and out of at different times.

Countryside for food

Outside of wilderness areas, humans and their artefacts to a greater or lesser degree dominate the Earth's surface. Population size means this is likely to continue, but human intervention must be much more natural.

Once we drop the assumption that money flows dominate what we do, our approach to the countryside becomes quite different. The obvious and necessary function of the countryside is to provide food for our huge population. However, the countryside could look very different if our food were seen as our principal connection to the rest of the natural world, and also as the key to our personal health, rather than simply as one more industry or a profitable leisure activity.

In the story of Pinecone Network (Chapter 3) Elderberry Farm illustrates the changed role of farming. Perhaps its most important characteristic is the provision of food mainly for the local population rather than for global agribusiness.

> **You** Is providing food for world markets such a bad idea?
>
> **Me** I'm afraid it is. I'm not saying that there should be no international trade in food. Far from it. It is just that food should come predominantly from local sources. There is a strong movement for organic food now, but the growing

movement for local food, though much less known, is at least as important.

The most obvious reason for food provision to be primarily local is freshness – for flavour, preservation of nutrients and health. It also removes the need for so much processing and packaging. Locally produced meat reduces some animal welfare issues. And for reviving the connection between people and the natural world there is nothing better than a connection with the food they eat.

Producing food for the global market shares many of the difficulties of globalisation of all products. For a start, there is a tremendous amount of extra transport. A typical plate of food in the US today has accumulated some 1,500 miles from source to table. In 1997 food transport was 20% of the total for US commodity transport. And that is just internal transport of food, not including imports, infrastructure costs or car trips to the supermarket.

It is not a matter of giving the consumer more choice. Equivalent products go both ways. For example, the UK imported 114,000 tonnes of milk in 1996 and exported 119,000 tonnes. A supermarket may supply half a dozen varieties of apples from around the world. Yet it probably offers no interesting local varieties because they aren't as suited to industrial scales of growing and handling.[1]

> "Americans import Danish sugar cookies, and Danes import American sugar cookies. Exchanging recipes would surely be more efficient."[2]

Food provision can be considered in terms of the high-level principles for sustainability listed above. First, regeneration and recycling: Elderberry Farm is a mixed organic farm, which includes crops, animals, woodland

and mixed grassland. It is a recycling centre for wastes, and supplies its own energy. It doesn't need external inputs such as fertilisers and pesticides or fossil fuels for its tractors. It is designed to fit into natural biological cycles.

The second principle is stability, resilience and self-repair. For a start, if food is produced locally, adapted to the local area, it is not susceptible to the ups and downs of the world commercial market. As to the nature of the farming, Elderberry Farm has a lot of perennial crops plus wild and semi-wild animals. That means it is a lot closer to self-regulation than conventional farms today. Because of its variety of species, it is not subject to the kind of diseases that can spread through monocultural agricultural systems. It uses a variety of biological controls for pests and diseases.

"In some cases, the farm itself mimics the wilderness, as in the traditional forest gardens of the Tamil Nadu highlands in southern India. These gardens produced a fantastic array of fruits, nuts, berries, roots and edible leaves, while relying on the forest's indigenous species – including micro-organisms, insects, wild animals and 'non-productive' plants – to maintain the garden's balance and health."[3]

217

Studies show that current farming practices are a principal cause of the loss of bio-diversity in the world today[4]. This reduces the stability of the biosphere. It is the combination of mixed, pseudo-natural farms and the preservation of the remaining wilderness areas that are the main eGaian means of stopping this loss.

Probably the most important effect of sustainable agriculture would be to halt the decline in soil fertility and the loss of topsoil. This is one of the most dangerous by-products of industrial agriculture. For example, it is estimated that five pounds of topsoil are lost for every pound of grain harvested in Iowa.[5]

You But surely this use of perennial crops, organic agriculture, and wild animals is much less productive than today's intensive farms. It sounds like a nice idea, but you have said we are going to have to feed nearly twice as many people as we do today.

Me I don't know precisely to what extent it is possible to change. Current research into sustainable agriculture systems points that way, but Elderberry Farm goes further than most of that research; it presumes several generations of research into food production that is designed for biological health and sustainability. Much of today's mainstream food research, such as most of that into genetically modified crops is motivated by a desire to improve money flows in agriculture.

The idea that sustainable agricultural systems are inherently lower yielding doesn't seem to be borne out by research. Jules Pretty writes about sustainable agriculture[6] characterised by:

- use of natural processes such as nutrient cycling, nitrogen fixation and pest-predator relationships

- reduction in external inputs

- more equitable access to productive resources

- use of the biological and genetic potential of plants and animals

- use of local knowledge and practices

- better match of cropping patterns to climate and landscape

- integrated farm management to conserve soil, water, energy and biological resources.

218

This is all very much consistent with the Elderberry Farm practices. Pretty describes the effect of sustainable agriculture in three different areas.

- In industrialised countries, about 1.2 billion people rely on agriculture with large external inputs (fertiliser, pesticides, transport, etc). Sustainable methods would lower yields by perhaps 10-20%, but remove the need for the external inputs. These are areas where the population is not growing and which currently have food surpluses.

- In the Third World, there are roughly 2.5 billion people whose food relies on 'green revolution' type farming methods – a few high yielding varieties which need a lot of water, fertiliser and pesticides. There, sustainable agricultural methods could match current productivity.

- In the poorest countries, there are about 1.2 billion people who use traditional agricultural methods, often on the poorest land (since the better land has gone into the global market). There, using the modern sustainable approaches Pretty describes could double or treble output.

219

> **You** Still, on that analysis, feeding the Earth's future human population doesn't look too easy.
>
> **Me** Not easy but not out of the question, which is how I see the whole transition to an eGaian world.

And what about the third high-level principle for sustainability – adaptability and creativity? Elderberry Farm used several networks to ensure that its practices were up-to-date and appropriate. It was monitored by its staff and linked into the scientific community to ensure that its results and its methods were the best practice available. And in a different sense of creativity, it was laid out with a strong sense of the aesthetic, so that it would have a visual appeal to the local population.

It is clear from the Elderberry Farm story that a lot of creativity needs to be put into the nature of food production if we are to move towards sustainability in that aspect of our lives. The growing popularity of organic food is only a small beginning. Supermarket organic food may not be grown with fertilisers and pesticides but it is still industrially grown and distributed food.

Urban and industrial areas

An eGaian world would still have urban and industrial areas, but they too would be changed significantly, towards a more organic form following the high-level principles for sustainability.

> **You** So you don't envisage a totally back-to-nature world then?
>
> **Me** No, that is not my vision. I grew up in a large city and understand their appeal as cultural and organisational centres. But I imagine that cities could actually be changed sufficiently so that they would fit in with an eGaian world.

Their food would come predominantly from the surrounding countryside for all the reasons given above. Some food would come from more distant places to provide interest and variety in people's diets, rather than because of market opportunities. In addition there would be a major expansion of urban garden-parks, to produce some of the local food, and – probably in some cities – the development of large market gardens within the city boundaries, as was the tradition in Beijing, for example.

Urban and industrial areas require enormous inputs of materials and finished goods, and large exports of the same. They have very large inputs of energy as electricity and as fuels and large outputs of waste heat and combustion products such as carbon dioxide and more toxic emissions. They have large outputs of wastes of all kinds. The following sections indicate how production and energy might be developed sustainably.

Making things sustainably

It should be clear by now that the eGaian image is in no sense a return to a low-tech, primarily rural pre-industrial world. But very dramatic changes in the way we make and distribute things will be needed to move towards sustainability. Over the past few decades a tremendous amount of research and thinking has been devoted to this subject. The eGaian image builds on this and projects it into the future, looking at what is desirable in physical, biological and social terms freed from the constraints of the present economic system.

Several parts of the Pinecone Network story illustrate this approach to sustainability, most especially the Pinecone Plastics factory, but also Apple Transport and the Transport Users Co-op, and the Pinecone Communications Workshop. As with food production, most products are made locally, customised to suit local needs. However, this is not done because of an ideological commitment to local self-sufficiency, but for practical reasons. If there are some products for which only a few high-volume production factories make more sense (for example, computer chips as opposed to computer assembly) than that is the strategy to adopt.

Local production dramatically reduces transport and the energy needed for it. It means that goods are designed for the needs of local people, not for some global mass market. The eGaian goal is largely local production but with global connections for ideas, advice and support.

The Pinecone Plastics factory illustrates and extends what is best in current environmental thinking about product design and manufacturing. The raw materials for its plastics come from local renewable resources (chemicals derived from wood and other organic materials). Its plastics are designed to be recycled and re-manufactured into other products when they reach the end of their life. This is a direct application of the first of the high level sustainability principles – regeneration and recycling.

Similarly, Apple Transport and Pinecone Communications products are designed so that their useful life can be extended by repair and updating of parts, with obsolete parts recycled and re-used.

These strategies reduce the amount of production needed, so reducing water and energy needs, raw materials and waste materials. As a result, they also reduce the workload of the organisations, giving their employees an easier life. Of course in our present economic system this would be a disaster for the three firms in question, as they would prefer to keep their production as high as possible to increase their income. Local production of long-life, customised recyclable products is good for the environment and all the people concerned but bad for an economy that is driven by producers' needs.

222

> **You** I must admit that this goes way beyond the kind of recycling of bottles, cans and paper I am used to.
>
> **Me** Yes, I hope it is clear why that is really just a token effort.

The strategies illustrated in Pinecone Network are part of what is now called 'ecodesign' or 'life cycle design' that aims:

> "to reduce and balance the adverse impact of manufactured products on the environment by considering the product's whole life cycle—from raw materials acquisition, through manufacture, distribution and use, to reuse, recycling and final disposal."[7]

Strategies include:

> "1 the selection of low-impact (eg renewable) materials
>
> 2 reducing the weight or volume of materials in the product

3 using cleaner (eg less wasteful, polluting) techniques for product manufacture

4 reduction of environmental impacts arising from the packaging and distribution of the product

5 reduction of environmental impacts arising from the use (eg energy consumption) and maintenance of the product

6 optimising the life of the product (eg by creating durable 'classic' designs)

7 reuse, remanufacture, recycling or disposal at the end of the product's life."[8]

Moving towards a sustainable world will involve reducing energy, water and resource flows, as well as waste and pollution generated, by anything from four to 20 times,[9] particularly in the more affluent industrialised countries. The strategies of ecodesign described above are only a part of what is needed. Roy talks about them as part of 'sustainable product-service systems'[10], which also include:

223

- systems designed to satisfy needs rather than provide products. For example, the Transport Users Co-op in Pinecone Network helps people with their transport rather than providing them with their own cars. Providing home insulation to keep people's homes warm rather than increasing the supply of gas or oil for heating is another example.

- sharing of services. Again, in the Transport Users Co-op, vehicles are shared so fewer are needed.

- product life extension services. This is very much in the model of Apple Transport or the Pinecone Communications Workshop, in which the organisation takes complete responsibility for the product (car or computer), from manufacture to maintenance to recycling.

- demand side management. Instead of taking the demand for something for granted and supplying it, a partnership between producer and consumer enables demand to be altered to suit conditions. For example, the Pinecone Plastics factory used renewable energy sources and adjusted its output somewhat according to how much energy was available. The Transport Users Co-op arranges shared transport for people so that for minor changes in their preferred travel plans large savings are made by sharing transport.

All of these strategies for improving the sustainability of producing and using things are much easier and more obviously desirable in a society which is organised for co-operation (as is assumed in the Pinecone Network) than in our current competitive market economy.

Sustainable energy use

This is probably the highest profile issue in current debates on sustainability because the carbon dioxide released by burning coal, oil and gas is the principal cause of global warming. However there are many other problems with our present use of energy,[11] including acid rain, oil pollution of the seas, radioactive wastes and the decommissioning of nuclear energy plants. Moreover, the concentration of fuel reserves in a small number of countries (especially in the Middle East) adds enormously to political tensions around the world.

In an eGaian future these problems would be eliminated through a variety of strategies. The most important of these is the reduction in the need for energy (but without reducing people's well being). Much of this has already been covered in the preceding sections. Local production of food and other goods plus the greatly increased use of shared transport hugely reduces the need for fuels for transport.

Much of the rest of the ecodesign and sustainable product-service systems also acts to reduce the need for energy. Some do this directly, as in more highly insulated buildings and other energy-saving techniques (low-energy light bulbs, better controls for heating systems, etc) Others do it indirectly. If the lifetime of products are extended through design, re-use and recycling of parts, much less need to be produced, saving the energy of production. Less raw materials need to be mined, quarried and transported, removing the energy needed for that. If things are shared and used more efficiently then less of them need to be produced, saving that energy.

There are also other, wider ways to reduce energy needs, such as the re-use of energy flows. Collecting the waste heat from electricity generation. and using it for heating buildings is one example.

225

From research done in the recent past, it looks likely that we could "accomplish everything we do today as well as now or better, with only one-quarter of the energy and materials we presently use."[12] In an eGaian future, when ecodesign would be central to social goals and thus much more highly developed, our needs for energy and materials could probably be reduced much further. (The changes resulting from the effort that has gone into improving computers and mobile phones are clues to what might be achieved.) For example, in an eGaian future there might be virtually no need to mine for more metals. The recycling and re-use of metal parts combined with mining our old rubbish might be sufficient.

You I thought this section was going to be about renewable energy, like wind power and all that?

Me Yes, I'm just about to get to that. This discussion of reducing our needs was necessary first.

Traditional discussions about energy concentrate on supplies – like how many more power stations would be needed. They assume continuing economic growth and energy needs and conclude that so much energy is needed that renewable sources could supply only a small fraction of them. But, once the possibilities of reducing energy needs are exploited, then there is no longer a problem in meeting all of humanity's energy needs purely from renewable sources.

For example, a United Nations study in 1992 concluded that "by the middle of the twenty-first century, renewable sources of energy could account for three-fifths of the world's electricity market and two-fifths of the market for fuels used directly."[13] This study assumed substantial economic growth and increased world energy consumption. With eGaian assumptions, there would easily be enough for all the world's energy requirements.

The Pinecone Network story gives a flavour of how this would work. There are renewable sources of energy in many places. Elderberry Farm has some large wind turbines to produce electricity. It also uses a certain amount of coppiced wood as fuel and takes in wastes that are processed into liquid and gaseous fuels. Pinecone Plastics and many other buildings have solar panels that produce electricity and heat.

The basic principle is to use whatever diverse forms of energy are available, whether direct solar energy, wind energy, energy from rivers and streams, biomass energy from wood and wastes, and in coastal areas wave and tidal energy and offshore wind energy.

You Does this mean that there would no longer be those horrible lines of electricity pylons marching across the countryside?

226

Me I'm afraid it doesn't, although they would be much smaller.

The principle here, as with food and goods, is that energy production is basically local, but connected globally. With energy supplies this is particularly important. There are still likely to be some larger sources of energy, such as the offshore wind and wave sources and some hydroelectric schemes where the energy needs to be distributed over an area. Also, renewable energy sources are very variable. By connecting them in a grid you average them out. A high wind in one place might provide more energy than is needed there, but will supply a place where there is no wind at that moment. At times when the variable sources are below requirements, the supply can be topped up with generators running on gas or liquid fuels (renewably made, of course). In a similar way, there could be gas distribution networks, as there are now, but supplying gas from a large number of local gasifiers fed using wood and wastes.

This approach to supplying energy locally but linked into a network follows the first two high-level principles. Energy is just one more part of the local regeneration and recycling system. Local but linked energy sources provide much more resilience than do large, centralised power stations. And of course there is no longer the problem of fluctuating fuel prices due to political events halfway around the world.

227

Towards a sustainable Earth

By looking at the use of land, especially for food, and at sustainable methods of producing goods and energy, it should be clear that sustainability is possible in physical and biological terms without the need to revert to a pre-industrial lifestyle. The obstacles to implementing these strategies are organisational and economic, not physical and biological.

Such obstacles are not inevitable, although they are major. They are of the form "changing the side of the road on which you drive" rather than "changing the law of gravity".

We don't need industrial agriculture to feed a growing world population. On the contrary, industrial agriculture is a major contributor to poverty and to the destruction of the environment. We need largely local organic food production that mimics natural ecosystems, but linked in a global human food web.

We don't need globalised production and distribution of goods to make the world prosperous. It serves the needs of global organisations but not the needs of the environment. It does a bad job for most of the human population. We need largely local production, tailored to local needs, designed for maximum re-use and minimum waste, but linked to a global information and support network.

We don't need more nuclear power stations and oil tankers to keep the lights on and to keep us supplied with goods. That serves the needs of those industries while creating pollution and destabilising the climate. We need largely local energy sources, exploiting whatever forms of renewable energy are available locally, but linked into regional grids.

The physical and biological side of sustainability is much easier to envisage than the social and economic. Growing a peaceful, collaborative world is the hardest part. If we can begin to get that established then sustainability will fall into place easily. And the possible steps in that direction are the subject of the next few chapters.

228

PART four

MAKING

eGAIA

HAPPEN

CHAPTER eleven

STARTING POINTS

"If humanity were to evolve into a healthy, integrated social super-organism, it would signal the maturation and awakening of the global nervous system." *Peter Russell*[1]

The twentieth century saw the development of the global cancer to its most destructive limits with globalisation, which at the same time, brought with it the possibility of a global-scale organism. Could it be that the progression to planetary organism has happened many times before elsewhere in the universe? And perhaps a common part of that process is that as life becomes increasingly complex it takes its planet to the very edge of destruction before it makes that final leap to unity.

If the Earth is to become a global scale organism, it will need:

• a communication system linking the various parts, leading to

- a global sense of identity, leading to

- symbiosis among the parts, so that they act in aid of each other and the whole rather than in conflict and competition with each other.

This chapter looks at recent and current starting points towards these three features including a review of some of the organisations whose work is heading in that direction. They rarely make the headlines and haven't affected the dominant trends, but are beginning to link up, so that significant changes may become visible within the next few years. Even this only scratches the surface of what is developing. In her classic book, *The Aquarian Conspiracy*,[2] Marilyn Ferguson chronicled many of those starting points, as they appeared 25 years ago. There have been enormous developments since then, especially because of the possibilities opened by the Internet.

A communication system

231

Communication has been a human strong point since the early stages of our evolution as 'the co-operative ape' when we developed language. Travel has given humans glimpses of cultures other than their own since ancient times. Conquests and migrations have long led to the mixing of cultures and languages. But only with the development of electronic communications in the last 100 years has our communication reached the stage where it could be the basis of a global nervous system.

The transition started in the late 19th century, with the invention of the telegraph and telephone, especially when undersea cables linked the continents. In the early 20th century, motion pictures and then radio linked the world much more closely. In the mid-20th century, with TV news sent by satellite, wars, famines and other crises became much more visible in homes around the world. Air travel became more widely available. With so much travel and the globalisation of business, English began to emerge as the first global language, spoken by at least some people everywhere. But it was the end of the 20th century, with the development of mobile telephones and the mass use of the Internet that provided the necessary infrastructure for a global nervous system. It now pervades the world. Even developing countries have rapidly growing Internet access, with access points in many small towns and even villages. Across the world, some 500 million people are on-line.[3]

You Are you saying that the Internet is the global nervous system?

Me No, it's not the Internet itself. That only provides the infrastructure. It is the way people are coming to use it, and could use it in the future, which might provide the global nervous system. The change has been so dramatic within my lifetime. When I was a child, my grandparents immigrated to

New York by ship, and air travel was a luxury. A long distance telephone call (to the one phone in the house!) was a rare and exciting event. Now, our children travel to such far-flung places as India and Guatemala and we worry if they don't email us from a cyber-café every few days. Friends with young children casually check up on them during the day, mobile phone to mobile phone. But this is only connection. It is the results of connection that could make a global nervous system.

A global sense of identity

The enormous growth of communications has lead to the beginnings (and we are still at a very early stage) of a global sense of identity. The availability of comparatively cheap long-distance transport has led to a world that is at the same time much more multi-cultural and much more culturally convergent. Small communities of foreigners are now much more common throughout the world, partially keeping their own languages and customs and partially adopting local ways. Food, clothing and consumer goods were once produced locally. Now there are familiar brands bought around the world.

There is at the same time a lot of cultural conflict in reaction to immigrant groups and the growth of tolerance and acceptance of different ways of living. The films, television programmes and advertisements of the 1940s and 50s show stereotypes of race, gender and cultural minorities that would be considered intolerable today. Tolerance has the backing of law in many countries and is enshrined in United Nations documents.

The realisation that human affairs are having a significant harmful effect on the environment entered mass public consciousness only in the 1960s, creating a strong sense that we are all connected on that level at

233

least. There have been various events that have so stirred the global consciousness that they could be called 'eGaian moments'.

- The first views of the Earth from space and the first moonwalks dramatically displayed the whole Earth as a single, closed system containing us all.

- The global aid events of the mid-1980s – Band Aid and Live Aid – showed how universal musical culture was among the young and was a global expression of concern for those people in the most need.

- September 11th was seen live on television – the second plane hitting and the collapse of the twin towers – by millions of people around the world. People were personally shocked by this in a global wave of emotion. Local papers everywhere reported on local people who had been involved. Amazing petitions circulated on the Internet in response, with signatures that leapt from nation to nation. eGaia felt pain and shock.

234

Symbiosis among the parts

The growth in a sense of the connectedness of all humanity and a global sense of identity has lead to many initiatives and to the creation of many organisations dedicated to resolving the world's problems. As with the growth of a global sense of identity, this is still at quite an early stage. At present their influence is very much smaller than that of the global cancer but it is growing rapidly.

The past few decades have seen a huge increase of non-governmental organisations (NGOs) which are neither commercial organisations nor governmental. Although they do not have much power, they have increasing influence, through very large numbers of supporters and good means of communications. They range from think tanks that propose policies and lobby governments to grassroots organisations taking direct action.

NGOs have become a new force in world governance, taking on a global role where governments are unable to. As a review of Julie Fisher's book on NGOs says:

"A living body of networking organizations has emerged to fill the niche produced by dysfunctional post-colonial governments. A plethora of unique interdependent organs assuming specialised functions which serve the whole have almost magically become the body that promises better life for the people in developing countries, and the whole Earth.

Grassroots Organizations (GROs) formed by the people in remote villages, have risen by the tens of thousand to solve local problems with local skills and local resources. They network horizontally with one another to provide mutual aid. Grassroots Support Organizations (GRSOs) have emerged independently in the cities, capitals and universities to answer their own need for social usefulness by providing information, material and services, to the remote and the disadvantaged GROs.

Overseas International NonGovernmental Organizations (INGOs) have recognized the failure of Governments and UN – run Development Decades" to provide "direct aid" to the people in their villages. This whole global Civil Society is a new phenomenon. It was not planned by the bureaucrats, not even by the participants themselves. It emerged and self-organized as a working whole within the last two decades. It is now composed of hundreds of thousands of new organizations each playing a unique role in the new body politic."[4]

The international search for peace

As technology advanced rapidly with the industrial revolution, so did the technology of war. The Great War of 1914-1918 so shocked the world that a global organisation, the League of Nations, was set up as a means of ending wars. Unfortunately, the world was not ready for peace. The second World War lead to a second attempt – the United Nations. The UN's peacemaking functions were severely limited before 1989 by the cold war. Its principal function was to provide a forum at which the polarised factions could shout across each other. However, it did at least establish the principle that there was a global forum and a legal basis for international actions for peace. Since the end of the cold war there have been various international attempts to intervene and defuse conflicts, with limited success. Old habits of power politics die hard. The newer approaches to conflict resolution described in Chapter 8 are only beginning to make an impact on international conflicts. There is a lot more to learn, but at least there is the beginning of intervention for the sake of resolving the problem, rather than simply to prop up one's allies.

Efforts to reduce poverty

While the political influence of the United Nations has been limited, its other agencies like UNICEF and UNESCO have had modest success in reducing poverty and improving health and education. Parallel to the growth of transnational corporations in the second half of the 20th century, there has been a growth in transnational aid agencies, such as Save the Children, Oxfam, Médecins Sans Frontières and many others. The Internet era has seen an explosion of smaller NGOs throughout the world dedicated to aid and development.

236

The International Federation of Red Cross and Red Crescent Societies is "the world's largest humanitarian organization, providing assistance without discrimination as to nationality, race, religious beliefs, class or political opinions. Founded in 1919, the International Federation comprises 178 member Red Cross and Red Crescent societies, a Secretariat in Geneva and more than 60 delegations strategically located to support activities around the world. There are more societies in formation. The Red Cross is used in place of the Red Cross in many Islamic countries."[5]

Looking after the environment

As awareness of our environmental problems grew, so did the attempts to do something about it. The first UN global conference on the environment was held in Stockholm in 1972. Twenty years later, at Rio de Janeiro, the UN Conference on Environment and Development (the 'Earth Summit') brought together policy-makers, scientists, media and NGO representatives from 179 countries in an effort to reconcile the impact of human socio-economic activities on the environment. The next Earth Summit in Johannesburg will be bigger still. Its potential to move us towards an eGaian Earth is the subject of this book's concluding chapter. In the environmental area there has been a particularly large growth of non-governmental organisations.

237

The Worldwatch Institute is "an independent, public policy research organization that aims to provide the information that brings about the changes needed to build an environmentally sustainable economy." It publishes an authoritative annual review. *State of the World 2002* includes chapters on climate change, farming, toxic chemicals, sustainable tourism, population, resource conflicts and global governance, with a special focus on the United Nations World Summit on Sustainable Development. The Worldwatch Institute provides a website for the public and a media centre to provide information to journalists.

Greenpeace International is "an independent campaigning organisation that uses non-violent, creative confrontation to expose global environmental problems and to force solutions which are essential to a green and peaceful future." When its campaign of public protest and boycott forced Royal Dutch Shell to reverse its decision to dump the Brent Spar oil platform in the north-east Atlantic Ocean the power of campaigning organisations was clearly shown.

The new economy

As the global market creates more and more problems throughout the world, many alternatives and experiments have arisen in reaction to it.

The ethical investment movement allows people to put their savings into banks and investment funds that have criteria other than maximising returns. This may mean as little as a stock market fund which avoids armaments and other harmful companies, or as much as the Triodos Bank which specialises in investments in social and environmentally beneficial enterprises. Micro-credit banks specialise in making very small loans to people in developing countries or deprived neighbourhoods in the West. These people would normally be unable to obtain any credit at all.

Movements for organic food have become very widespread in many Western countries, and there are also moves towards local food, in farmer's markets and other forms. The principle of 'fair trade' is growing as an alternative to trade that simply seeks the lowest price. Instead it is concerned with a different kind of relationship, including paying a fair wage, providing healthy and safe working conditions in the local context, engaging in environmentally sustainable practices and being open to public accountability.

> The Fair Trade Federation (FTF) is "an association of fair trade wholesalers, retailers, and producers whose members are committed to providing fair wages and good employment opportunities to economically disadvantaged artisans and farmers worldwide.
>
> FTF directly links low-income producers with consumer markets and educates consumers about the importance of purchasing fairly traded products which support living wages and safe and healthy conditions for workers in the developing world. It also acts as a clearinghouse for information on fair trade and provides resources and networking opportunities for its members. By adhering to social criteria and environmental principles, Fair Trade Organizations (FTOs) foster a more equitable and sustainable system of production and trade that benefits people and their communities."[6]

239

New currencies

There have been many experiments with local or complementary currencies. These circulate only within a defined group. This encourages members of that group to patronise other members. They are often set up so that people can also get credit in the local currency at no interest, often when the same people would be unable to obtain credit elsewhere, or only at exorbitant interest rates.

> Time Dollars are "a new, tax-exempt kind of money that empowers people to convert their personal time into purchasing power by helping others and by rebuilding family, neighborhood and community. An hour helping another earns One Time Dollar.
>
> From child care to karate lessons to phone companionship, to being a juror on a youth court, the ways of earning Time Dollars are endless. Everyone's contribution is valued the same: an hour for an hour.
>
> Time Dollars are a tool to recognize, validate and reward doing 'the right thing' for others. For the elderly, Time Dollars look like a new kind of extended family. For teenagers, Time Dollars provide a setting where kids can level with kids and say: Don't do something stupid. For residents in public housing, they mean doing what neighbors used to do for neighbors.
>
> Time Dollars express four core values: 1. everyone has strengths and assets; 2. raising children and building community is valuable work; 3. mutual support is more powerful and empowering than one-way helping; and 4. trust is the basis for community."[7]

New communities and co-operatives

New forms of community and co-operatives would be the social basis of an eGaian world. Taking a long view of human history, this can be seen as a return to the kind of social support that shaped human evolution and to which human minds and personalities are adapted (as discussed in Chapter 5, The co-operative ape). More recently, there have been many experiments with communities and co-operatives such as:

- the pioneering efforts in the 19th century co-operative movement in Britain
- the *kibbutz* movement in Israel
- the hippie communes and communities in the 1960s and 70s.

A review article in 1994 on the history of the co-operative movement said:[8]

"In 1844, ... 28 workers in northern England formed the first successful co-operative... the Rochdale Equitable Pioneers Society, taking their name from the town they lived in, Rochdale, which is 12 miles north of Manchester. ...Their idea established the fundamental principles of modern co-operation which were eventually borrowed by 700 million people in nearly 100 countries.

The co-operative form is flexible and endlessly adaptable, and in the 1990's co-ops provide almost every imaginable product and service a person could ever need, from the cradle to the grave. There are co-ops that sell bicycles, furniture, camping equipment, appliances, carpeting, clothing, handicrafts, and books. There are co-operative wholesalers, like those in the hardware, grocery, and natural foods businesses. There are co-operatives that disseminate news and co-operatives for artists. There are co-operative electric

241

and telephone utilities. There are co-operatively managed banks, credit unions, and community development corporations. There are thousands of farm co-ops, along with co-ops that provide financing to farm co-ops.

And every day in the rest of the world, another 600 million people demonstrate that co-operation is truly an international phenomenon ...In many cases, in fact, co-ops are the dominant players in their industries. Co-ops control 100 percent of Uganda's cotton-ginning capacity, 99 percent of Sweden's dairy production, 95 percent of Japan's rice harvest, 75 percent of western Canada's grain and oil seed output, 65 percent of India's sugar production, and 60 percent of Italy's wide production. A co-op in Shanghai is considered a world leader in waste management and recycling techniques, and a co-op in Argentina is one of South America's major book publishers.

... particularly in developing nations – smaller co-ops are making a major difference in people's lives. In India, for example, the Shri Mahila Sewa Sahakari Bank is a co-operative owned by and for self-employed illiterate rural peasant women who earn their living as street vendors and seamstresses. Before Sewa was established, in 1973, these women couldn't obtain even rudimentary financial services. Today well over 25,000 poor women have a place to build savings and get loans to buy equipment."

The Global Eco-village Network (GEN) – "Ecovillages are urban or rural communities of people, who strive to integrate a supportive social environment with a low-impact way of life. To achieve this, they integrate various aspects of ecological design, permaculture, ecological building, green production, alternative energy, community building practices, and much more.

Ecovillages typically build on various combinations of three dimensions:

- Social/Community
- Ecological
- Cultural/Spiritual.

Today, GEN counts the following members:

- 100 members for GEN Europe and Africa
- 80 members for GEN Oceania
- There are 500 in North America, 700 in South America.
- The GEN South Asia subregional secretariat is currently communicating with 40 ecovillages outside Sri Lanka, and is located at the headquarters of the Sarvodaya Movement in Sri Lanka, with 10,000 member villages."[9]

Ross Jackson says of GEN: "It unites North and South in a common agenda that cuts across all cultural, racial, and religious differences. It is a remarkable fact that the builders of ecovillages often have more in common with each other than with their respective local cultures, no matter where they come from. A common, global vision is emerging that has the power to change the world."[10]

243

A case study: The Federation of Damanhur

"New forms of society are possible and practical. They are the indispensable pathway to the creation of a new planetary balance in social, economic, human and cultural terms."[11]

Most GEN members have goals that are very much in line with eGaian principles. They are trying to create sustainable communities along co-operative lines. One, however, the Federation of Damanhur in northern Italy, is especially interesting because of its highly developed social structure. Damanhur has developed a collaborative, supportive, responsive, organism-like social structure for its members that has many of the qualities described in the eGaian Guide. This has enabled them to move much further towards sustainability than their Italian neighbours. At the same time, examination of Damanhur shows up some of the limitations of eGaian principles in terms of what is possible in today's world.

> **You** Are you saying that your eGaian principles aren't really practical?
>
> **Me** eGaia is a long-term vision. I think that some aspects aren't possible as first steps, starting from where we are now. The interesting thing about Damanhur is that it shows how far it is possible to go socially while it is perhaps less possible to go as far in terms of sustainability.

The group was formed in 1975, encouraged by the teachings of Oberto Airaudi, who remains Damanhur's spiritual guide. In 1979 they inaugurated their first community village. "The village was conceived to be a miniature state through which it would be possible to demonstrate...self-sustainability."[12] It has developed since then into a federation of communities, largely spread around the Valchiusella valley in the foothills of the Alps north of Turin. It has around 1,000 citizens, most of whom are resident in the communities. Those who are not are closely associated with it.

The Earth is seen as a living thing which the people are expected to look after. Damanhurian society is mutually supportive and organism-like rather than competitive. From the beginning it was seen as a spiritual community whose basic principles were:

- "the school of meditation as a spiritual and ideological prime mover
- the value of service attributed to managerial and political roles
- importance of the group and of others
- respect for Nature and the forces that inhabit it
- care of children
- solidarity
- positive thought and common sense
- value of work
- study and research"

In many ways Damanhur appears much like a conventional, reasonably prosperous Italian community. The people dress quite smartly, carry mobile phones, have cars and neat homes and work very hard at their jobs. They run about 50 businesses (mostly co-operatives) including farms, restaurants, guest houses, builders, web design, and many more, but especially creative crafts such as jewellery, hand-made fabrics, mosaics and stained glass.

A closer look reveals some of the differences from their Italian neighbours. Most of their buildings are decorated inside and out with paintings (some walls have murals of giant painted plants and animals). Statues, altars and various other works of art are placed around their

245

grounds. Damanhur has built a magnificent underground temple, its walls covered with murals, floors with mosaics and ceilings with stained glass. It has to be seen to be believed. Notices on walls and bulletin boards announce games, theatrical and musical events and courses of all kinds. There is a strong sense that creativity and the arts have replaced the drive for material consumption.

While Damanhurians are Italian citizens (and they seem very Italian), at the same time they have overlain this with their unique culture. They have their own customs, laws, social institutions and constitution that each individual member has agreed to follow. While not in any way challenging the Italian state, Damanhur provides social services such as education, security and conflict resolution which replace those of the Italian state for its citizens. Damanhur remains within the conventional Italian state, and without significant conflict with it. (That has not always been the case: it took Damanhur quite a long time to be accepted by the authorities.) In fact, Damanhurians are now members of some local councils and one is the mayor of a local town.

Damanhur's citizens are responsible for their personal maintenance, while being part of a community based on sharing and solidarity. Much of what is important to them – food, homes, jobs, social life – comes through the community. They live in household groups of 10-20 people which they call *nucleos*. These include parents and children, single people and elderly people, as they believe in mixing different ages. Sometimes teenagers will live in a different *nucleo* from that of their parents, to everyone's mutual satisfaction. Within a *nucleo* all the adults share responsibility for the children (but without replacing the special relationship with their parents). Adults take turns feeding the children, seeing that they do their homework and putting them to bed, so that the parents are much freer to do other things than in most western societies. Each *nucleo* has its own arrangements about how much income its members must contribute, and jointly plans expenditure.

Groups of *nucleos* make up a community. Damanhurians believe that beyond 200 or so people, it is difficult to relate well to everyone. So as Damanhur grew larger it split into two communities, and now has reached five, which together form the Federation of Damanhur. Each *nucleo* elects a head (*capo nucleo*) who represents them at the level of the community and the Federation.

At the Federation level there are various organisational bodies, generally elected in various ways including a College of Justice and two king-guides (usually one man and one woman elected for six months at a time from the more senior Damanhurians). There is a constitution for the Federation and detailed rules at the level of each community, determined by the community.

At all three levels – nucleo, community and federation – the needs and interests of the individual, the group and the needs of the Earth are the driving force for decision making. From the individual's point of view, they live in a local democracy without political parties or significant factions, a democracy which is genuinely responsive to their views and needs.

One especially interesting feature of Damanhur is their emphasis on change:

> "Damanhur is a way of living and thinking based upon experimentation, play and transformation, whose aim is to overcome limiting habits and to open up new empowering visions of reality."

They have built in various institutions to ensure that they don't get stuck in rigid ways of thinking. Their constitution and social structure have

247

changed many times as their society has matured. If they make a decision that doesn't work out, they have no problem with changing it. All of this is very much in line with the eGaian principles of a social structure with many feedback mechanisms to ensure it is responsive to its members.

Serious personal conflicts are quite rare and crime non-existent. This is effected by a combination of their spiritual philosophy, the intimate and deep connection between individuals and their supportive community and educational system.

> "Human beings are gregarious mammals and find harmony and well-being through relationships with others. Feeling accepted, loved and satisfied with our place in society gives us a lust for life and an openness towards the new."

Communication, conflict resolution and seeing from another's perspective are an important part of Damanhur's educational principles. Where problems do arise they are dealt with informally. On those rare occasions when it is necessary, the College of Justice intervenes using an approach of restorative justice aimed at healing the social breaches rather than punishment, just as suggested in the eGaian Guide.

Economically, the various businesses of Damanhur function as autonomous profit-making enterprises and are generally quite successful. Most of the Damanhur businesses are run as co-operatives by their employees. Although largely autonomous, they are subject to the principles of the Damanhurian philosophy and Constitution. They are not in competition with each other. Rather, each has its own niche and role in Damanhurian society. "Damanhur's economic system is fundamentally based on the idea of sharing." Businesses serve the needs of Damanhur as well as that of their external customers. They provide for much of the physical needs of Damanhur as well as bringing in money from outside. Damanhur has its own complementary currency system, the *Credito*, which is currently pegged in value to the Euro. This helps to encourage Damanhurians to patronise their internal businesses rather than external ones.

However, as Damanhurians still buy a proportion of their goods from the outside world, they rely on the commercial success of their businesses and are subject to external competitive pressures. They have made their economic niche the sale of high-quality crafts and art works, sold to affluent buyers throughout the world. Their prosperity depends upon the health of that market and not just on the quality of their work.

> **You** And you say that in Damanhur they still do use money, even if it is a complementary currency. That is not in line with your eGaian guide or your Pinecone Network.
>
> **Me** True, but Damanhur is operating now, in a world where people are used to money and expect to be paid for what they do, not in an eGaian future. Nonetheless, Damanhur's strong social structure enables them to resist commercial pressures to quite a remarkable degree even in today's world. I consider a moneyless economy to be desirable at quite a late stage. The development of an information-based economy needs to develop before it is possible The use of local currencies is very appropriate for the first stages.

249

Damanhur is very advanced in its communication system, by any standards. It produces a daily newspaper that is distributed to all Damanhurians and an extensive web site in several languages. It also has an internal network of computers in all the businesses and residences. As an example of its use, they have regular discussions with their spiritual teacher, Oberto Airaudi, which are broadcast on their internal network and on the

Internet so that people can participate even if they aren't physically present. Thus Damanhur has the physical infrastructure in place for an information-based economy such as in the Pinecone Network. Although it doesn't currently use its network for those purposes, Damanhur does have a system of evaluation for individual, *nucleo* and national consumption, agricultural production at all levels, and currency circulation. It regularly runs statistical analyses of national consumption.

Sustainability is a major goal for Damanhur. Although quite advanced compared with the Italian society that surrounds them, they still have a very long way to go. The Damanhurians do a lot more recycling of their glass, cans and plastic than their neighbours, but then Italy doesn't do much recycling yet. But this is very far from the complete use of renewable materials and the total use of waste streams as inputs to other processes described in the eGaian Guide. Damanhurian buildings are relatively well-insulated and they are experimenting with the use of solar photovoltaic electricity, but much of their fuel use is conventional. They also do a lot of travelling which must add significantly to their ecological footprint. By living in larger households than is conventional they are able to share many appliances, which keeps their consumption relatively low.

Damanhur is planning to become self-sufficient in food by 2003 and in clothing and energy within the next few years. This will require an heroic effort, but if successful it will not only reduce their ecological footprint very dramatically, but will also help isolate them to a significant degree from the twists and turns of the larger economy. To become fully sustainable, Damanhur would either have to become self-sufficient in everything they use (impossible for a technologically sophisticated community) or become part of a much larger network of communities which live sustainably as described in the eGaian Guide. The latter seems to be their preferred strategy, and so they are taking a very active role in the Global Eco-Village Network and are forging links and offering help to other groups with similar aims.

One clear lesson from Damanhur is that it is possible to live much more sustainably when you are part of a community that acts as a whole towards sustainable ends than it is for an isolated individual. They have created a co-operative bubble within the larger competitive world. This frees them to move towards sustainable living.

Finally, and perhaps most important of all, Damanhurians have moved a long way towards the kind of extended sense of self described in the eGaian Guide. To the Damanhurians, being a Damanhurian is a dominant part of their sense of self. They see themselves as 'a People', with a distinctive culture. Their philosophy gives them a purpose in life and a sense of connection to the Earth and to all life.

251

eGaian
co-operative networks

This chapter discusses starting points towards one kind of co-operative network that would be a foundation of an eGaian world. This chapter is practical, not Utopian like the story of Pinecone Network in Chapter 3. It looks at the initiatives that can be started now, in the world we inhabit. This vision of eGaian networks builds on the principles in the eGaian Guide. It is an attempt to re-invent community in a way which enables people to lead lives which are more sustainable and co-operative. It provides starting points for an economy based upon trust where the pressures of the commercial marketplace are significantly reduced. It builds on the ideas behind eco-villages but without requiring people to give up their existing homes and livelihoods and move to a new community. It builds on experience with existing on-line community networks but adds an economic dimension. It builds on experience with existing complementary (local) currencies but adds organised co-operatives so that the whole plays a significant rather than a marginal role in peoples' lives.

> **You** So this is it. Your big idea of how to move towards your Utopian vision. You've got it all worked out.
>
> **Me** Well, sort of. I have thought long and hard about it but I wouldn't say I have it all worked out. I see this as starting points, as far as I've got with it, ready for the details to be worked out, applied and tested by any group who wants to try it.

Essentially, an eGaian co-operative network is a group of like-minded people coming together to support each other in ways like obtaining local food, sharing transport, child care, health care or whatever is appropriate for them, using a computer network as an aide to organising themselves. They may do this for each other as an exchange of favours, or through use of their own local currency, as well as through paying each other in the national currency.

The eGaian vision differs from many current local currency systems or community networks in that it:

253

- actively promotes co-operation and support through sub-groups that organise food, transport, childcare etc for its members

- is actively concerned to maintain a basis of trust and connection among its members

- uses the immediacy of the computer network to match wants and needs on a daily basis.

Although the computer network is a central part, this is not a virtual network where people meet only online. Most contact would be in person.

The computer network provides organising facilities like notice boards, sign-up sheets, discussion forums, accounts and polls for decision making. In a traditional small community or a modern eco-village, people could see each other daily and co-ordinate their activities easily. Today, people who want a more co-operative life are likely to know others who do also, but they will live scattered in a larger geographical community. The on-line tools are to enable them to keep in touch more easily.

> **You** So you have to have a computer, know how to use it, and know how to get on-line to be part of these networks.
>
> **Me** No, that's too strong. I think a lot of the members would need to have computers. The rest would need access to a computer, either through another member or through a public computer in a library or cyber-café. A lot could be done by telephone or word of mouth. But if networks like this start being successful it will provide a reason for people without computers to get one.

254

The computer is there as infrastructure, to make things easier, in the same way that email is simpler and faster than writing a letter. You don't have to look up someone's address because the address is automatically inserted when you type the first few letters of their name. It is that kind of low-effort co-ordination that these networks need to provide.

An eGaian network would allow its members to exchange goods and services with people they trust, and pay for these using on-line accounts. The on-line cheques, like email, would be much simpler to use than paper cheques. They would also offer very low-cost credit, in some cases to people who couldn't otherwise get credit.

Members could sign up on-line for a shift at a shared garden or co-operating local farm, or for a shift driving an informal taxi service or for whatever work was needed. These would function as flexible part-time jobs chosen to suit a member's interests and free time. Moreover, these shifts would be opportunities to provide a service needed by the community, rather than jobs done just to provide a monetary income. Signing up for these on-line is much easier than the normal hassles of arranging a part-time job.

The function of the computer network is to enable people living separate, dispersed lives to co-ordinate their activities easily. However, no matter how good the on-line service or how easy it is to use, it will probably not be the main factor which determines whether an eGaian network will succeed or fail. That is likely to depend upon the kinds of relationships its members form with each other. They will need effective means of maintaining trust, of making decisions, of coming to consensus on important issues, and of handling conflict when it arises, as discussed in the eGaian Guide. They will need to find areas in which their members want to work co-operatively (food, shared transport, childcare, health care, etc) and to organise themselves appropriately.

255

The success of a network will depend upon whether it offers its members immediate, personal benefits, and must be set up with that in mind. Particularly in the early stages, their larger effects on the world will be extremely small and must be secondary.

Starting an eGaian co-operative network

An eGaian network is meant to be much more than a way for its members to live more sustainably. It should provide a sense of community, including social activities, support of various sorts, effective means of conflict resolution, and also provide the basis of an economy based upon trust.

Thus the relationships between its members will always be central to its effectiveness. This is particularly important when it is being formed.

If a network is formed from a random group drawn from the general public, a lot of effort will be required in its early stages to build trusting relationships. This is an issue its organisers will need to take seriously. An alternative is to grow the network from existing informal friendship networks, so that a good relationship and a basis of trust are already there. Another strategy would be for an eGaian network to grow out of an existing group which already shares some of its characteristics and simply takes on extra dimensions.

> **Me** To help bring these networks alive, and to add some detail and colour, I shall again resort to fiction. Pinekernal Network might be the grandparent of Pinecone Network described in Chapter 3.

The birth of Pinekernel Network

Pinekernel Network was the brainchild of Marilyn who had heard about them from her cousin, who was in one. Marilyn began talking about it with her friends, and found a few that were also enthusiastic about it. Each of them then began to canvas further friends who in turn invited others until they had a nucleus of about 30 people interested. Their first efforts were devoted to gathering information about the first few eGaian Networks, and about other communities and eco-villages. Marilyn's cousin arranged for one of her network's organisers to come to an early Pinekernel meeting.

The meetings and discussions were usually quite lively,

and since the group had been assembled on the basis of friendships, coming to their initial agreements was not that difficult. Meetings often involved shared meals and tended to drift into social events. The birth of Pinekernel Network was as much a social opportunity as it was of practical benefit to its members.

In its formative stages an eGaian network needs to consider a variety of issues. One is the areas in which they are interested in supporting each other (food, transport, childcare, etc). Each area will need a significant amount of effort and organisation. Another set of issues is to do with how the group organises itself. Do they want to set up their own currency? Perhaps there is a local LETS, Time Bank or other similar local currency that they can use already. How will they handle membership? How will they deal with conflict? How big do they want to grow? Are there other, similar networks they want to connect with? What about making links with local farms or shops? What will they do about issues of tax and benefits on their transactions? How will they go about finding or setting up the on-line software support they need?

Together, these issues will create a formidable challenge to the earliest pioneer networks. Once a few are started, many lessons will be learned, precedents set, and software developed. The second and successive waves of networks will find it much easier to get started and become viable, building upon the experience of the pioneers.

The set of areas in which members of a network can support each other is likely to depend very much on the members' interests and available time. It might be quite different in an inner city area and in a country area, or among the members of an existing organisation.

257

Food

The issue of food is so fundamental to existence that it is likely to be included in any eGaian network. The opportunity to obtain locally grown, very fresh, organic food could be a very appealing platform around which to organise. It effects health and makes a difference to sustainability. It has natural extensions to transport and social life. The sharing of food is a fundamental part of all traditional societies and is at the heart of all human cultures. Most eGaian networks are likely to want to set up a sub-group to look after food.

At its simplest, those members of the network who like gardening could agree to share whatever surpluses they have with other members. A next step would be for members to help out in each other's gardens or to take on shared gardens or allotments. This would provide only a small amount for the members, but that food would be very fresh and would be a morale-boosting start. It would also offer many social opportunities.

The next steps would be to seek out other sources of local food. A sub-committee could systematically check out local farmers' markets. They could look for local farmers who would be interested in supplying an organised group. In exchange for a preferred status as food suppliers, some farmers might offer discounts or accept part payment in the group's local currency. They could use that currency to pay members to do occasional work on the farm. A related approach would be to look for local shops that were already outlets for locally grown produce. As with the farmers, the group could try to make special arrangements – either discounts or part payment in the group's local currency.

If the food available becomes more than marginal, then the issue of distribution arises. The use of local shops may be one way of handling this. Another is for the group to do its own distribution in an organised fashion.

This offers the prospect of modest amounts of work opportunities for group members. It could be one of the basic functions of a transport group, should the group wish to start one.

The food group could organise a lot more than just basic raw foodstuffs. Cooked meals and shared meals are likely to be very useful. Some members may enjoy cooking more than they need for themselves and could offer it to other members, either freshly-cooked or frozen as an alternative to a take-away or frozen supermarket meal. Where it suits people socially, eating together could be on offer. For the cooks, this could be useful as a part-time job. The food group could canvas members to find out who was willing to prepare food, either on a regular basis or on request. The on-line bulletin boards would be used to match cooks and eaters.

This first example of food shows much of the potential of an eGaian network. It gives members the opportunity to give and receive something from each other in a way that reduces their need for money and builds relationships between them. Eating local fresh food is a move towards sustainability that goes well beyond tokenism. It can also contribute to the regeneration of the local economy by supporting local farms and shops.

259

The Food Co-op in Pinekernel Network

When Norma first became interested in Pinekernel Network, she knew that the food side would be her main interest. She loved both cooking and gardening and was a good organiser. She enjoyed visiting the farms around her town, seeking out those interested in organic production. She started with one that already supplied a local wholefood shop and arranged for a discount for Pinekernel members.

The farmer now emails Pinekernel Network weekly with a list of what she has available, and people collect what they want at the wholefood shop. It has increased the business of both farm and shop. Norma emails the farmer regularly with comments and requests from the members. Thus the relationship between farmer and members is beginning to be determined by information rather than just by money flows.

Norma also now has a regular arrangement to provide food for several people in the network. The children of one family come to her for dinner once a week while their parents attend an evening class. Two others collect food she has prepared and frozen once or twice a week.

Transport

Transport is likely to be a promising area for eGaian networks. Arranging transport is often a burden to people, whether it is the ferrying of children to their many activities, transporting furniture or other bulky items, simply getting about if you are elderly or unwell, or taking long journeys on your own. Co-ordinating transport could make a significant difference to people's lives both socially and in terms of the sustainability of their lifestyles. Again, it can provide flexible opportunities to provide service for others in the group.

At its simplest, the transport sharing could be nothing more than an on-line bulletin board in which people give their transport needs and offer their services. Who has a van or large car that could be available to move large items? Are there any regular journeys which people can share? Could someone take me to the airport next week? Collect my children from their after-school club on Thursdays? Take me shopping tomorrow? Take us home after the party on Saturday night? Distribute the food from the farm to those members who had ordered it?

An active transport group could take this further than just a bulletin board. They could maintain a register of people with vehicles to share or lend, or who would be willing to drive people when desired. The transport group could be the contacts for such information.

A further step would be to have something like an informal taxi service. The transport group could poll the members to see if there were any times when people were particularly likely to need transport. Is there a need for morning or afternoon school runs? What about evening social times? A few drivers could sign up for regular shifts when they are available.

> **You** Surely telephone contact would be better for this than your computer network.
>
> **Me** Yes, I agree. The computer network isn't there as a matter of ideology. Phones and mobile phones are a much better way to organise a taxi service.

261

The transport group could also make arrangements with local taxi firms, or may have taxi drivers among their members. As with food, they could make special arrangements, offering preferred status in exchange for use of local currency. If there is sufficient demand from within the network, it might be able to support a taxi business that served the general public as well as its members. This would especially benefit members who didn't own cars and might allow families who had two cars to give up the second one.

Finally, there is the servicing and repairs. Having your car serviced by someone you trust could be very attractive to many people. The network might include people who have the skills to do basic vehicle servicing. It could make special arrangements with local garages. This could include feedback from members to the garage and other members on the quality of the service received, made public on-line to other members. This would establish a relationship where trust is maintained by information and feedback and goes beyond monetary exchange.

Transport Co-op in Pinekernel Network

Olga is one of the organisers of the transport group in Pinekernel Network. Her serious arthritis has left her unable to drive. She was tired of always asking friends and relatives to do her favours by driving her places. By acting as a transport organiser for the network, she feels she can then use its services freely. Olga has a list of about 20 members she can ask to drive when it is needed. Between them they deliver and collect a lot of children to the local schools, to the great relief of their parents. She has two retired mechanics and several young people who work with them who do a lot of the servicing for network members' cars.

She doesn't get out much on her own, but seems to spend half her life on the phone, matching people's needs to driver's availability. She prides herself on being able to combine trips for different people, by convincing them that a small change in their plans will make a large difference to the sustainability of their lifestyle.

Her biggest coup was to recruit a local used car dealer, who was an old friend of hers, as a member. He has been accepted as thoroughly honest and reliable by the members (proved by their ratings of him). He is known for his willingness to put right all faults or to take back a car that its new owner doesn't like. Pinekernal Network now makes up a large part of his business, which makes it a lot more secure.

Childcare

In our fragmented modern societies, where we have lost the extended family and often the nuclear family, looking after children can often be a tremendous burden on their parents as well as a source of joy. A re-invented community offers many possibilities for reducing this burden. There is a big difference between asking friends and family for favours (if any are available) and being part of a larger group which is set up explicitly to make it easy for people to arrange to do things for each other on a reciprocal basis.

An organised childcare sub-group of an eGaian Co-operative Network could canvas its members' needs on issues such as baby-sitting, advice and support on health or behavioural problems, help with schoolwork or even home education. It could then seek solutions from its members. A minimal effort might be sign-up sheets for a basic baby-sitting circle. For childcare, perhaps more than any other area, the trust between members will be a crucial asset to an eGaian network.

263

Services

Any group of people has within it a wide range of skills and abilities which can be of use to each other. This is the basis of most local currency systems. These may include DIY skills, repairs, gardening, office skills, counselling or advice on anything from health to relationships or legal matters, temporary accommodation, lessons and tuition, massage and whatever.

These should certainly be included in any eGaian network either in an organised manner, or at the least, as an on-line database of available skills.

A network might simply include listings for whatever skills its members have to offer. Alternatively, a services sub-group could actively investigate what it is people want and then find ways of providing that. As with food and transport, this could include making arrangements with external firms for special status in exchange for discounts. The extra eGaian element in this would be the two-way exchange of information, perhaps including ratings, to maintain a basis of trust.

Problems/crises

The real test of a co-operative group is how it handles problems and crises for its members. In the days when we all lived in close-knit communities, emergency support would have been taken for granted. Whether the emergency is physical, medical or emotional, people like to know that there are other people around to whom they can turn for help when it is needed. It may be much easier for people to turn to a friend or a friend of a friend than to the law or social services when they are having serious problems with a relationship or with children. If a relative is ill or dies and you have to leave suddenly, it helps to know there are people who can step in to cover for you in whatever ways are needed. One of the significant sources of pressure on public health services is from people who need to stay in a hospital for relatively minor illnesses because they have no one to look after them at home.

At the very least, an eGaian network can have an on-line bulletin board with prominent space for emergency needs. This could be the first thing people see when they look at it. It allows anyone to offer help if they can. Beyond that, there could be a problem/crises sub-group that thinks

264

through the kinds of problems that are likely to arise and seeks out suitable resources. This may include lists of emergency plumbers, counsellors, carers, accommodation, cleaners, or whatever. People who are prepared to help sort out whatever problems arise could be on call on a rota basis.

Shopper's guide

Even if an eGaian co-operative network provides a significant amount of the food, transport, etc for its members, most of their consumption will be through the usual commercial sources for some time to come. Nonetheless, the network can help to put some of that on a better basis of trust and also help its members to keep the environmental impact of their shopping low. A shopper's guide can help with that.

People are usually faced with a choice of shops and a choice of brands within them for goods, and with a choice of tradespeople for services. It is always useful to know what your friends' experience has been so that you can buy on the basis of their recommendations. A simple way of providing this is through an on-line database giving member's local experience. If you buy an appliance or use a plumber or a lawyer, you fill out an on-line form rating the results for the item or the firm. Before you buy you can look through the database to see what other people have thought of local choices. The database could also list the entries for any local firms with which any of the other groups had made special arrangements.

If the network sets up a shopper's guide sub-group there is a lot more that can be done. There are various sources of information on the social and environmental impact of consumer products, such as *The Green Consumer's Guide*[1] and *Ethical Consumer*[2] magazine , plus various web sites. The sub-group can use these sources to identify the greenest products, find out where they are available locally, and add them to the shopper's guide database.

The overall purpose of the shopper's guide is to give network members some basis for choosing goods or services other than cost (although cost can be included in your guidance). It can build up systematic ratings of local firms and products both by its members and through information obtained from other organisations.

Social events

Social events are the glue which hold a community together. Enjoying yourself regularly in the company of people you like is one of the keys to a good quality of life. As a minimal effort, network members could simply put notices of social events on an on-line group bulletin board. If there are people who wish to be pro-active, they could organise events to suit members' interests, and notify them of public events of interest in their area.

Exchange issues

The type and nature of the exchanges between members of an eGaian network are likely to be one of the key points in its success. On what basis are members giving their time and effort to all the areas discussed above? Is this purely voluntary? Are they to be paid in some way? Do they pay for what they receive and if so, how?

In conventional society, people either exchange formally using money or informally through gifts and favours. In the Pinecone Network story, and as discussed in the eGaian Guide, exchange is guided by real costs such as ecological footprint and other physical and biological implications of consuming, and the number of hours and conditions of work of the human input. Exchange in an eGaian network is meant to include steps in that direction, to the extent that its members find comfortable. Ideally, it should offer opportunities to exchange using the national currency, an internal,

266

local currency and also simply through gifts and favours. By combining all three, the network can start with the current needs of members and evolve gradually towards much less use of conventional money.

Members who are in full-time employment are likely to have relatively little spare time to put into the various network areas, but will be able to pay in national currency. For them the network offers a sense of community and common purpose and a much greater degree of trust in their transactions rather than an opportunity for part-time employment. By spending their money preferentially with other members, they are providing support to people who, through the network, are supporting them.

Members who are partly employed or unemployed will appreciate the opportunities the network offers to reduce their need for conventional money and also to obtain both conventional and local currency through contributing to the various network areas. (And they too will appreciate the sense of community and trust.)

For an eGaian network to set up its own local currency, with its own on-line cheques and accounts, is relatively straightforward. For it to combine the local currency with national currency on the same on-line cheques is not so straightforward. It could provide an internal accounting system for its members in the national currency. The difficulty would be in getting money into and out of its members' (conventional) bank accounts. Doing this would require a link to the conventional banking system, as well as credit limitations and charges. This might be arranged through one of the ethical banks or through a credit card company, but that is really beyond the scope of this book. In the early stages, transactions between members using conventional currency would have to be made using conventional means.

When setting up the network, members would have to decide on a

267

name and a unit for their internal currency. They would decide which of the various forms of local currency to use and what form the fees to cover overheads would take. All of these decisions could be kept under review through membership polls and discussion, so that it remained open to change over time as the network matured. Is the currency meant to represent hours of effort? Is this a strict rule, or are some hours worth more than other hours?

Exchange in Pinekernel Network

The founding members decided to have an internal currency, which they called the "Kernel". They decided that as a guideline, 5 Kernels should represent one hours' work, but that this needn't be strictly adhered to. For example, two hours caring for some active children in an afternoon isn't the same as babysitting for the same children in the evening when they have gone to bed. This decision took a lot of discussion and was very controversial, and came with the recommendation that people should have good reasons for deviating from the 5 Kernels per hour norm.

They set up a Community Account with a flat annual fee plus a small excess charge for anyone whose account was either very heavily in credit or in debit to encourage people to be active. Members had the option of paying the annual fee in national currency or in Kernels.

For transactions in the national currency, they joined in a scheme that had been pioneered by an earlier eGaian Co-operative Network in connection with the credit card arm of one of the ethical banks. All members who wished to use it needed to have a credit card on record with Pinekernel Network. Each month their credit card is either debited or credited with the net result of their transactions with other members.

Membership issues

When it is formed, an eGaian network will have to consider various issues to do with its membership. Will there be a limit to the number of members? Will it be open to anyone or just by recommendation of existing members? What approaches will it take to conflict resolution and to decision making? Will there be elected organisers?

Membership issues in Pinekernel Network

The founding members of Pinekernel Network decided to limit their membership to 100 people. Beyond that size they might split into two groups. Membership was to be only by recommendation by an existing member and subject to the approval of the existing membership.

They set up a conflict resolution sub-group whose members were to be elected annually and who were expected to have skills or training in mediation, counselling or similar areas. Any conflicts that arose were to be handled by mediation and through the principles of restorative justice, if appropriate. As a condition of membership in Pinekernel Network, people were asked to agree that any conflicts arising from their membership or with other members were to be referred to the conflict resolution group.

269

Deciding how to make decisions was one of the most difficult discussions the founding group faced. They were torn between habits of thought that demanded group involvement in all decisions on the one hand, and the amount of effort they were finding in coming to agreement on the other. They decided that for the first year or two they would try what they called 'elected benevolent dictatorship plus consensus'. There would be two 'Chiefs' to be elected annually, one male and one female (following the model of Damanhur). All significant decisions were to be open to discussion by all members, with polls to determine the state of members' views. If conflict arose, the Chiefs were to try to find solutions that most nearly obtained consensus, but in the end, they made the decisions based on their own views as to what was best for the community.

270

External links

The eGaian model may strongly emphasise local production and local community, but it is in no way a return to the ideals of self-sufficiency of the 1970s or of early human settlements. It is an essential part of the picture that groups are connected to others of all sorts, ultimately forming a global nervous system.

There are various types of links the organisers of an eGaian network will probably need to consider: links with similar networks, with commercial organisations, with national and global NGOs concerned with the environment and social change, and with their governments. If there are several eGaian networks in the area, it would make sense for them to co-operate closely with each other. If one network gets too large, so that people have difficulty knowing each other and maintaining trust, it may choose to split or to bud off a new group. Overlapping memberships are a good way of spreading trust between networks. They may choose to share a local currency or have some convertibility between different ones.

The members of an eGaian network are likely to include a fair number who are also activists in the major organisations working for environmental and social change, especially in their earlier days. These organisations may provide support and information and the local networks may reflect their concerns.

Any organisation that has an economic function will need to consider its position on tax and benefits and that will involve its local or national government. For example, the Australian government has agreed that activities in LETS are not subject to tax, and the UK government is actively promoting a Time Bank scheme which they have agreed is similarly free of tax and benefits considerations. However, a government could, for example, decide that active members of an eGaian network who were on benefit were not seeking work and thus should lose their benefit. This would probably exclude all members on benefit.

271

However, if these networks are ever to play a significant economic role in their member's lives, it is not desirable that their activities should be entirely separate from tax and benefit considerations. If they are regenerating a community, they should reduce their members' needs for benefit. They should make a contribution to the larger community services currently provided by taxation. Anyone who sees them as a tax dodge or as an extension of the black economy is missing the point.

Various sensible strategies can be imagined.

- There might be a clear division between those activities that members are doing as extensions of their normal working life, and those that are more in the nature of informal favours or gifts. Only the former would be considered for tax and benefit purposes.

- A network could give the local government an account and contract to undertake various services in lieu of some portion of its members' taxes.

- Graded systems of benefit reductions could be negotiated at rates comparable to national tax levels. With sufficient network activity a person might come off benefit entirely.

The software

The availability of good supporting software is likely to be one of the keys to the success of eGaian networks. It needs to be easy to use by people with little aptitude for computers. Moreover, it needs to be exciting, something that people look forward to using because through it they are in touch with the people and events which matter to them. Would email ever have become popular if it hadn't been easy to use?

There is no software currently available that could support an eGaian network in full, but there is quite a lot which supports aspects of it. First there are the eGroups. There are various public web sites that allow people to set up an on-line group. Perhaps the largest is Yahoo[3], which provides a large number of public discussion groups on almost any conceivable subject. Moreover, any group, club, organisation which wants to use the Internet to support their activities can set up a Yahoo eGroup very simply, and without charge, provided they don't mind the advertising they will get.

The main feature of an eGroup is group email that is provided in the form of a mailing list. Members address their email to the eGroup's address and it gets sent automatically to all other members. Egroups offer other facilities, such as on-line chat, space to post photos and files, databases, polls and group calendars. All of this comes automatically when the group is set up. Setting up a new eGroup involves little more than filling in an on-line form with the group's name, purpose and then listing the members' email addresses. There are various group settings such as whether the group should be private or open to the public.

In a similar way, software to support an eGaian network might be made available on some public sites. Perhaps it could be hosted by some of the larger environmental organisations, such as Friends of the Earth or Greenpeace. In some places, they may be hosted by progressive government

273

organisations, seeking to regenerate an inner city or a declining rural area. Of course, the physical location of the software is quite irrelevant to the place where it will be used. When a group sets up their software, they would automatically get a range of facilities, as with the eGroups. This would include:

- an account system for transactions between members, complete with local currency and on-line cheques

- a database set up for a shopper's guide, complete with links to the local currency system to allow ratings of products and services

- blank bulletin boards ready to take news of various areas like food, transport, childcare or whatever the group wanted

- discussion spaces and polling facilities.

Another web site of relevance to this discussion is 'Slashdot, News for Nerds, Stuff that matters.'[4] It is an on-line hangout space for the community of people who are interested in such subjects as the Free Software Movement, Open Source Software, the LINUX operating system and the Apache web server. One way of looking at Slashdot is as an interactive community newspaper. Many people can add stories and there is a discussion and perhaps a poll attached to each story.

Slashdot serves that part of the software-writing community that believes software should be written co-operatively and distributed freely. The convention within that community is that the source code of a programme – ie the author's original work – should be distributed freely so that anyone with the relevant skills can see how it was produced. That is why it is called open source software. Of course, *Slashdot* itself is built as open source software. This has enabled a small group of developers to take it and modify it for other uses. Some of these look very different on the surface, and versions are available in very many languages. These groups are in touch with each other and help each other. Thus as *Slashdot* develops, a whole cluster of similar software follows it.

That is very much the approach that would suit the development of the software for eGaian networks. (In fact, the *Slashdot* source code might be a useful starting point for parts of it.) It should certainly be developed as open source software. There should probably be a number of variants each tailored to the needs of the groups using it, but sharing ideas all round. What is important is that the software evolves rapidly. We cannot know exactly what will be needed at the beginning.

Pinekernel Network On-line

Paula is checking to see what's new in Pinekernel Network this morning. She notices two new receipts in her accounts. To enhance security, when a Pinekernel cheque is written, a receipt is sent by email to the person who wrote it. The cheque is credited only when the sender confirms that it is correct.

She notices that Glenda needs help, and makes a note to phone her a little later. She then has a look at some of the news stories. She subscribes to several news sources that give the kind of news analysis she likes and covers the topics that interest her. She then has a browse through the Flea Market looking for second hand children's clothes. Besides the on-line notices, the Flea Market organisers hold a monthly event at which Pinekernel members bring their old things along to exchange with each other. It also is an excuse for the Food Co-op people to show off their best cooking, and the Pinekernel musicians tend to turn out in force.

Paula has a quick look at what is currently on offer by the Food Co-op and, simply by marking a few boxes, puts in her order for the week. She has been thinking about buying a new vacuum cleaner and so looks to see what is in the Shopper's Guide. She finds one that is recommended by a couple of people in the network. There is a link to a review of it, which says that its manufacturer is relatively good with its suppliers and makes efforts to build parts that can be re-cycled. It is available in a shop in her town that is associated with Pinekernel Network and will accept 20% payment in Kernels.

Summary on eGaian co-operative networks

An eGaian co-operative network could make a difference in people's lives which may start small but has the potential to be quite significant, if its members wish it to. Their initial benefits are likely to be largely social and economic. They are a step towards the re-invention of community, and with it, the basis on which to grow a peaceful world. Members will be practising and developing their skills of working in a self-organising co-operative organisation and skills of conflict resolution. These are the key skills for an eGaian world and are not very advanced in many human cultures.

The initial impact of eGaian Co-operative Network on the sustainability of their members' lifestyles is likely to be noticeable and worth doing, but nowhere near full sustainability, as described in the eGaian Guide.

- More of their food will be locally grown,

- more of their transport will be shared,

- more of their purchases will be informed by environmental considerations,

- more goods will have their use shared and lifetimes extended, thus lowering members needs to purchase more.

The most important impact of eGaian co-operative networks will come as they grow in number and become linked to each other. This will increase their members' sense of connection with those other members of humanity who are trying to grow a peaceful, sustainable world. They may begin to feel that the transformation is happening.

277

CHAPTER thirteen

TOWARDS AN eGAIAN EARTH

"One of the most important effects of 11 September has been to
highlight the fact that we are living in one world, and
that no part of that world can afford
to ignore the problems
of the rest."
UN Secretary General
Kofi Annan [1]

This preliminary edition of *eGaia* is intended specifically to help people and organisations prepare for the World Summit for Sustainable Development to be held in Johannesburg, in August/September 2002. The Summit is an extremely important opportunity for humanity. It could mark an important step towards an eGaian Earth and hence this concluding chapter is devoted to it.

The Johannesburg Summit

The Johannesburg Summit is being organised by the United Nations, which is expecting over 60,000 people to attend, substantially more than the Rio Earth Summit in 1992. A few thousand of those will be governmental delegations. They will include many of the world's heads of state and high-ranking ministers and will be the focus of the world's news media. Many people are very cynical about the likely outcomes of the Summit. That is because they see the outcomes of the Summit in terms of what the government delegations will produce, and are not expecting the dramatic breakthroughs which most people think are needed.

The Rio Earth Summit produced Agenda 21, a "comprehensive plan of action that was to be taken globally, nationally and locally by organisations of the UN System, governments, and major groups in every area in which humans impact the environment".[2] Agenda 21 is a marvellous document that has produced many initiatives from governments all around the world. It has produced a useful change in global consciousness. But compared to the strategies for sustainability in Chapter 13, its practical accomplishments (eg widespread recycling schemes for glass, cans and paper) have not much been much more than token. Since then our impact on the environment has continued to worsen, as have problems of entrenched poverty, hunger and ill health on a global scale as outlined in

279

Chapter 2, Humanity as a global cancer. The official view, from UN Secretary General Kofi Annan is that: "Progress towards the goals established at Rio has been slower than anticipated and in some respects conditions are worse than they were ten years ago." The official goals of the Johannesburg Summit are to get Agenda 21 implemented more meaningfully.

It is extremely difficult to get detailed agreement, particularly if it needs to be approved by pretty well all of the world's governments. If the government delegations involved allow the commercial needs of their national industries to take precedence over the needs of the environment and development, strong regulatory treaties are very unlikely. How many members of those delegations accept that the present economy is fundamentally flawed, or envisage the alternative described in Chapter 12, A co-operative economy?

Fortunately, most of the people attending the Johannesburg Summit will not be part of government delegations. They will be from a wide range of organisations committed to principles of sustainable development and social justice. The aims and goals of most of them will be broadly similar to those in this book – a peaceful, sustainable Earth. These delegates are not likely to be as inhibited as the governmental delegates. Moreover, this Summit is different from previous summits in some vital respects.

Its UN organisers officially recognise that there are useful outcomes other than governmental treaties and pronouncements.

> 'At Johannesburg, governments will agree on a common plan of action. But the most creative agents of change may well be partnerships – among governments, private businesses, non-profit organizations, scholars and concerned citizens such as you.' Speech by UN Secretary-General Kofi Annan, delivered by Mrs. Nane Annan, New York, 14 May 2002

280

There are two types of Summit outcome planned – Type 1: negotiated outcomes for adoption by all member states and Type 2: non-negotiated outcomes, which the UN envisages as coming from 'multi-stakeholder' coalitions, and the many groups that have been part of the planning process for the Summit. And of course, there will be many unofficial outcomes of the Summit, due to the presence of the non-governmental delegates who are organising many meetings of their own in parallel with the official meetings.

Moreover, this is the first Earth Summit of the Internet age. That opens the possibilities of groups of people around the world co-ordinating their actions locally and globally in ways that this book has been describing. It opens the possibility of attending groups planning their input in advance with each other, and with the general public through web portals such as Earth Summit for All[3]

Possible projects for the Johannesburg Summit

What sort of initiatives could become part of the Type 2 outcomes and the informal outcomes at the Summit? Very many are being developed and proposed by the organisations attending. The six described below are examples of projects that would embody the principles in this book. They may or may not become part of the Summit outcomes, but are meant to implement the basic eGaian principles described in Chapter 2.

> **You** So this is your personal plan for the Johannesburg Summit?
>
> **Me** Well, I will be there, and my personal goals before and during the Summit are to get these six projects (or something equivalent to them) taken up and agreed.

They are designed to create a sense of global identity and community, using electronic communication tools. They aim to use these tools to promote links and mutual understanding within groups of people and between different cultural groups. They are designed to create the beginnings of a globalised economy that is no longer out of control, in which trade is subject to the needs of the environment and social development.. The six projects are:

- Global green information networks with green ratings
- The Co-operative and community networks initiative
- Fair trade networks
- Global emergency aid and development fund
- Media initiatives for peace
- Education for sustainability

The six projects are each worthwhile in their own right, but they also interact and would be much more effective as a co-ordinated set. The outlines that follow need to be fleshed out through the sorts of discussions intended on the Earth Summit for All web portal.

Global green information networks

These networks would provide information of three types:

- green consumer information and ratings on products and companies at both local and national/transnational levels
- green ratings of non-commercial organisations, including national and local governments
- tools for creating personal green ratings, to enable people to evaluate their own lifestyle.

The major purpose of this initiative is to provide the public with a buying guide so that consumption choices can include knowledge of their impact on the health of the environment and social well-being. Getting the best price should not be the main much less the only criterion. It is a first step towards an economy that is driven by information about the real costs – social and environmental – of consumption rather than just on conventional economic considerations. It is the basic tool for growing an economy based upon co-operation and trust.

Information would be provided by many different organisations and also by individuals, at a local level, based upon their own experiences. There is a huge amount of collective information the groups attending the Earth Summit have about the environmental impact of different products, of the social conditions under which they have been produced, and of the political pressures which shape those conditions.

In the early stages of the project, ratings and information would be in many different formats, some incompatible with each other and perhaps contradictory. Over time, standards will emerge and evolve. It is far better to start with the large amount of information already existing and to develop common standards than it is to attempt to establish standards at the start, when the needs are not yet known.

For commercial organisations and products, ratings would incorporate separate evaluations in areas such as life-cycle environmental impact, conditions of employees and contributions to local and global community well-being. These would be represented in a simple graphical form using separate icons and also combined into an overall green rating. League tables highlighting best and worst would be included.

At the local level, information would be provided on the availability of high rated and low rated products. Information would come from the

283

general public and from members of the organisations co-ordinating the network. It would also provide personal ratings of local firms by customers, somewhat like the rating systems of on-line auctions such as eBay.

For other organisations, such as local and national governments, the ratings would have components including environmental policies and actions, democracy and civil rights and openness. Again, league tables would be included at various levels.

For individuals, the tools would enable people to calculate their ecological footprint through simple software that is already widely available. In addition, tools could be developed to estimate a 'personal connection index'. It would give a crude comparison, in hours, of what an individual gives to the community compared to what they receive from it. It would calculate the hours an individual contributes to the community – by paid work or other activities – to the hours provided by others in the goods and services they consume. This is a personal green index in which wealthy, large consumers come off badly. Its purpose is primarily in support of fair trade.

Co-operative and community networks

If a peaceful, sustainable world is to become a reality, it will need to build on co-operative and community groups to a much greater extent than today. The purpose of this initiative would be to promote and support such groups. They are likely to take various forms: from community co-operatives in cities providing local regeneration; to farming, craft or industrial co-operatives in the developing world strengthening the prospects for fair trade.

Community co-operatives take the form of like-minded people coming together to support each other in ways like obtaining local food, sharing transport, child care, health care or whatever is appropriate for them. Chapter 12 described in detail one form of such groups, applicable in areas where a significant fraction of the population have access to a computer. In poorer areas, a single computer might serve one or more whole communities. Where there is a lot of face-to-face connection, there might be much less need for a computer.

The initiative could promote such co-operatives and set up secondary co-operatives to provide advice and support and to fund development workers to get them off the ground. On-line links would share best practice and provide mutual support. For producer co-operatives, micro-finance agencies could be set up.

Fair trade networks

The principle of fair trade is trade that takes into account the social needs of the producers and which respects the environment. It presumes that these considerations take priority over simply getting the best price. This initiative builds on that principle and extends it considerably, even to trade within the more affluent parts of the world.

285

This initiative links closely with the previous two. It would seek links between co-operatives and other groups in different areas, to create a relationship between groups that leads them to trade preferentially with each other, even if the cost may be somewhat higher. It would take the form of a global, on-line market linking groups world-wide. The basis of trade would be that the price enables the producers to live in modest comfort, in terms of the standards of their own culture. Working conditions would be expected to be reasonable by the standards of those affected. Production would be expected to respect the environment.

Producer groups would be encouraged to include information about themselves and their products to establish the fair trade nature of their offerings. This might include a breakdown of the costs of their products and the wages of those employed. It should also include personal information about their community to help build a relationship with consumer groups. A major part of this could be through school children, making links with each other as part of cross-cultural education.

Information about participating groups would be part of the global green information networks to assist contacts and links between groups. The fair trade principle is consistent with obtaining high green ratings.

Global emergency aid and development fund

The purpose of this initiative is to set up a new channel for aid, outside of existing governmental aid and world financial institutions, to bypass the usual complaints of the developing world. Projects would be led by recipients, without conditions and ties to spending specified by the donors. Aid would normally be in the form of grants, but with repayment if conditions make that possible.

A multi-sectoral consortium, probably led by businesses with a green commitment, would raise funds. Contributions to this fund – including from governments and private individuals – would afffect donors' green ratings. The other initiatives listed in this chapter would be used to publicise and promote the campaigns of this fund.

Allocation of funds would be on the principle of priority to the most needy. Two early, high profile campaigns for this fund might be Food Security for All – tackling regions of endemic malnourishment; and Advancing Africa – An African-led campaign to reduce the environmental, social and political problems of the region.

Media initiatives for peace

This initiative would target parts of the world that are sites of endemic inter-ethnic conflict. It would target attitudes such as that of the Israeli official who was asked about the 'continuing spiral of violence' and said "There is no spiral. The Arab terrorists are attacking us and we are retaliating." It will promote the view that promoting peace means seeing how both sides are involved in continuing the conflict, rather than seeing your own side simply as the victim of the other.

This initiative will use a variety of mass media, local contacts and events to present to each side in a conflict the realities of life on the other side and how their side is affecting the other. It will promote the global value that mutual understanding is a necessity of peace. It will seek to transform the view of conflict from 'us versus them' to 'those who seek mutual understanding versus those who don't'.

The mechanism for this project might be a UN-sponsored annual media peace initiative award: a sort of Academy Awards for Peace. Media organisations would submit their work, which could be judged both by panels of specialists and public voting on-line. The on-line public voting should include members of the communities affected.

The initiative could also provide grants to artists proposing projects of the type that could be entered for an award.

Education for sustainability

The focus of this initiative is to encourage schools and school children around the world to take responsibility for monitoring and preserving the natural environment around them. It has the dual purposes of substantially increasing the attention paid to issues of sustainability in schools, and of

287

promoting an approach to éducation through active involvement and project work. It should also include a heavy emphasis on cross-cultural contact between children. An additional benefit would be to bring issues of sustainability to the attention of the parents and local communities.

The initiative would provide sets of tools, largely on-line, for use by schools wishing to undertake local projects. These might take the form of looking at local wildlife diversity, air and water pollution, local energy use, sustainable practices in local businesses and industry, creating wildlife sanctuaries etc. It would provide regional databases into which children could add the results of their investigations, to be compared with those of their peers locally and around the world. It would include facilities for cross-cultural discussions between different schools to explore these comparisons.

The beginnings of an eGaian Earth

Only some and perhaps none of the six initiatives described above are likely to succeed. But suppose that these six did become part of the official or unofficial outcomes of the Summit and became well established. What would be the results?

The first three – Green information networks, Co-operative and community networks and Fair trade networks – are the basis for the beginning of a globalised economy which is under the control of social needs and the needs of the environment rather than being driven by random, disconnected money flows.

The next two – Global emergency aid and development fund and Media initiatives for peace – are ways of easing the most serious crises facing humanity in the short term. Humanity taking responsibility for humanity is the essence of creating a sense of global identity and community.

The final initiative – Education for sustainability – looks to the future, by pointing children in the direction of a peaceful, sustainable Earth. The cross-cultural aspects enhance the most fundamental of all human social skills needed for an eGaian world, seeing through another's eyes.

All are different ways of linking up humanity to look after itself and the Earth. These six together would be sufficient to be considered the beginnings of a global nervous system.

And what might be the emergent properties of such a global nervous system? The coming to self-awareness of a being of planetary scale – a self-aware eGaia?

289

NOTES

CHAPTER 1

1 *Living Planet Report 2000*, World Wide Fund for Nature, at www.panda.com.

2 This is the Gaia Hypothesis as promoted by James Lovelock in *The Ages of Gaia*, Oxford, 1988 and other books. Much research has filled in details, such as in *Gaia, the Thesis, the Mechanisms and the Implications*, ed. Peter Bunyard and Edward Goldsmith, Wadebridge Ecological Centre, 1988.

3 William Rees, "Revisiting Carrying Capacity: Area-Based Indicators of Sustainability", *Population and Environment*, Vol. 17, No. 3, Jan. 1996, Human Sciences Press, Inc.

4 Ward, Peter D., Rivers in Time, *The search for clues to Earth's mass extinctions*, Columbia University Press, New York, 2000, p.82.

5 Reuters, 4 Oct. 1997.

6 2000 IUCN Red List of Threatened Species

7 World Resources Institute, Washington, D.C.

8 *A Guide to World Resources 2000-2001, People and Ecosystems, The Fraying Web of Life*, World Resources Institute, Washington, D.C. 2000.

9 *ibid.*

10 *ibid.*

11 Third Assessment Report of Working Group I of the Intergovernmental Panel on Climate Change (IPCC), Summary for Policymakers, January 2001

12 United Nations Research Institute for Social Development, Environmental Degradation and Social Integration, Briefing Paper No. 3, World Summit For Social Development, November 1994

13 *SIPRI Yearbook 2000, Armaments, Disarmament and International Security*, Stockholm International Peace Research Institute..

14 *Annual Report 2000*, Amnesty International.

15 Mayhew, P. & Dijk, J.J.M. van. (1997), *Criminal Victimisation in eleven Industrialised Countries, Key findings from the 1996 International Crime Victims Survey*, The Hague: Ministry of Justice, WODC.

16 Tony Thomson, "Crime is costing UK £60bn a year", *The Observer*, 23 April 2000.

17 Ignacio Ramonet, "The politics of hunger", *Le Monde Diplomatique*, November, 1998.

18 *Poverty Report 2000*, United Nations Development Program.

19 *Human Development Report 1998*, United Nations Development Programme, New York, September 1998.

20 *ibid.*

21 Cherlin, A., Marriage, *Divorce and Remarriage*, (2nd ed.). Cambridge, MA: Harvard University Press, 1992.

22 Glick, P. C. (1988). "The role of divorce in the changing family structure: Trends and variations." In S. A. Wolchik & P. Karoly (eds.), *Children of Divorce, Empirical Perspectives on Adjustment*. pp. 3-34). New York: Gardner, 1988.

23 Executive Summary of the WHO/FIGO Pre-Congress Workshop, Elimination of violence against women 30 – 31 July 1997.

24 *The New English Bible*, 1970.

25 Bernard Lietar, Beyond greed and scarcity. On-line interview at http://www.resilientcommunities.org/Articles/Curriencies.htm.

26 for example, the Japanese government gave out vouchers to encourage people to consume. J. Watts, "Even free money fails to tempt Japan's shoppers", *The Guardian*, 1 Feb. 1999.

27 I am old enough to remember when this was not the case. Beautiful old buildings, like New York's Grand Central Station were designed simply as efficient railway terminals.

291

28 Richard G. Dudley, "The Rotten Mango: The Effect of Corruption on International Development Projects", Eighteenth International Conference of the System Dynamics Society "Sustainability in the Third Millennium". August 6-10, 2000. Bergen, Norway.

29 United Nations Research Institute for Social Development, Geneva, Switzerland, http://www.unrisd.org/engindex/publ/list/bp/bp2/bp02-02.htm.

30 H. Speight, *Economics, The Science of Prices and Incomes*, Methuen, London, 1968, P.106.

31 That may be changing. The Linux operating system and software which runs on it are part of this general movement, and have been cited by Microsoft as potential serious competition, as part of their claim not to be a monopoly.

32 See http://www.gnu.org/fsf/fsf.html.

33 see http://www.gnu.org/copyleft/gpl-howto.html.

34 The Internet as a whole was built on co-operative principles, a legacy of this early period in computing history. That is a major reason for its culture of free content and for its robustness.

35 see for example, the special issue of *Oxford Review of Economic Policy*, Volume 15 Number 3, Autumn 1999, Financial Instability, Edited by Colin Mayer.

36 See http://www.twnside.org.sg/title/crises-cn.htm. Chakravarthi Raghavan is the Chief Editor of the South-North Development Monitor (SUNS) in which the quote first appeared.

37 Reform of the International Financial Architecture, Speech by Dr. Eisuke Sakakibara, Japanese Ministry of Finance, At the Symposium on Building the Financial System of the 21st Century, Kyoto, Japan, June 25th, 1999.

38 "Central banks and financial system stability in an uncertain world", An address by Donald T Brash, Governor of the Reserve Bank of New Zealand to the Belgian Financial Forum, Antwerp Region, Brussels, 6 June 2000.

39 World Resources Institute, "Population Growth -- Stabilization," at http://www.wri.org/wr-98-99/popgrow.htm.

40 Nicholas Eberstadt *What if it's a World Population Implosion?, Speculations about Global De-population*, American Enterprise Institute, Harvard Center for Population and Development Studies, March 1998

41 Ignacio Ramanet, "The politics of hunger" *Le Monde Diplomatique, op. cit.*

42 Eckholm, Erik P., *Losing Ground, Environmental Stress and World Food Prospects*, Pergamon, 1976, p.181.

43 Ignacio Ramanet, "The politics of hunger" Le Monde Diplomatique, *op. cit.*

CHAPTER 2
1 Peter Russell has been developing this image for a long time. See his *The Awakening Earth, Our Next Evolutionary Leap*, Routledge & Kegan Paul, London, 1982.
2 James Lovelock, *The Ages of Gaia, A biography of our living Earth*, Oxford University Press, 1988, p. xvi.

CHAPTER 4
1 Margulies, Lynn, *The Symbiotic Planet, A New Look at Evolution*, Basic Books, 1998.
2 Lynn Margulies and Dorian Sagan, *Microcosmos, Four Billion Years of Microbial Evolution*, Allen and Unwin, 1987, p.47.
3 I am using the word 'period' in its everyday sense. To a geologist, the most fundamental divisions of geological time are called 'ages' or 'aeons'. The Hadean Age is the oldest, followed by the Archaen, Proterozoic, and Phanerozoic. Ages are divided into 'eras' which in turn are divided into what geologists call 'periods'.
4 *op. cit.* p. 71.
5 Sorin Sonea and Maurice Panisset, *The New Bacteriology*, Boston, Jones and Bartlett, 1983, p.22
6 Margulies and Sagan, *op. cit.*, p.97
7 Margulies, Lynn, *The Symbiotic Planet, op. cit.*
8 *ibid.* p. 45.
9 *ibid.* p.10.
10 Ward, Peter D., *Rivers in Time, The search for clues to Earth's mass extinctions*, Columbia University Press, New York, 2000 is the source for this and the following discussion.

CHAPTER 5
1 Desmond Morris, in his classic book, *The Naked Ape*, made this point very well.
2 From Helen Fisher, *The Sex Contract, The Evolution of Human Behaviour*, Granada, 1982.

3   Frans de Waal, *Chimpanzee Politics,* Jonathon Cape, 1982., p. 41.

4   *op. cit.* p. 19.

5   There is a very good discussion of this in Helen Fisher's *The Sex Contract, op. cit.*

6   Fisher, *op cit.* p. 79.

7   Brody, Hugh, *The Other Side of Eden, Hunter-gatherers, farmers and the shaping of the world*, Faber and Faber, London, 2001, p. 255.

8   *ibid*, p. 308.

9   Morrison, James, *The Journal of James Morrison*, London, Golden Cockerell Press, 1935, p. 170 (report from 1784).

10 Levy, Robert I, "Tahitian gentleness and redundant controls", in Montague, Ashley, *Learning Non-Agression*, Oxford University Press, 1978, p. 224.

11 Liedloff, Jean, *The Continuum Concept*, Futura, London, 1975., pp. 78-79.

12 *ibid.*, p.95.

13 Norberg-Hodge, Helena, *Ancient Futures, Learning from Ladakh*, Rider, 1991, pp. 46-47. I am including Ladakh because it is such a clear example of the kind of culture I am describing even though it is not an example of a gathering/hunting lifestyle, and as a Buddhist culture, it developed much later than the others.

14 Sorenson, E. Richard, "Cooperation and Freedom among the Fore", in Montague, *Learning Non-agression, op. cit.*, p. 14-15.

15 Mead, Margaret, *Sex and Temperament in Three Primitive Societies*, Morrow, New York, 1935.

16 Montague, *op. cit.* , p. 7.

17 *op. cit.*

18 Harper and Row, 1971.

19 This is the title of a chapter in the classic book on exchange in hunter-gather societies by Marshall Sahlins, *Stone Age Economics*, Tavistock, 1972.

20 *ibid* p.1

21 *ibid.* p. 17.

22 *ibid.* p. 21.

23 *ibid.* p. 35.

24 Lee, Richard B., "What hunters do for a living", in Lee, R.B. and DeVore, I. (eds.) *Man the Hunter,* Chicago, 1968, p. 33.

25 Malinowski, Bronoslaw, "The primitive economics of the Trobriand Islanders", *The Economic Journal*, March, 1921.

26 *ibid.* p. 7.

27 Malinowski, Bronoslaw, "Kula; the circulating exchange of valuables in the archipelagoes of Eastern New Guinea", *Man*, July, 1920, pp. 97-105.

28 Sahlins, *op. cit..* "On the sociology of primitive exchange", pp. 185-277.

29 *ibid.* p. 195.

CHAPTER 6

1 Wesphal, Sylvia, "Smart Bullets", *New Scientist*, No. 2319, 1 December 2001, p. 31-32.

2 Ponting, Clive, *World History, A New Perspective*, Chatto and Windus, London, 2000, p. 51.

3 Wilkinson, Richard, *Poverty and Progress, An ecological model of economic development*, Methuen, London, 1973.

4 Ponting, *op. cit.* p. 51.

5 Randerson, James, "Too old to take it", *New Scientist*, no. 2326, 19 January 2002.

6 McMichael, Tony, *Human Frontiers, Environments and disease*, Cambridge University Press, 2001, p.33.

7 *ibid.* p. 72.

8 *ibid.* p. 102.

9 Abram, David, *The Spell of the Sensuous*, Vintage Books, 1997. A wonderful book!

10 *ibid.* p. 71.

11 Herodotus, *The Persian Wars,* Book 1, Clio, 93, translated by George Rawlinson, Modern Library, New York, 1942, p. 53

12 Ponting, *op. cit.* p. 646.

13 *ibid.* p. 642.

14 From *Stow's Annals of 1631*, quoted in Ponting, *op. cit.*p. 648.

15 *ibid.* p. 668.

16 *ibid.* p. 790.

17 Lietar, Bernard, *The Future of Money*, Century, London, 2001.

18 Keynes, John Maynard, *The General Theory of Employment, Interest and Money*, Macmillan, London, 1936.

CHAPTER 7

1   Theodore Zeldin, *An Intimate History of Humanity*, Vintage, 1998, p. 437.

2   This is drawn from my experiences at a variety of events at camps and festivals in the UK, and isn't meant to describe any one of them in particular. They were the inspiration for the social side of Elderberry Farm in the Pineapple Network story.

3   Quoted in Peter Russell, *The Awakening Earth*, Our Next Evolutionary Leap, Routledge & Kegan Paul, 1982.

4   *ibid.*, p. 98.

5   A wonderful book describing the body, and especially the brain, as a control system, is William T. Powers, *Behavior: The Control of Perception*, Wildwood House, London, 1974.

6   Peter Russell, *op. cit.* p. 115.

7   J. Scott Turner, *The Extended Organism*, Harvard University Press, 2000.

8   This is a superficial introduction to a very deep subject. For a very clear discussion of the primacy of consciousness see Peter Russell's *From Science to God, The Mystery of Consciousness and the Meaning of Light*, ISBN: 1-928586-03-1, 2000.

CHAPTER 8

1   Theodore W. Kheel, *The Keys to Conflict Resolution*, Four Walls Eight Windows, New York, 1999, p. xi.

2   Jeanmarie Pinto, "Peacemaking as ceremony: the mediation model of the Navajo Nation", *The International Journal of Conflict Management*, 2000, Vol. 11, No. 3, pp. 267-286.

3   Zion, J.W., (1994, Spring) Stories from the Peacemaker Court, *In Context* [www.context.org/ICLIB/IC38/Yazzie.htm], quoted from Pinto, *op. cit.*

4   This example is based upon, and quotes extensively from chapter 2, "We have to live together" in Helena Norberg Hodge, *Ancient Futures, Learning from Ladakh*, Rider, 1991, pp. 45 – 54.

5   This example is based upon Klaus-Friedrich Koch, "Pigs and politics in the New Guinea highlands: Conflict escalation among the Jalé", in Laura Nader and Harry F. Todd, eds., *The Disputing Process—Law in Ten Societies*, Columbia University Press, New York, 1978, pp. 58.

6   Bassam Abu-Sharif and Uzi Mahnaimi, *Tried by Fire, The searing true story of*

two men at the heart of the struggle between the arabs and the jews, Little, Brown and Co., 1995.

7   quoted by Michael Bond, "This is how we live", *New Scientist,* no. 2342, 11 May 2002, p. 42.

8   David Grossman writing in *The Guardian, G2,* 8 Feb. 2001, p. 4.

9   Michael Bond, "This is how we live", *op. cit.* p. 43.

10 Abu-Sharif and Mahniami, *op. cit.* p. 140.

11 See http://searchforcommonground.org/ for the various quotes I have used.

12 Dudley Weeks, *The Eight Essential Steps to Conflict Resolution,* Tarcher, Los Angeles, 1992, p. ix.

13 *ibid.*

14 *ibid.* p. 33.

15 Arrow Business Books.

CHAPTER 9

1   The many books of Hazel Henderson, such as *Building a Win-win world, Life beyond global economic warfare,* Berrett-Hoehler, San Francisco, 1996, are a good example, but also the work of the New Economics Foundation, James Robertson, Bernard Lietar, Richard Douthwaite, and numerous others.

2   My objection here is in terms of centralisation and authoritarian control.

3   For example, D. Pearce, "The practical implications of sustainable development", in P. Ekins & M. Max-Neef, *op. cit.,* pp. 403-411, or Ernst vonWeizsacker, Amory B. Lovins, L. Hunter Lovins, *Factor Four, Doubling Wealth, Halving Resource Use,* Earthscan, London, 1997.

4   T. Jackson and M. Jacobs, "Carbon taxes and the assumptions of environmental economics", in T. Barker (ed.), *Green Futures for Economics,* Cambridge Econometrics, Cambridge, 1991,p. 62.

5   This example is loosely based upon my experiences at various events over the past 10 years, but especially at Dance Camp East, which ran for 9 years in Norfolk, England from 1992 until 2000, but unfortunately, is no longer held.

6   Published by Ethical Consumer Research Association, Manchester, England.

CHAPTER 10

1   Helena Norberg Hodge, Todd Merrifield and Steven Gorelick, *Bringing the food economy home,* International Society for Ecology and Culture, October, 2000, p. 11.

2   Daly, Herman, "The perils of free trade", *Scientific American,* vol. 269, no. 5, Nov. 1993, p. 51.

3   Norberg Hodge, et. al. *op. cit.* p. 17.

4   Korneck, D. and H. Sukopp., "Rote Liste in der Bundesrepublik Deutschland ausgestorbenen, werschollenen und gefahrdeten Farm- und Blutenpflanzen und ihre Auswertung fur den Biotop- und Artenschutz?., Bonn, 1988, found in Norberg-Hodge, *op. cit.*

5   Norberg-Hodge, *op. cit.,* p. 20.

6   Jules N. Pretty, *Regnerating Agriculture,* Earthscan, London, 1995.

7   Robin Roy, "Sustainable product-service systems", *Futures* 32 (2000), p. 290.

8   *ibid.* p. 290-291.

9   Ernst von Weisacker, Amory Lovins A, and L. Hunter Lovins, *Factor Four. Doubling wealth, halving resource use,* Earthscan, London 1997.

10 Robin Roy, *op. cit.*

11 Alexander, Gary, "Overview: the context of renewable energy technologies", in Boyle, Godfrey, *Renewable Energy, Power for a Sustainable Future,* Oxford University Press, 1996, pp. 19-26.

12 von Weisacker, et. al, *op. cit.,* p. xxi.

13 Johansson, T.B., Kelly, H. Reddy, A.K., and Williams, R.H. (eds) *Renewable Energy: Sources for Fuel and Electricity,* Island Press, Washington, D.C., 1993.

CHAPTER 11

1   Russell, Peter, *The Awakening Earth, Our Next Evolutionary Leap,* Routledge and Kegan Paul, London, 1982, p.211.

2   Marilyn Ferguson, *The Aquarian Conspiracy, Personal and Social Transformation in the 1980s,* Tarcher, 1980.

3   see the NUA Internet surveys at:
    http://www.nua.com/surveys/how_many_online/index.html.

4   From a review at http://www.permacult.com.au/community/ngo.html of Julie Fisher, *Nongovernments: NGOs and the Political Development of the Third World,* Kumarian Press, 1997.

5 Quoted from their website at http://www.ifrc.org/

6 From the Fair Trade Federation website at
   http://www.fairtradefederation.com/.

7 From the Time Dollars website at
   http://www.timedollar.org/101/x1Question_one.htm.

8 From "A day in the life of cooperative America" published by National
   Cooperative Bank, US, found at
   http://www.wisc.edu/uwcc/icic/def-hist/history/1994.html.

9 From the Global Eco-village Network website at http://www.gaia.org/.

10 Ross Jackson, "The Global Ecovillage Network", *Communities Magazine*
   (Summer 1996)

11 From "Constitutzione della Federazione di Damanhur", Dananhur, 1999 (in
   4 languages), p.157.

12 *ibid*. p.125-6.

CHAPTER 12

1 John Elkington & Julia Hailes, *The Green Consumer Guide*, Gollancz,
   London, 1988.

2 Published by Ethical Consumer Research Association, Manchester.

3 See http://yahoogroups.com.

4 See http://slashdot.org.

CHAPTER 13

1 From the UN Secretary-General's report on progress on Agenda 21 as part of
   the preparatory process for the Johannesburg Summit.

2 From the IISD's Introduction to Johannesburg Summit 2002. See
   http://www.iisd.ca/wssd/background.html

3 See http://earthsummit.open.ac.uk. This site is sponsored by the Open
   University and was set up by the author.